Transvestites and Transsexuals

Toward a Theory of
Cross-Gender Behavior

PERSPECTIVES IN SEXUALITY
Behavior, Research, and Therapy

Series Editor: RICHARD GREEN
University of California at Los Angeles

THE CHANGING DEFINITION OF MASCULINITY
Clyde W. Franklin, II

GENDER DYSPHORIA: Development, Research, Management
Edited by Betty W. Steiner

HANDBOOK OF SEX THERAPY
Edited by Joseph LoPiccolo and Leslie LoPiccolo

IMPOTENCE: Physiological, Psychological, Surgical Diagnosis
and Treatment
Gorm Wagner and Richard Green

NEW DIRECTIONS IN SEX RESEARCH
Edited by Eli A. Rubinstein, Richard Green, and Edward Brecher

THE PREVENTION OF SEXUAL DISORDERS: Issues and Approaches
Edited by C. Brandon Qualls, John P. Wincze, and David H. Barlow

PROGRESS IN SEXOLOGY
Edited by Robert Gemme and Connie Christine Wheeler

SEX EDUCATION IN THE EIGHTIES: The Challenge of Healthy
Sexual Evolution
Edited by Lorna Brown

THEORIES OF HUMAN SEXUALITY
Edited by James H. Geer and William T. O'Donohue

TRANSVESTITES AND TRANSSEXUALS: Toward a Theory of
Cross-Gender Behavior
Richard F. Docter

Transvestites and Transsexuals

Toward a Theory of Cross-Gender Behavior

Richard F. Docter

California State University
Northridge, California

PLENUM PRESS • NEW YORK AND LONDON

Library of Congress Cataloging in Publication Data

Docter, Richard F.
    Transvestites and transsexuals: toward a theory of cross-gender behavior / Richard
F. Docter.
        p.   cm.—(Perspectives in sexuality)
    Bibliography: p.
    Includes index.
    ISBN 0-306-42878-4
    1. Transvestism—United States—Psychological aspects. 2. Transsexuals—United
States—Psychology. 3. Sexual behavior surveys—United States. I. Title. II. Series.
HQ77.D63   1988   88-19586
305.3—dc19   CIP

© 1988 Plenum Press, New York
A Division of Plenum Publishing Corporation
233 Spring Street, New York, N.Y. 10013

Printed in the United States of America

Preface

The objective of this book is to propose a theory of transvestism and secondary transsexualism, and to provide information concerning these behaviors. My view of these topics is much like that of Benjamin (1966) and nearly all other gender researchers. It holds that a syndrome of similar behaviors can be identified, ranging from fetishism through transvestism, transgenderism, and secondary transsexualism. But description is one thing and explanation of causes is another. I agree with other gender researchers (e.g., Green & Money, 1969; Stoller, 1985c) who have concluded that the causes of transvestism and transsexualism remain largely unknown. But the fact that we cannot fully explain the origins of transvestism or secondary transsexualism does not mean that a comprehensive theory is impossible. Indeed, excellent theoretical statements have been proposed concerning each of these topics (Bancroft, 1972; Buckner, 1970; Buhrich & McConaghy, 1977a; Money & Ehrhardt, 1972; Ovesey & Person, 1973, 1976; Person & Ovesey, 1974a,b; Stoller, 1968a, 1974, 1985c). It is with considerable respect, therefore, that we acknowledge both the strong shoulders on which we stand, and also the more practical fact that we have drawn heavily upon the many contributions of these researchers.

The approach I have adopted has the same scientific difficulties that confronted all of these previous workers. For example, the ideal way to study these behaviors would be through long-term longitudinal observation starting in very early childhood, but that technique is not available to us for several reasons. Our study is based on survey and test data from 110 heterosexual transvestites and some of their wives, together with follow-up correspondence with most of them over a 5-year period. We have also had the opportunity to follow 40 TVs more closely during this time period, interviewing and observing them regularly, and attending many of their meetings in various parts of the nation. Fifteen of

these have participated with me in counseling activities, often together
with their wives.

A difficulty with this topic is that transvestism, much more than
transsexualism, is taboo behavior in our culture. The population of
transvestites, therefore, is neither clearly definable nor readily available
for study. Our sample, like all the others, must necessarily draw from
those individuals willing to take a step or two out of the "closet"—at
least far enough to give a history and complete a packet of research
materials. Wherever possible, we attempted to follow-up these cases
through establishing, at the least, major changes in patterns of behavior
over time, but this has not always been feasible. As limited as this
procedure may be, it represents the best we have been able to do within
the applicable constraints. From a scientific perspective, transvestism
has been much less extensively explored than transsexualism. Our focus
has been upon heterosexual transvestites, and although we will discuss
transsexualism throughout this book, it is a minor theme. As we shall
see, there is good reason to believe that secondary transsexualism is
based on a long preparatory period of cross dressing.

There are two major assumptions which run throughout this book.
First, is the idea that cognitive determinants are critical factors in the
structuring of behavior. It is the beliefs, the expectations, the self-ap-
praisals, the gender perceptions, the information processing, and the
sexual script of a person which can lead toward unusual presentations of
self, as in transvestism. Second, we assume that transvestism and secondary transsexualism represent the product of extensive change and
development across the life of an individual, and therefore, a developmental perspective or life span view is imperative to understanding this
behavior. Too often, we shall argue, transvestism has been described as
if it were a stable behavior pattern rather than a changing process. In
Chapter 8, we present a multistage theory of heterosexual transvestism
which relies heavily on the life span or developmental view of this
behavior. Our theory attempts to account for secondary transsexualism
as the product of the developmental struggles of some transvestites. We
shine the spotlight upon cognitive and developmental factors, because
in our view, these have been historically understated. There can be no
question, however, that in transvestism the behavior of cross dressing is
closely tied in with sexual excitement, the alteration of mood, and pleasurable changes in general arousal level. More than anything else, it is a
way of generating satisfying affective experience.

We shall take *self theory* as the overarching theoretical framework to
explain how the behavior described here is organized and carried out.
Self theory has been part of psychological and sociological theory for
more than a century, and with the rise of cognitive psychology and

humanistic psychology over the past several decades, the self is now well-established as a hypothetical construct. The concepts of identity, gender identity, and cross-gender identity will be conceptualized as subsystems of the self. We shall necessarily take a few excursions into self theory in order to deal with the apparent capacity of the self to share control, and even to be "overthrown" by subordinate units of the self, as in dissociative states and hypnosis (Hilgard, 1977). This capacity for a duality of the self, to use Hilgard's term, has been extensively described in transvestism. Prince (1976), for example, has strongly pressed the idea of a "second self" or an "alternate self," and Money (1974) has described dissociative-like dual personality in the transvestite, as have many others. We agree with this description of "the feminine self"; our effort will be to fit the idea into a theory consistent with current views of how the self seems to operate.

The concept of a "feminine self," or better, of a cross-gender identity (Freund, Steiner, & Chan, 1982) is extremely important in both transvestism and transsexualism. We will attempt to trace the formation of this temporary reversal of gender identity in transvestism arguing that it occurs after extensive fetishistic cross dressing has been learned and practiced. As we see it, the cross-gender identity is formed the same way any other aspect of identity is shaped: Through social learning and social feedback. We will stress that it is the social presentation of the transvestite's "feminine self" in semipublic or public social situations which is critical to the development of a cross-gender identity.

In brief, we propose the following theory about the process of transvestism: The management of the cross-gender identity by the self system is the determining factor in the stability, or, alternatively, the "progression" of transvestism into some other behavior pattern, such as transgenderism or secondary transsexualism. In most cases of the transvestites who have been most extensively described—the club members—the cross-gender identity is gradually integrated into the self system and it functions there as an obedient, managed, reasonably responsible and subordinate component. Only when cross dressed does the typical transvestite experience an intense sense of being in both the opposite gender role and of having a cross-gender identity (or feminine self, as TVs prefer to say). It is in the rare cases wherein this process of integration and management of the cross-gender identity is not satisfactorily resolved that sustained conflict, anxiety, and ultimately for some, transsexual urges become intense. Although this is rare, there appears to be increasing support for the view that much, if not most, transsexualism is secondary, and that such transsexualism follows an extensive career in either a transvestite or a homosexual form (Person & Ovesey, 1974b).

Stoller (1985c), in his most recent summation of a career of psycho-analytic studies of gender deviance, expresses little satisfaction with the terminology and pseudo-precision in differential diagnosis along the spectrum of gender identity. He speaks of both transvestism and transsexualism as "wastebasket" terms. Stoller may be correct. He is definitely correct in poking holes in the simplistic conceptualizations which have too often passed as theory concerning transvestism and transsexualism. But although we have no hesitation in helping Stoller punch a hole here and there, we will be realistic about using the diagnostic categories for transvestism and transsexualism in the *Diagnostic and Statistical Manual of Mental Disorders* (DSM-III-R) of the American Psychiatric Association (1987). Because this is the internationally accepted standard for description and categorization of psychiatric disorders, we will relate our work to the definitions provided in that manual. To do otherwise would invite huge communications difficulties concerning our subject matter. Note that we do not assume that either transvestism or transsexualism ought to be conceptualized as disorders. Such a view stems from a medical model of illness which does not clarify the understanding of these behaviors. However, we are not going to debate here the value judgment involved in deciding whether either of these behavior patterns should or should not be viewed as a psychiatric disorder. That is not central to our present effort. Therefore, although we use the DSM-III-R, we will remind our readers that we see both good and harm in using this medical model terminology. In Chapter 2, we offer a bit of history concerning the origins of these diagnostic terms, and we urge the inclusion of transgenderism as part of the gender spectrum. It seems to be a behaviorally definable landmark or plateau intermediate between very intense transvestism and secondary transsexualism.

However modest one's efforts as a behavioral scientist, it is imperative to draw together the knowledge base for any subject matter of interest, to evaluate this knowledge, and to assess the constructs that have been used in theory construction. Ultimately one must judge whether the observations support explanatory theory. In the most elementary sense, this is the scientific process for the refinement of knowledge. There is a considerable challenge in attempting to bring together the extensive literature concerning both transvestism and transsexualism. In attempting to do this, we hope enough information is provided in Chapter 3 to help the reader extract what others have said.

In Chapter 4, we review the concepts of self, identity, gender identity, and cross-gender identity, using the model of cognitive psychology to illustrate how our expectations and thinking processes participate in the management of our behavior. We rely heavily on the line of reasoning set out by Kelly (1955) with his theory of personal constructs. This line of thinking is linked to Chapter 5 by treating sexual scripts as highly integrated networks of personal constructs—preferences, fantasies, expectations—all with erotically charged overtones. And in Chapter 5, we also review the topic of fetishism, noting its great significance as a starting point for heterosexual transvestism.

Chapter 6 presents data from our survey of 110 heterosexual transvestites, mostly members of cross dressing clubs throughout the United States with a few from Canada. Also given in Chapter 6 are the results from the Bem Sex-Role Inventory (Bem, 1981a), from a measure of TVs' preferred explanations for their cross dressing, and from an experimental cross dressing inventory. Chapter 7 presents the results from a survey of 35 wives of transvestites. They tell us how this behavior impacts the family and the marital relationship. For the most part, we let the wives speak for themselves.

Many individuals have helped me with the conduct of this project and with the writing of this book. None of this would have been possible without the cooperation of 110 transvestites who have trusted me with their histories and, in many cases, with confidential and personal information reflecting intimate aspects of their experience. The members of a southern California group, Chic, have been very kind in helping me, as have many individuals who are affiliated with the Tri Ess organization. I also want to thank the 35 wives of TVs who were willing to participate in this research. They too have shown courage and trust in making their beliefs and feelings known.

Sandy Thomas has been exceptionally helpful in several ways. Early in this project he took initiative in urging the participation of other individuals and groups. This kind of help is virtually imperative when an outsider seeks the cooperation of a very private minority group. Sandy has also been helpful in reviewing the ideas, the interpretations, and the theoretical scheme which emerged.

I have received much assistance from the libraries of California State University, Northridge. Helen Bennett, Don Reed, Dennis Bakewell, and many other staff members have given me substantial professional help. The Special Collections department of the library at California State University, Northridge, has responsibility for the Vern and Bonnie Bullough Collection. This collection consists of several thousand volumes pertaining to human sexuality, including many rare historical materials dealing with transvestism and transsexualism. It is one of the largest collections of its kind in the world. I have made considerable use of these resources, especially as a source for the extensive writings of Virginia Prince, who has contributed much to the study of transvestism and gender theory. I should also like to express much gratitude to my fellow psychologists at CSUN, Richard Coleman and Robert Redding, who helped me immeasurably with the factor analytic aspects of data management.

Finally, my wife has shared responsibility for many aspects of this project. Her sound judgment has been invaluable, but more important, her insights into human behavior and her loving encouragement have made her both my best friend and my closest collaborator.

Contents

Transvestites and Transsexuals

Chapter 1

Introduction

There have been three main approaches to the topics of transvestism and transsexualism:

The Biological or Medical Model.   This approach views these behaviors as based in our physical constitution; they are viewed as expressions of sexual, identity, or personality disorders. Major hypotheses emphasize neurophysiological or neurological factors—possibly stemming from early fetal development, hormonal variables, genetic determinants, chromosomal uniqueness—all of these, and much more, would comprise the subject matter of greatest interest. We shall discuss some evidence that transvestites and transsexuals differ from control subjects in some of these biological dimensions, but in general, there is little compelling data to support biology as a major causal factor. Because all behavior involves biological processes, biology is basic to all behavior. Further, because both transvestism and, in some cases, transsexualism involve intense sexual arousal, we must not ignore the realities of such biologically based systems as motivation and reinforcement. But the point is this: If we try to explain transvestism or transsexualism as the product of unique biology or physiology we soon run into a dead end. These individuals do not seem to differ much from anyone else relative to most of the biological variables that have been explored.

The Intrapsychic/Psychodynamic Model.   This model takes infancy and early childhood as its principal subject matter, giving special emphasis to how the dynamics of personality evolve. For transsexualism, the hypothesis is that in very early childhood an overly close "symbiosis" with the mother sets the stage for gender identity distortions (e.g., Stoller, 1968a, 1974, 1985c). The best of the psychoanalytic models of transvestism (Ovesey & Person, 1976) describe this as a disorder of the self stemming from major difficulties in early object relations. Women's

1

clothing are said to become symbolic ties with the mother and to serve as transitional objects, providing security and anxiety reduction. This line of theory seems more in harmony with the developmental behaviors of the transvestite than the earlier "phallic woman" model that drew mainly on castration anxiety and the oedipal complex as explanatory theses.

The Developmental/Learning Model.   This view attempts to explain transvestism and transsexualism based on the principles of learning and the process of socialization. The idea is that these behaviors are acquired through classical conditioning, operant conditioning, and modeling and imitation, just as are so many other behaviors. According to this approach, it is experience which shapes not only the sexual preferences of a person, but the entire set of complex cognitive determinants that guide behavior. Transvestism and transsexualism just happen to be significantly different from the behavior of most persons.

As we see it, none of these conceptual models ought to be ignored; there is richness in each of them and each makes vital contributions. And so we join with practically all gender researchers in saying that the behavior of interest ought to be viewed as multidetermined and as involving interactions across all three of the above orientations. One disadvantage of this is that a confusing array of constructs may be invoked to account for behavior. One study discusses the temporal lobe, the next deals with the separation-individuation process, and another with how particular sexual stimuli come to be effective in promoting arousal. For the present, there is no way to avoid this complexity. No general systems theory can rescue us yet. But one thing we can do is refine our thinking to the absolute minimum number of constructs we consider essential to explain transvestism and secondary transsexualism. This will give us a focus, a conceptual structure which will run throughout this book.

Four Thematic Constructs

There are four constructs we shall use throughout this book as organizing themes to unite the subject matter. They are:

1. *Sexual arousal and sexual excitement* are terms we define as synonymous. Sexuality is essential because as Benjamin said, " . . . to take sex out of transvestism is like taking music out of opera" (1966, p. 37). Sexual arousal is innately reinforcing and the intermittent reinforcement of fetishistic cross dressing almost certainly guarantees long-term per-

sistence of this behavior. It is a serious error, however, to think that either transvestism or secondary transsexualism are exclusively motivated by sexual feelings, or that erotic reinforcement explains all. The story line is far more complex, and different reinforcers seem important at different stages across the life span.

2. *Pleasure*, like all subjective experience, is a problem for the behaviorist. But both transvestism and transsexualism are heavily loaded with mood-altering power, and we must therefore give prominence to the affective side of these phenomena. By cross dressing and adopting a cross-gender role, these individuals generate one of their most significant sources of joy and comfort.

3. *Sexual scripts* account for the consistency of human sexual preferences. But they represent more than mere cues for action. They are the network of ideas, expectancies, knowledge, judgments, and memories which guide complex behavior. We think of these cognitive schema as subsystems of the self, all part of the management system of human behavior, and we attempt to give examples illustrative of possible learning experiences which might favor development of cross-gender sexual scripts.

4. *Cross-gender identity* must be a fourth construct, for somehow we must account for the fact that many transvestites and all secondary transsexuals, when cross dressed, report something akin to an altered sense of gender identity. But this is selective. It is switched on and off by the processes of cross dressing and going into public settings in the cross-gender role. We think for many individuals this identity is nothing more than a causal attribution; it may not be an identity transformation at all. But for others, the cross-gender identity seems to grow stronger with practice and with social reinforcements of the pseudowoman. In unusual cases, the end result is a kind of revolution within the self system. The balance of power shifts in favor of the cross-gender identity with consequent disorganization and conflict within the self system. One result can be a quest to resolve the tension through sexual reassignment procedures or hormonal feminization. It is the outcome of this developmental process involving the cross-gender identity which is central to secondary transsexualism.

These four constructs may, in fact, offer the organizing focus and the conceptual framework which will help us to unravel the complexities of this subject matter. But as with most scientific effort, we shall no doubt soon want to revise them, restructure them, or get better constructs which lend themselves to better operational definition. But for now, let us see if these four variables can help us think clearly about this very complicated and multidetermined behavior.

Gender, Gender Identity, and Cross-Gender Identity

The chances are good that many people will see transvestites and transsexuals on television programs, for in recent years such individuals have often been invited to explain themselves and respond to questions from a curious audience. But the chances are not very good that the average person will ever get to know one of these individuals. Most of us, I think, will tend to be heavily influenced in thinking about transvestism and transsexualism by the moral values and gender training we absorbed throughout the socialization process. Two things are involved here. First, our society experiences discomfort with anything that is strongly sexual. Despite the so-called sexual revolution, ours is a sex-negative society, full of value judgments and inhibitions whenever sexual topics arise. It is this reticence which makes sex in movies, in literature, and in music videos so attractive an outlet for some. A fear of sex leaps over into a fear of transvestism and transsexualism. Not only are TVs and TSs believed to be taking their sexuality into the public streets, they are also different from most people and therefore suspect. Second, the TV and TS violate society's rules requiring gender conformity. These rules do not bend much in our culture, and we shall therefore examine them more fully.

Social Rules Governing Gender Presentation

One of the most explicit social rules of our society is that you are expected to present yourself in public situations in a manner consistent with your anatomical sex, and such presentation is expected to be unambiguous. There is an implicit assumption (only partially correct because pseudohermaphrodites certainly exist) that everyone has a single, unambiguous anatomical sex. That is, you are either a man or a woman. Depending upon the rules of a given culture, each sex is provided its unique pattern of socialization and sex role training. When we observe individuals in our culture, in virtually any setting, it is usually easy to identify each one as either a man or a woman. If this is even slightly unclear, as in the case of an unusually masculine appearing woman or vice versa, such ambiguity is likely to stimulate social exchanges of surprise and questioning. We tend to seek clarification of our perceptions of others concerning ambiguous gender status. Children learn to present themselves clearly as either boys or girls and to state publicly through their appearance and body language: "I am male," or, "I am female." Considerably greater latitude is accorded preadolescent children in their gender presentations than is later the case, especially in informal or family settings, and this seems more true for girls than for boys. Males are strongly expected to avoid any effeminate behaviors in all kinds of social settings.

How does gender identity comes to be established and sustained? Are there biological foundations which underlie gender identity, such as gender systems within the brain? These are questions which, until very recently, have been taken up quite superficially and perhaps with misleading results. First, few would argue that boys and girls are socialized differently in many families and treated differently by peers throughout their developmental years. This so-called sex role learning has been extensively studied during the past several decades. It can be stated with confidence that social learning processes are very important in the formation of gender identity and gender role, and that all kinds of socialization experiences contribute to this. But it remains unclear whether prenatal hormonal factors, *in utero*, may prepare the nervous system and other body components to facilitate either masculine or feminine gender identity formation. Contradictory evidence exists to support both sides of this question (Diamond, 1982; Hoenig, 1985). In brief, Money and Ehrhardt (1972) have provided strong evidence from studies of hermaphrodites showing that social learning is even more important in gender identity development than chromosomal sex. The critical factor, as they see it, is the assigned gender role as experienced by the very young child—from about eighteen months through the third or fourth year. This experience of being treated as a boy or as a girl—regardless of actual chromosomal sex—is believed to cement gender identity in place.

Milton Diamond (1965,1977), together with many others, believes that gonadal hormones of the intrauterine fetus may play a crucial role in the neurological programming of gender. He cites cases which seem to contradict the social-learning position of Money and Ehrhardt. But the final word in this debate has yet to be given. An excellent summary of the research bearing both on animal and human studies of gender formation has been provided by Hoenig (1985). He concluded that, "In spite of an increase in our knowledge of these matters, it must be admitted that it would be premature to consider that the question of how psychosexual characteristics come about in humans is settled" (1985, p. 29).

The Complexity of Transvestism

About 75 years ago, Magnus Hirschfeld described several patterns of cross dressing in men and named this *transvestism*—literally, cross dressing. Perhaps most of us have seen cross dressed individuals on television, at Halloween, as part of the punk rock scene, or at a female impersonation show. But there is a different kind of cross dressing, usually by heterosexual men, which seems not only strange and mysterious to many, but may generate feelings of revulsion or fear. Until a decade or so ago, most psychological and psychiatric texts gave prominence to the idea, for example, that transvestism often was based on a homosexual orientation. This is now known not to be the case. Today, in fact, the definition of transvestism requires a heterosexual orientation. Strong emotional reactions to cross dressing can be expected, for when men dress like women they violate not only our own expectations of socially acceptable behavior, they also violate one of the basic rules of our culture: Men shall not present themselves as women. This rule is suspended only in social situations wherein tacit approval of cross dressing has been given, such as costume parties or mock weddings.

Why then, do some heterosexual men repeatedly dress as women and report that this is among their most pleasurable activities? This is the central question of this book. Many answers have been suggested, and no one explanation is likely to apply to all. A major common element, at least in the beginning, appears to be that cross dressing is associated with sexual excitement and that it may be an elaborate foreplay preceding masturbation. This is often very important at the beginning of a cross dresser's experience; however it is not the whole story. Our thesis is that the understanding of heterosexual cross dressing must move beyond the two main explanations which have become most prominent. The first of these is that cross dressing can be explained mainly (or even entirely) as a way to achieve sexual arousal. The second is that transvestism is part of a personality struggle stemming from trauma and conflict.

The understanding of heterosexual cross dressing, we shall argue, must also encompass the study of how identity and gender identity are formed, how arousal and pleasure are generated, how sexual scripts are learned and rehearsed, and how intense envy and fear of women may contribute to becoming a transvestite. Each of these motivating factors, together with sexual arousal, seems to contribute to the strong expectancies of pleasure which the cross dresser describes. Additionally, social reinforcers also play an important part in sustaining cross dressing behavior. Here we refer to friendships and group membership, the taking of a new and different social role, perceiving oneself as a more socially attractive person and behaving accordingly, and the "role relief" which accompanies becoming a "different" person—a pseudofemale person who adds excitement, enjoyment, and extraordinary delight to life. As we shall see, for many transvestites the enactment of fantasies is not only fun in itself, but, for some, enhances social relationships as well.

Transsexualism in History

From Greek mythology and Roman times throughout the Middle Ages and into the Renaissance, all periods of history have included examples of transvestism and transsexualism (Bullough, 1974, 1976a,b, 1987; Green, 1969). But such examples stand out as unusual, even rare behaviors in most cultures. Perhaps there is some kind of biological imperative which encourages clearly defined and separate genders. For example, Mellen (1981) proposes that gender specificity may stem from the survival value associated with having clear-cut differences in the roles and responsibilities of men and women. But just as we seem to need to make this distinction and to enforce it through cultural standards, some persons have always needed to function in the gender role opposite their biological sex. Behavioral evidence of this gender role switching has been reported across scores of different cultures. But despite this extensive history of transvestism and transsexualism, the scientific study of these phenomena has barely begun. Although Hirschfeld (1910) described several forms of transvestism three-quarters of a century ago, and Ellis (1936) reported cases of what we would now call transvestism and transsexualism, very little scientific work on either topic was initiated until after World War II. A major stimulus for transsexual studies came from the Christine Jorgensen case (1967). But 30 years earlier, in Germany, the first "sex change" operation is believed to have taken place—almost certainly for the wrong reasons.

The first medically authorized sex reassignment (transsexual surgery) is believed to have been performed in Germany in the early 1920s. The year may have been 1923, as suggested by the account of the Einar Wegener case (Hoyer, 1933), but this starting point is not well documented. Wegener, born a male, married when he was about 20 but progressively came to think of himself as a woman and took the name Lili. There is no satisfactory account of how he was evaluated medically or psychiatrically at that time, or of exactly what surgical procedures were completed, but there is no doubt that he not only considered himself to have become a woman, he also lived full-time as a woman. By the time Wegener reached his forties he felt he could not go on living unless his "female" self could be fully expressed. He consulted with many physicians, some of whom considered him homosexual, although others apparently attributed his transsexual motivation to biological causes. Wegener went to Berlin, had his testicles and penis removed, considered himself to be a woman, and behaved accordingly. He was issued a Danish passport in the name of Lili Elbe.

The Berlin of the 1920s offered a medical capability and a cultural perspective wherein this earliest transsexual surgery could be carried out. The city at that time was unusually tolerant toward the expression of sexual diversity. Prostitution was openly solicited by males and females and by the young and old. Magnus Hirschfeld was very outspoken in defense of the rights of homosexuals, and he operated a kind of free clinic and sexual research center. Benjamin (1966) recalls seeing many transvestites upon visiting Hirschfeld's clinic, most of whom were obtaining documents to help them obtain police permission to appear in public cross dressed. However, with the rise of Hitler in the 1930s, the libertine subculture of Berlin was destroyed. Beginning with the actual burning of the books from Hirschfeld's library, Hitler ordered a program of violence, murder, imprisonment, and finally extermination of thousands of homosexuals. These men became the first mass-victims of the death camps (Rector, 1981). Hitler had invented the final solution to the "homosexual problem," a solution to be applied later to the "Jewish problem."

We know of no systematic research concerning transvestism or transsexualism during the 1930s and 1940s, other than Havelock Ellis' case reviews, but this changed quickly during the summer of 1952 when George Jorgensen became Christine Jorgensen. Danish physicians had been interested in endocrinological studies of hermaphrodites and in related gender topics. It was this work which led Jorgensen to seek their help in his quest for gender reassignment. Born and raised a male in a middle-class immigrant family from Scandinavia, Jorgensen had grown up in New York City. His childhood was not remarkable except for the retrospective report that he had always felt he should have been born a girl. No cross dressing was said to have occurred during childhood or adolescence. The story of this historic transformation is described in her book (Jorgensen, 1967) and also, in part, by the medical team which carried out the surgery (Hamburger, Sturup, & Dahl-Iverson, 1953). Upon returning to the United States, Christine Jorgensen became a sensational news story. A feature film was made describing her life. The impact of this case upon public awareness of transsexualism was unprecedented. Christine Jorgensen went on to enjoy a career as an entertainer and has often appeared on national television programs. She has never married.

Next we move on to a more orderly consideration of terminology and diagnostic categories. Although naming a thing does not explain it, setting differences straight may at least help to limit our examination to one set of issues at a time. As we turn to Chapter 2, Stoller's (1985c) criticism of simplistic categorization should be kept in mind. The spectrum of gender differences contains much behavior with very similar underpinnings, therefore, let us not be so dazzled with diagnostic divisions that we forget we are actually dealing with what may be different developmental stages of a single phenomenon.

Chapter 2

The Spectrum of Cross Dressing

We begin this chapter with a review of five heterosexual behavior patterns involving cross dressing: fetishism, fetishistic transvestism, marginal transvestism, transgenderism, and secondary transsexualism (TV type). The latter part of this chapter will describe four homosexual behavior patterns involving cross dressing: primary transsexualism, secondary transsexualism, so-called drag queens, and female impersonators. Our goal is to describe each of these terms and state what we see as the essential differences among them. The terminology is not our invention; it has been in use for many years. Stoller (1985a) has reviewed problems relating to classification and diagnosis in transvestism and transsexualism. Unfortunately, the knowledge base necessary to support a system of classification is only now beginning to take shape. When the definitions of "types" are unclear, research reports may be difficult to interpret for they may include persons drawn from two or more "types" of cross-gender behavior. There are many potential harms which may arise from the assignment of labels and classifications to individuals, but from a research perspective, it is necessary to say as clearly as possible what behavior is being studied. Our present emphasis is upon the etiology and course of heterosexual transvestism—a phenomenon believed to be found almost exclusively in men. Hence, most of what we say here pertains to males. Females are involved only with reference to primary transsexualism. Another clarification: When we use the word transvestism without specifying either the fetishistic or marginal type, we are referring to the combination of these two types. Similarly, when we use the word transsexualism without specifying either the primary or secondary variation, we are referring equally to both.

Fetishism

Fetishism that involves cross dressing needs to be distinguished from fetishistic transvestism. Confusion sometimes results because these behavior patterns overlap, making a sharp line of separation difficult, but important differences do exist. We urge these definitional restrictions: While the *fetishistic transvestite* cross dresses so as to impersonate a woman, dressing fully and using makeup and suitable hairstyling, the *fetishist* is concerned only with separate components of this stimulus array. In the fetishist, cross dressing is partial, never complete, for if it should be complete we would then classify this as fetishistic transvestism. The fetishist's entire motivational objective is sexual excitement. He never cross dresses in an effort to "pass" in public as does the fetishistic transvestite. His partial cross dressing does not involve feelings of a cross-gender identity; when the sexual response cycle has been completed he has no further use (at that time) for his sexually excitatory clothing or other sexually arousing stimuli. As set out here, this classification corresponds to Benjamin's Type 1 "pseudo-transvestite" (Benjamin, 1966).

The psychoanalytic theory of fetishism (Bak, 1953; Stoller, 1976, 1985b) relies heavily upon a trauma-conflict-mastery model of behavior. Fetishism is seen as compensatory for a partially damaged sense of masculine identity. The behavior is viewed as part of an ongoing struggle to master and overcome the humiliation and anxiety associated with past traumatic events. We see the possible roots of such humiliation in the case of Fred, presented below. But note that the traumatic incident he describes involving both a form of assault and cross dressing was superimposed upon a preexisting pattern of fetishistic masturbation. This may be highly significant in understanding his reaction to what was, for him, a very distressing high school experience. This individual's fetishistic behavior has changed somewhat throughout the course of his life, yet the central theme remains the same. It is very important to note that this person did not "progress" from fetishism to transvestism despite the fact that he has long incorporated women's clothing into his fetishistic fantasies and behaviors.

The Case of Fred

Fred has been married to his first and only wife for 30 years and they have three children. He owns and operates a small automotive parts distribution business and has taken an active role in community affairs. He is 58 and in good health.

I felt turned on by girls' shoes and dresses since I was 5 and I used to try these clothes on about twice a month—that means I've been cross dressing more or less regularly for 50 years! I don't know why. I just like the moment when the feelings of femininity come over me. It's like all of a sudden I can experience the feelings that a woman has. I know I'm not a woman, but just the chance to dress up once a month lets me build all kinds of fantasies and mental trips which I really enjoy.

He has never been a very sexually active person, often abstaining entirely from marital sex over a period of many months: "Then, all of a sudden we'll both get the idea at the same time and we'll really enjoy having sex— but ordinarily, we don't even talk about sex, not even after we both read *The Joy of Sex*." He began masturbating at 14, always with a slip, a bra, or a pair of panties and this occurred regularly at the rate of about twice a month until he was married at the age of 25.

A frightening but very exciting event took place shortly after his fetishistic masturbation began:

A strange thing happened to me just before I entered high school. I'd seen this bunch of guys being initiated and it really scared me. They'd been stripped of their clothes, forced to put on dresses, and they made 'em go to school like that all day! The fear of it never left me—I never forgot that scene, although it never happened to me. I completely stopped cross dressing and masturbating for maybe 2 or 3 months, then when I tried it again I noticed it was even more exciting than before!

One of Fred's emotional outlets is his correspondence with other cross dressers. Nearly every day he uses his lunch-time to answer a letter or two, but it is unusual for him to meet these men.

I can't explain my desires about cross dressing but I guess it's got something to do with my early childhood. I grew up in a happy family and my mother and dad always told folks I was "all boy." I think for me, somehow, this cross dressing all became a humiliation trip of some kind, and what I try to do is to act very ladylike so that it won't be humiliating. But whatever else may happen, I'll be a closet TV and no more. I don't even think about passing in public.

Fetishistic Transvestism

Following the lead of Buhrich and McConaghy (1970, 1977b), we will distinguish between two main groups of heterosexual transvestites: fetishistic transvestites and marginal transvestites. Our goal here is to emphasize the differences between these groups, but there are major similarities as well as important differences. Each of these behavior patterns is believed to develop out of earlier fetishistic behaviors, growing more elaborate with years of practice. It is not entirely clear what determinants govern the formation of either pattern.

All of the major contributors to the study of transvestism are in general agreement with the criteria for transvestism given in the Diagnostic and Statistical Manual of Mental Disorders (DSM-III-R), (American Psychiatric Association, 1987), although this description is not fully satisfactory. In our view, the greatest deficiencies are in the inadequate treatment of changes in the behavior of transvestites with age and experience, and in the absence of recognition of fetishistic and marginal types of transvestism. The contributions of many researchers both support the DSM-III-R criteria and suggest possible limitations (Benjamin, 1966; Bentler, 1976; Bentler & Prince, 1970; Brierley, 1979; Buckner, 1970; Cauldwell, 1956; Croughan, Saghir, Cohen, & Robins, 1981; Ellis, 1936; Feinbloom, 1976; Freund et al.,1982; Gosselin & Wilson, 1980; Green & Money, 1969; Gutheil, 1954; Langevin, 1985a,b; Lukianowicz, 1959; Money, 1974; Ovesey & Person, 1973, 1976; Podolsky & Wade, 1960; Prince, 1976; Stoller, 1968a, 1971, 1974, 1985c; Talamini, 1982; Wise & Meyer, 1980).

In DSM-III-R, transvestism is designated as *fetishistic transvestism*. Using the DSM-III-R definition, this term encompasses both what we are calling fetishistic transvestism and marginal transvestism. This diagnosis is used when a heterosexual male experiences (over a period of six months) intense and recurrent sexually arousing fantasies and sexual urges associated with cross dressing, and when he has either acted upon these transvestic urges or is distressed by them. Transsexualism must be ruled out. We have noted that as general guidelines these criteria are on target, but they leave much unsaid. The diagnostic criteria fall considerably short of operationally defined variables, although some progress in that direction is being achieved (see especially, Blanchard, 1985a,b).

Concerning the DSM-III-R criteria for transvestism, we consider it imperative that the criteria for fetishism be exceeded as, for example, in expecting complete rather than partial cross dressing. Further, the cross-gender identity seen in these men is highly variable, both when cross dressed and otherwise, but given several years of experience, such cross-gender feelings are typically shown. It is predicted that if a cross-gender identity is experienced it is to be expected primarily, or according to some, exclusively (Freund et al., 1982), when the individual is cross dressed. Different intensities of motivation to cross dress are seen, both across individuals and within the life-career of each person. There is usually a progression over the years toward increased transvestic behavior as the opportunity to cross dress increases with retirement and greater privacy. Passing in public is highly valued. Additional observations concerning the behaviors we believe are most important in the assessment of the heterosexual transvestite are given later in this chapter. Several intensities of fetishistic transvestism remain to be sorted out.

Fetishistic transvestites constitute the subgroup of transvestites that has been most extensively described, at least in general terms, through observations of cross dressing club members (Brierley, 1979; Buhrich & McConaghy, 1976; Feinbloom, 1976; Langevin, 1985a; Prince, 1976; Talamini, 1982), through survey research (Bullough, Bullough & Smith, 1983; Gosselin & Wilson,1980; Prince & Bentler, 1972), and through case studies (Benjamin, 1966; Stoller, 1968a, 1974, 1985c). This group corresponds to what Benjamin called Type 2 and Type 3 transvestites. Buhrich and McConaghy (1977a,b) have termed this type the "nuclear transvestite" group. Most of these men marry, and they are usually said to be without major psychiatric or personality problems other than those directly related to the stress and strain of their cross dressing. The main behavioral characteristics of the fetishistic transvestite are these (Buhrich & McConaghy, 1977b):

- History of strong sexual arousal to cross dressing
- More strongly heterosexual in orientation than the marginal TV group
- Stronger personal adjustment history than the marginal group
- Less gender discordance than the marginal group
- Cross-gender identity is facilitated by cross dressing but is egosyntonic
- Seldom elect long-term hormonal usage for feminization
- Do not seek major cosmetic surgery or sexual reassignment
- Never lives full time as a woman
- With years of experience, "passing" in public becomes highly valued
- Cross dressing is periodic

Cases of Transvestism

The following cases exemplify the marked diversity of origin, development, and style of enactment of fetishistic transvestism, despite common features. For all cases we cite, names, ages, family data, occupations, locations and other identifying information have been changed. Care has been taken, however, not to delete or alter anything which would distort the case history. Information has been drawn from interviews, research materials, and correspondence.

John: A Fetishistic Transvestite

John is a 34-year-old caucasian male who was married for 6 years. He has an impressive occupational history and a wide circle of friends, most of whom have some interest in cross dressing or cross-gender activities. At the open house of his TV club he is impressive as "JoAnn" with his own hair fashionably styled. "I was born on Vancouver Island and my dad worked for a public utility company. Dad travelled frequently and was not highly involved with the family," he explained. John's first cross dressing was at age 6 when he put on his mother's underwear and "it just felt good." The rate of cross dressing was once or twice per week. At age 13 he discovered some boxes of his mother's clothing in the basement, tried some on, and experienced his first orgasm. Thereafter he cross dressed more frequently, usually masturbating. "It was relaxing and sensuous . . . I felt taken care of . . . pampered . . . like I was a different person." These weekly episodes often lasted two or three hours and they continued until he was about 17 when he moved into his own apartment. For the first time he began to purchase his own feminine wardrobe. "Throughout those years—in fact, until I was 23—this was all partial dressing. I had never had a complete outfit or a wig, and I had never gone out in public."

In high school he wasn't performing up to his academic potential but excelled as a member of the golf team. He didn't feel comfortable around girls, never felt part of the in-group, and generally disliked high school. Shortly after moving into his own apartment he concluded nearly every day with what became a cross dressing ritual and masturbation. It relaxed him and produced a "good feeling, a glow" that was a pleasant ending for the day. He began college without any clear occupational plans but seemed most interested in business and economics courses. Much changed when he met Lois, an attractive commercial artist, and she later moved into his apartment. At first, she knew nothing of the cross dressing; John had sealed his TV books and pictures in several carton boxes. But Lois discovered them and was confused about seeing pictures of John cross dressed. At first she thought he surely must be a homosexual, but knowing him very well, this didn't seem likely. When she asked him for an explanation he gave it to her as best he could, describing the whole story.

Lois never really appreciated the cross dressing scenes which meant so much to John, but she noticed that he was especially sexually aroused after pulling on some of JoAnn's clothes, so she decided to make the best of this peculiar situation. She began to be a little helpful, especially concerning the use of makeup. As a consequence, JoAnn began to emerge as a more passable "woman." They began to shop together. He commented: "Practically every day I was thinking about what I could do to have fun with JoAnn—buying new clothes, make up, wigs or shoes—thinking where I could go and what I could do." Throughout the years, from ages 6 to 27, his cross dressing was solitary; he had very little association with any other transvestites.

A few months later, however, after Lois departed, the most significant thing in John's cross dressing life occurred: He attended an 8-day convention of TVs at a resort location, and he met Beth, who was one of the instructors. "I fell in love with her right away," he said, "although when we first met I was dressed as JoAnn." Beth knew a lot about clothing and makeup and as their relationship developed she began a complete transformation of JoAnn from a somewhat fussy looking transvestite into a remarkably passable young lady. John's confidence grew. His dreams of doing more as JoAnn in public were finally being fulfilled. Beth and John were soon married. Often, John would hurry home, transform himself into JoAnn, and then show Beth the latest "look" when she arrived home from work. Beth was very supportive of JoAnn, for the most part, and throughout these years John's occupational success was soaring. However, after 3 years of marriage some conflicts began to surface. JoAnn felt strongly about spending two evenings a week at a gay bar which was a center for TVs and TSs and Beth enjoyed these outings as well. But for JoAnn, having Beth along destroyed the fantasy of being JoAnn—he felt like John in a dress. He asked her to stay home and she did, but this became one of several wedges which seemed to separate the closeness they had once enjoyed. They were divorced after 6 years of marriage, but not primarily because of cross dressing.

At 34, John has been in and out of several relationships with women, never feeling really committed to any of them. He still cross dresses and visits the bar twice a week. His sexual satisfaction has not been reduced by the divorce: "For a lot of TVs the dressing and masturbation is a lot more enjoyable than heterosexuality . . . you have only yourself to think about and you can do the whole thing exactly the way you want to." John sees JoAnn as a "playgirl without real-life worries . . . just enjoying the fun and pleasure . . . while John has to worry about relationships with people. But the biggest problem is that cross dressing has been the reason behind my breaking up all my relationships with people I've cared about. Girls want togetherness and I don't. Mostly, I want to go out as JoAnn."

Three years after providing this case history, John was married to a young lady he had known for many years. They had spent part of the preceding year developing ways of adapting both to the requirements of marriage and to John's desire to be JoAnn and attend his favorite cross dressing activities about twice a week.

Comments on the Case of John

This case is very typical of the predominantly or exclusively heterosexual fetishistic transvestite. He begins cross dressing a little earlier than most, at the age of 6, and shows the usual expansion and elaboration of transvestism before, during, and after adolescence. What is not brought out in the history is the erotic tension which existed between John and his mother. She is remembered as having fondled and stroked her son in a loving way but of withdrawing and becoming rejecting when her son let her know he experienced this as erotic. It is possible that her actions were part of an effort to compensate for the absence of a supportive husband. But whatever did occur in John's earliest years, it seems likely that a close bonding with the mother was not achieved.

Another important point is that in his several romantic relationships following his divorce he appeared to enter and then terminate these relationships when it became clear that he was loved and needed by a woman. Their dependency feelings were threatening to him. His behavior suggests difficulty in establishing and maintaining intimate relationships and in sustaining lasting commitments. External demands and the threat of controls from others are distressing to him. These are seen as forms of entrapment from which he must flee. Such fears, however, are not apparent thus far in his second marriage.

The facilitation of his cross dressing and his skillfulness in role-playing a woman also came about in ways which are often seen in transvestites. These behaviors require patient practice and rehearsal, in his case, in association with helpful women. These learning steps are based on social learning processes with much imitation and modeling. John has functioned very effectively as a businessman and seems largely successful in fitting his JoAnn role into carefully selected times and places. He states, however, that cross dressing is a "constant" background theme in his daily experience and that he has occasionally experienced persistent fantasies of living full time as a woman. This he has never attempted to do, even when excellent opportunities to do so were available. Such fantasies are very common in fetishistic transvestites, but few act upon them when given the chance.

Mark: A Fetishistic Transvestite with Some Marginal Type Behaviors

Mark is a 50-year-old caucasian male raised by his natural parents whom he describes as showing average warmth toward their three children. He has an older brother and a younger sister. Mark's father was the purchasing agent for a small manufacturing company. After growing up in a large southwestern city, Mark graduated from college with a B.A. in business administration. He has been married for 23 years. There are no children. His wife knows very little about his cross dressing although several years ago he attempted to discuss the topic with her. Here is his story in his own words:

My cross dressing began during grade school, at about age 12, and consisted mainly of experimenting with my older sister's lingerie (girdle, bra, nylons, and heels). This was done while no one was at home and happened at least twice a month and sometimes more. Let's say that I tried on her lingerie at every opportunity that presented itself. There was no makeup involved and each session involved a full-length mirror and much parading back and forth in front of this mirror. To this day, I still prefer a girdle or corset and would rather wear nylons versus panty hose. I do remember that in about the fourth grade a teacher was a single gal. One of the games I played was trying to look up her dress while she was giving individual instruction to the students seated ahead of me. One of the striking memories was her pink or white girdle with nylons attached. This too was done at every opportunity and was quite thrilling. Finally, I was caught in the act and was reprimanded. It was shortly after this that on a whim I first tried on my sister's girdle, bra, and nylons and experienced my first orgasm. I was 13.

A session usually lasted an hour and was always followed by masturbation, sometimes with a pillow between my legs as though I was really being made love to by another person. Through my senior year in high school, during college, and while I was in the service I didn't dress at any time. I really didn't know what transvestism was, but I had the feeling that something was wrong and should be suppressed. I saw my first drag show while in the service and found it very exciting. Also, I came across literature concerned with transvestism and found that I wasn't alone in secretly desiring to dress in women's clothing. Up to about the age of 25 I thought that I was strictly homosexual but very much interested in girls. I completely suppressed this desire to dress until I got my first apartment, alone. One day, while in a department store, I bought my first pair of nylons and could hardly wait to try them on.

What brought this about was the chance to experiment with the clothing in the privacy of my apartment. The thrill of shopping was almost as great as dressing and I could hardly wait to get home and to try the new things on. This need to dress just came about overwhelmingly when I knew I could dress in private and not be caught. I lived in a big city and by now was completely aware of other transvestites and also knew about drag shows. There wasn't a great amount of literature available at that time, but through conversation with other people in drag (mostly at the drag shows), I knew that I wanted to dress completely from head to toe as a woman. About this time in my life, at age 28, I met and married my wife. Everything pertaining to women's clothes or transvestism went out the window. The only remaining activity which I continued was to buy TV magazines and the *Female Impersonator News* which were becoming more available on newsstands. I was interested in both the organizations which were described and the personal ads which appeared in their magazines. About eight years ago, when I was 41, I started running an ad about myself. I also joined a TV club, began to meet other TVs, corresponded with TVs, and developed a more professional approach to my looks, my clothes and my feminine appearance.

My wife is more or less aware of at least some of my TV interests or activities because she has attended several drag shows and knows that I have a more than passing interest. As a matter of fact, two or three years into our married life, on the pretense of adding spice to our love life, I tried on her panty hose, panties, shaved my legs, and got her to buy me a sexy nightgown. It reached the point where I am sure she really knew I was interested in women's clothes. At this point she became a little disturbed by all this so I quit this and really began to dress completely as a woman. Wigs, makeup, jewelry, and so on. I'm sure she is aware of things, but not quite sure how much. Long fingernails and plucked eyebrows have raised a few questions. Dressing and masturbation have definitely had an effect upon our sex life. Each dressing session is followed by masturbation, and then by a small amount of guilt in that I am denying her some pleasure that should be enjoyed by both husband and wife. The pleasure of dressing is much greater and more thrilling than having intercourse. I would really prefer to be Maureen while making love to my wife. Some all-time peak experiences for me have been receiving mail for the first time as Maureen and being made love to by a man while dressed as Maureen. There was something special about being attractive enough to a man to have him pursue me as far as the bed. It was beautiful to be undressed and to manipulate him into having an orgasm.

I get a very pleasurable feeling anytime I am dressed and can answer the telephone, type, or act the part of a secretary. This is one fantasy that has become real. I love to correspond with other TVs while dressed. The first time I met with another TV and went shopping was extremely pleasurable. My own theory of why I do this goes back to the incident when I was peeking up the teacher's dress. The picture is still very vivid in my mind, with her legs encased in nylons, the garters, girdle, with or without panties, and her sexy heels. I think she knew what was going on and encouraged me to look up her dress. This was just before puberty and somehow this precipitated my first attempt at wearing women's clothes.

To dress now is almost a compulsion and does release tension and anxiety. I can hardly wait for the feel of breasts, the sway of my hips, the rustle and feel of a slip against my body, and the general good feeling of applying makeup and doing my nails. It feels so good to dress because I know I will finish with masturbation and a very intense orgasm. I don't think I've ever dressed by myself or with another when I haven't had an orgasm. It seems that all the preparation, the shopping, the dressing, is all rewarded by something that brings great pleasure. Another interesting happening is that after orgasm I can't wait to take off my feminine things and return to my normal male clothes. It leaves one with the feeling of having gotten away with something without being caught.

Comments on the Case of Mark/Maureen

As a teenager, Mark experienced his first orgasm while cross dressed. This is common in transvestites and provides support for a learning model to explain this behavior. He entered adolescence believing he was a homosexual which is also common in TVs. He doesn't say so, but such a self-image may contribute to restriction of dating and other teenage sexual-role learning experiences as noted by Buckner (1970). While predominantly heterosexual, Mark has experienced some incidental homosexual contacts in his role as Maureen.

There has been a positive correlation between his cross dressing and masturbation; this appears to have reduced his marital sexual activity. He clearly values his cross dressed sexual activity more highly than heterosexual contact. Again, this is often the story with transvestites. High value is accorded fetishistic scenes that provide variety and spice. Intense fantasy supports this source of pleasure-getting.

And so we see in Mark a typical history and development of fetishistic cross dressing with cross-gender identity restricted to the period when cross dressed. What we do not have is information to help clarify what variables contributed to cross dressing in the first place. Whatever they may have been, the resulting pattern of cross dressing has been a great source of pleasure, exhilaration and delight for Mark. It is clearly at the center of his erotic and pleasurable experience. An imaginary person—Maureen—has become one of his closest allies. To the extent that a cross-gender identity comes forth with cross dressing, it is an ego-syntonic component of personality.

Marginal Transvestism

Benjamin (1966) described what he called a latent transsexual type of transvestite having much in common with the marginal transvestite of Buhrich and McConaghy (1977b). He saw these men as nonfetishistic and as often manifesting a long-standing gender dysphoria. But Benjamin believed a sharp distinction between the fetishistic transvestite and what we now shall call the marginal type is not always possible. Just as we shall urge that transvestism be viewed as a multistage, progressive phenomena, Benjamin also believed that a long-standing gender dysphoria is at the root of changing patterns of transvestism. Buhrich & McConaghy (1977b), through long-term observation of a transvestite sample in New Zealand have extended and clarified the earlier impressions of Benjamin and we shall use their term, "marginal transvestite," to designate the TVs with these attributes:

- History of sexual arousal to cross dressing
- Weaker heterosexual orientation than in the fetishistic group
- Possible bisexual or homosexual preference
- Persistent feelings of gender dysphoria
- Seeks and achieves hormonal therapy for feminization
- Seeks information concerning possible transsexual steps
- Experiments with transgender living but is not a transgenderist
- Seeks transsexuals as role models, mentors, or tutors
- Values marriage less than the fetishistic group but more than the transgenderist
- Cross dressing is periodic

Summary of Fetishistic and Marginal Transvestism

We shall attempt to spell out more completely what we believe is most important as defining attributes of fetishistic and marginal transvesitism. By listing these summary points, it is hoped we may further clarify both the similarities and differences we have with the DSM-III-R criteria:

1. Periodic cross dressing is always linked to a history of sexual arousal although this may give way to less fetishistic cross dressing after several years. This point has been made by Prince (1976), by Stoller (1968a), and many others. In the later years of cross dressing, social gratifications while in the feminine role may become highly important sources of reinforcement, together with intense nonerotic pleasure and feelings of exhilaration.

2. Cross dressing in heterosexual transvestites who have had several years of experience is almost always ego-syntonic. There is no request for psychiatric or counseling assistance except in response to life crises, and if this occurs at all, it will usually be during the earlier years of cross dressing. Such crises usually involve strong feelings of aversion for cross dressing as perceived by a wife or other significant other. Less commonly, problems may be secondary to actual or threatened employment difficulties brought on by cross dressing (as in steps to terminate a security clearance or dismissal from employment).

3. When cross dressing is associated with masturbation, orgasm greatly reduces or eliminates the immediate motive to remain cross dressed. There is a brief period of strong resurgence of the masculine self and a disinterest in the feminine.

4. Whether cross dressed or not, the transvestite reports that he maintains an accurate self-perception of his masculine self and sustains his primary identity. However, when cross dressed he typically reports feeling much more feminine. The meanings of such causal attributions have often been assumed to be gender-related, but many other possible meanings and combinations of meanings are possible. Intense feelings of gender dysphoria are not reported although joyful longings of becoming a woman are common daydreams and fantasies. There is nothing "dysphoric" about such imagery and rumination. It is these feminine feelings—however ill-defined in behavior—that are key indicators of the cross-gender identity of transvestites.

5. Progression to living full time as a woman is rare. No definitive statistics are available, but it is our impression that fewer than 5% of transvestites who meet the DSM-III-R criteria for fetishistic transvestism ever live in a transgender or transsexual mode.

6. A predominantly heterosexual orientation is imperative, by

definition, but in fact, there are definitely fetishistic transvestites who are strongly bisexual. It is important to comment on the nearly universal fantasy of the heterosexual transvestite which deals with seduction of the "female" (the transvestite) by a male. Such fantasies, or even the enactment of sexual activity with a male by a transvestite while in the feminine gender role, appear to incorporate stimuli (primarily clothing) which the respective partners interpret as heterosexual signals. We have never met a transvestite who described such a sexual encounter as homosexual. The matter awaits clarification.

7. There is a strong desire to wear all or some transvestic accoutrements in connection with heterosexual encounters. Most transvestites are reported to have done so (Croughan *et al.*, 1981) but it is also true than a high percentage of wives resist or dislike this. Although data are lacking, we believe that when heterosexual relationships do not allow some cross dressing, the probability of "dating" men and subsequent sexual activities with male partners may be increased.

8. It is common to seek beard reduction through electrolysis, but cosmetic surgery is rare. Body feminization through female hormones is also rare although many fetishistic as well as marginal transvestites experiment for a short time with such hormones.

9. The amount of fetishism and the frequency of orgasm associated with cross dressing is highly variable both across individuals and across the life span of transvestites.

10. Frequency and duration of cross dressing sessions tend to increase with age providing there is increased opportunity to cross dress.

Transgenderism

In our view, transgenderism is a behavior pattern, an elaboration, very closely associated with the marginal transvestism group. The category is useful to distinguish between different patterns of cross dressing, and presumably, different intensities of cross-gender identity which may underlie such conduct.

The term *transgenderism* does not appear as a diagnosis in DSM-III-R but it has been recognized as a category intermediate between transvestism and transsexualism for many years. Prince (1976) created the term while publishing *Transvestia* magazine (Prince, 1980), but our use of the word differs from hers. We define transgenderism as full-time living in the cross-gender role in the absence of sexual reassignment surgery, with oscillation, however rare, back and forth from one gender role to the other. Without such oscillations, the full-time cross-gender living would qualify in our definition as transsexual behavior. Sexual orientation may be heterosexual, bisexual, or homosexual. These individuals may represent cases in transition toward secondary transsexualism. However, full-time living in the cross-gender role as part of an extended real-life test preliminary to possible sex-reassignment surgery should not be described as transgenderism. We prefer the term, *preoperative transsexual*, simply to indicate that reassignment procedures are anticipated. Time spent in each gender role is highly variable across cases. The transgenderist usually seeks female hormone prescriptions and such cosmetic and dental treatments as may be considered helpful. This category has major similarities and some important differences to Benjamin's Type 4, or nonsurgical transsexual (1966). Marked individual differences in life-style are seen among transgenderists. We know of individuals who reverse gender roles daily, working as men and functioning entirely in a feminine gender role each evening and usually on weekends. For others, the duration of time in each role is measured by weeks or months, and less commonly, some function in a cross-gender role for years with very rare reversion back to the male role.

Everett: A Transgenderist

Everett is 22 and has never been married. His feminine name is Angela. The youngest of five children, he was raised with his four older sisters by his natural parents whom he described as supportive and close. For the past year he has been working at the order desk of a small company. Cross dressing began at age 6 at the rate of once weekly. He described this as " . . . a period of getting used to it . . . practicing with makeup, bras, panties. . . ." There was a marked increase in cross dressing from age 11 to 14 with a weekly rate of from two to five times; each session included masturbation. He was then discovered cross dressed by one of his sisters: "I was so embarassed that I didn't dress again until I was 18." He then "rediscovered cross dressing." During his teenage years he considered himself to be bisexual "although I had never been to bed with a man. I got tired of being bisexual . . . discovered men . . . joined a group of TVs and TSs . . . and went gay." He was by then cross dressing from 15 to 25 times monthly, usually followed by sexual activity. There is a long history of feminine identification but without full rejection of his masculine identity: "I was always, from the earliest childhood, disappointed that I had had the bad fortune of being a man, so I resolved to do as much as possible to correct that. I found that by wearing women's clothes and attempting to be as feminine as possible, I could do it." Continuing, he noted: "After puberty, I discovered the pleasures of making love to men as a woman, but the basics haven't changed."

He perceives himself as being able to set his masculine identity aside and of even having two different styles of handwriting, one masculine and the other feminine. A typical cross dressing session includes such activities as attending his TV-TS club meeting or going to a gay bar and finding someone to go home with for the night. In a series of letters Angela describes his/her behavior as follows:

> First off, let me reiterate that I have not had a heterosexual relationship or experience with a woman in over 2 years. During this same time I have had many male lovers. My current lover is a preoperative transsexual. So, I guess, in a practical sense, I am gay. However, my desires experience phases or swings which I cannot control. My usual pattern has been to go through 3 to 6 months of exclusively homosexual desires, then 2 or 3 months of exclusively heterosexual desires during which I abstain from sex or have unsatisfactory homosexual encounters. I feel weird actually having sex with women. Then I go through 2 or 3 months of bisexual desires again, then it begins repeating. I am apparently in the bisexual phase heading toward heterosexual. Isn't this weird?
>
> When I cross dress my real name disappears and Angela is all that's left. Therefore . . . I see myself as a woman and not as a man "in drag." Obviously, it's hard to remain in that mood when naked with a lover, but I sometimes do. It depends on the guy. If he can accept and respect Angela, I remain as Angela. If not, my male persona may again take over. From my experience with my many TV friends I know that exclusively heterosexual TVs generally never actually "feel" like women—or if they do, they often consider their femme persona to be lesbian, and they usually have no, or very limited, transsexual leanings. As I began to identify more with Angela as I grew older, and less with Everett, I began to feel more and more uncomfortable with "lesbianism" and decided to concentrate more on lovers who could satisfy Angela. Up until I was about 14 I identified exclusively with my Angela portion. Then, when I was discovered at 14, I consciously changed and tried to be as much Everett as possible with no Angela. It obviously didn't work. At about 18 I again began cross dressing, and at 21 I began experiencing "homosexual" relationships. So you see, it's not that Everett invented Angela, but that Angela was forced to invent Everett for protective reasons. I plan to begin hormone treatments soon, but still continue working as Everett while living more and more as Angela. When I can pass better I will begin working as Angela. Except for my periodic mood swings I would say that everything is proceeding according to plan.

Comments on the Case of Everett

This young man now has well-organized homosexual preferences but his history has been bisexual. He is also much younger than most of the heterosexual TVs in our study. His goals of living full time as a woman and of obtaining sexual-reassignment surgery are distinctly different from those of the transvestite. This pattern of transvestism-in-process-to-transsexualism has been described by several researchers and is believed typical of the pretranssexual for whom a transvestic stage is simply one of the steps in a transsexual process (Buhrich & McConaghy, 1977b; Wise & Meyer, 1980). It is of importance to note the virtual absence of self-described feelings of gender dysphoria; such feelings, if they exist at all, can only be inferred from his behavior and his stated transsexual goals. It is by no means certain that such feelings actually exist. This is an example of how the construct of gender dysphoria can be applied as a causal attribution without actual behavioral evidence that such dysphoria is experienced. His behavior and changing sense of self are consistent with the impression of a secondary transsexualism process. It is not possible to say with confidence whether this is of the transvestite type or the homosexual type, as components of each pattern seem present in the history.

We have considered four behavior patterns of cross dressing: fetishism, fetishistic transvestism, marginal transvestism, and transgenderism. Before proceeding to consider several other categories it may be helpful to examine Figure 1, which presents a schematic arrangement of all nine behavior patterns comprising the spectrum of cross dressing. The arrows in Figure 1 are intended to suggest likely changing patterns of behavior and the direction of change. Importantly, such changes are not shown by all persons in any given category. For example, the upper half of Figure 1 suggests that from the population of fetishists arise fetishistic TVs, marginal TVs, and transgenderists. Secondary transsexuals (TV type) are seen as coming out of the transgenderist group. The upper half of Figure 1 is also intended to show various intensities of heterosexual or bisexual preference, with exclusive heterosexuality at the top. The lower half is intended to show various intensities of homosexual preference with exclusive homosexuality (Primary Transsexualism) at the bottom.

Primary and Secondary Transsexualism

Primary Transsexualism

This category describes individuals who have presented a lifelong history of gender dysphoria, a history of cross-gender identity, and an absence of fetishism associated with cross dressing. It is imperative that early childhood roots of major gender discontent are revealed. Sexual preference is usually homosexual from an early age. There usually will have been a history of cross dressing. The critical component that sets this category apart from all others is the necessary history of lifelong

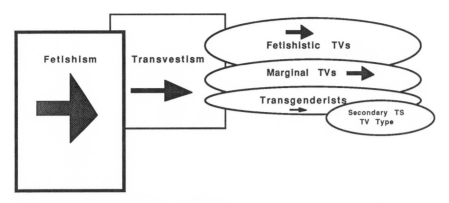

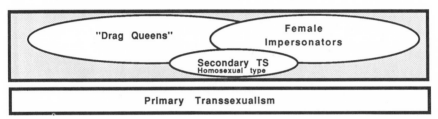

Figure 1. Schematic representation of heterosexual and homosexual variations of cross dressing behavior. From a population of heterosexual fetishists there emerge much smaller groups of fetishistic and marginal transvestites. Some marginal transvestites become transgenderists. A very few transgenderists "progress" to secondary transsexualism (TV type). Among the homosexual variations, many secondary transsexuals (homosexual type) are believed to have functioned previously as drag queens or female impersonators. The pattern of primary transsexualism is believed to be founded on cross-gender identity and gender dysphoric feelings rooted in the earliest years of childhood.

gender dysphoric feelings. Stoller (1985c) considers the term transsexualism as little more than a "wastebasket" category. For him, the male primary transsexual (whatever he may be called) is an extremely feminine male who has never functioned in typically masculine roles and who has a feminine "core gender identity," possibly due to fetal feminization of the brain.

Transsexualism has been said to be the only major surgical procedure carried out in response to the unremitting demands of the patient. While this may not be entirely correct, it is true that the currently accepted definition of transsexualism rests, quite insecurely, upon the reported subjective feelings, beliefs, and self-perceptions of the person involved. In adults, the key diagnostic criteria for transsexualism given in DSM-III-R are these: A profound unhappiness with one's anatomic sex, and a preoccupation (for at least 2 years) concerning the changing of primary and secondary sex characteristics (American Psychiatric Association, 1987). The intense gender dysphoria must not be merely an expression of situational stress.

Stoller (1985c) has commented that these are loosely stated criteria which need to be reduced to operationally-defined terms. We agree, and we also need a complete set of criteria for secondary transsexualism, which is not included in DSM-III-R. All forms of transsexualism are heterogeneous with many differences observed in the course of development, motivation for sexual reassignment, daily style of living, personal adjustment, and accompanying symptoms of personality or behavioral difficulty. The demand to live in the gender opposite to one's anatomic sex is the essence of transsexualism. The idea that such motivation is unremitting and irreversible has come to be one of the myths of transsexualism. In clinical settings serving so-called transsexuals, it is common to see such individuals change their minds and their behavior. The attitudes and values communicated in such settings, together with role models and mentor relationships, probably play a critical part in such decision-making.

From psychological and psychiatric perspectives, there is extensive agreement on the general features of primary transsexualism (Bentler, 1976; Freund *et al.*, 1982; Green & Money, 1969; Koranyi, 1980; Pauly, 1969; Person & Ovesey, 1974a; Steiner, 1985a; Stoller, 1968a, 1974, 1985c). Primary transsexualism occurs in both men and women, possibly in equal numbers, although these statistics leave much to be desired. It is estimated that there are between 6,000 and 10,000 postoperative transsexuals (combining both the primary and secondary variations) in the United States, but precise numbers are not available. It is not known how many individuals may be living in a full-time cross-gender role who do not seek sex-reassignment surgery, but we believe the number is far greater than the surgically reassigned group. The nonoperative group remains relatively silent and invisible to mental health services and to gender identity clinics, hence it has never been adequately studied or described. These "uncounted" transsexuals often live on the fringes of the gay community and the ones we have interviewed differ from traditionally defined primary transsexuals only in the absence of their desire for reassignment surgery. This is obviously a major difference because the DSM-III-R criteria are built around gender dysphoric feelings and the quest for surgical reassignment.

The causes of primary transsexualism remain unclear. An extensive discussion of theories of causation from several perspectives has been provided by Steiner and her associates (1985a) at the University of

Toronto, and by Blanchard, Clemmensen, and Steiner (1987). One thing that has become clear is that there are both heterosexual and homosexual transsexuals—using these terms relative to chromosomal sex. Blanchard (1985a,b) notes that, although the question of the number of types of transsexuals has not yet been settled, there is strong evidence pointing toward these two groupings. Using questionnaires to measure erotic attraction, he studied 163 male-to-female transsexuals who had been divided into four groups: heterosexuals, homosexuals, bisexuals, and asexuals. He found that the bisexual and asexual groups are best classified as subtypes within the heterosexual grouping; hence, the two major categories—heterosexual TSs and homosexual TSs—appear to be clearly identified. The clinical significance of this is not clear, as Blanchard notes, because so-called secondary transsexuals (who may be either homosexual in type or heterosexual in type) and so-called primary transsexuals all seem to benefit at least to some degree from sexual-reassignment surgery (Bentler, 1976; Laub & Fisk, 1974). Although case histories vary greatly, the critical factor in primary transsexualism is the necessity of very early self-awareness of a desire for gender change, a feeling of not "being in the right body," and actual behavior which is more appropriate for the opposite gender. What follows is a case which meets most of the these criteria.

Janice: A Primary Transsexual

Born in Texas oil country, Janice was raised almost entirely by his physically abusive mother. His father had divorced when Janice was three. "By the time I was 7 I realized I wanted to be a girl and I tried to pull my penis off . . . my mother kept telling me to straighten up and be a man." There was no cross dressing during these early years. He experienced strong feelings of wanting to be a girl and prayed for this change. During adolescence he alternated between feeling certain that such a change was his proper destiny and the certainty that he must function as a man. "I had these romantic little girl fantasies. I dreamed of the clothes I'd get, and I wondered what it would be like to be kissed by some of the men I idolized. But I seldom cross dressed because I was disgusted by seeing a man in the mirror dressed as a girl."

"My main interest then was in motorcycles and I drove trucks in the oil fields. When I was 17 I joined the Navy, and this gave me a lot of time for introspection. At about 19, I saw Canary Conn (a transsexual) on television and I came to idolize her. She's responsible for me being a TS today as much as anybody . . . so I wrote away for tapes about TS from *Psychology Today*. I began to collect books and to study about transsexualism. . . ." By the time he was 20 he had been promoted to a very high security job, but he was also tired of Navy life and was discharged after revealing his transsexual longings to medical personnel. He returned to the oil fields where he had worked as a youngster. This was to be a heterosexual period during which he dated women exclusively. As happy as he had ever been, he married at 21 and attended college, earning high grades. Soon thereafter, he and his wife moved to California where, he states, " . . . I was just bursting with transsexual feelings and I started the transition to living as a female." Soon the marriage had broken up. He describes a growing "romantic feeling" associated with being in the full-time role of a woman. His main difficulty was that he had little money. He had saved $1500 by the time he was 24, and with the help of a friend he was able to raise a total of about $6500 for reassignment surgery. "There is a beautiful, romantic and wish-fulfilling quality to it. Maybe that feeling wouldn't be so strong if it were not forbidden and so expensive. It's very hard to achieve this for a poor person."

Following the surgery, Janice returned to the same office job she had previously held. She felt elated and happier than ever before. "Surgery of this kind is not healing, but it facilitates adjustment—you can be happier with your own body—but personality change requires additional work." Janice continued her college studies and is accepted by students and faculty as a woman. Living with three girls in the rented house has not raised problems or suspicions. She has greatly enjoyed dating and her sexual relations with boyfriends. A careful observer, Janice commented on the TV/TS scene in this way: "TSs tend to look down on TVs—they see them as all screwed up—but most TSs have major personality disorders as well! I've seen a lot of severe introversion in TSs . . . they can't let themselves open up . . . ."

Comments on the Case of Janice

This may be an example of primary transsexualism with a long history of intense envy of women and a desire to be a woman, but there are some contradictions. For example, Janice seems to have functioned satisfactorily in several vocational roles often held by men, and for a short time she was married. As frequently observed, there is a history of disliking the male genitalia. However, Janice experienced a pubertal period of strong strivings to function as a macho male. Marriage, however unstable, is not unusual in TSs and may be part of an effort to establish a more conventional life style. There is no history of fetishistic cross dressing in this case, and this is consistent with primary transsexualism. Janice may have been a victim of unstable and rejecting parents and of complete abandonment by the father. The physical abuse delivered by her mother might have added to feelings of basic insecurity and to the mobilization of separation anxiety. The separation anxiety theory of gender dysphoria is highly regarded by many theorists (Person and Ovesey, 1974a,b) and we will consider it later.

Secondary Transsexualism (Transvestite Variation)

Two patterns of secondary transsexualism have been identified (Person & Ovesey, 1974b). One is based on a career as a transvestite and the other is based on a prior career as a homosexual. It is because of these preceding career life styles which may be considered primary that the subsequent change to transsexualism is called secondary. It is essential that one of these preceding patterns of behavior be identified and that there be an absence of long-standing gender dysphoria. Several researchers have identified progression through a career as a transvestite culminating in application for reassignment surgery (Lothstein, 1979; Meyer, 1974; Newman & Stoller, 1973; Prince, 1978; Stoller, 1968a, 1974, 1985c; Wise & Meyer, 1980), and similar long-term development was noted earlier by Benjamin (1966). It is generally believed these men function adequately as transvestites or homosexuals until, in their later years, some life stressor or change destabilizes them. They then insist that transsexual change is imperative to continue their lives. The main characteristics of the secondary transsexual (transvestite type) appear to be:

- History of some sexual arousal to cross dressing
- Progressively stronger history of gender dysphoria which may be stress related
- Less ego integration than in transvestites
- Seeks sexual-reassignment surgery after career as transvestite
- Absence of lifelong gender dysphoria
- Lives full time in cross-gender role, with or without sexual reassignment
- Strong features of narcissistic or borderline personality

Albert/Agatha: A Secondary Transsexual (Transvestite Type)

Albert is in his late fifties and has earned national recognition as a department head in a large company. Raised mainly by his mother with his father returning to the family on weekends, he is the second born of three sons. In his early years he was very close to his mother but in later childhood he grew emotionally distant from her while becoming far closer to his father. He began school as the only male youngster in an all-girl school and was much distressed 2 years later when he was required to transfer to a coed school. Before the age of 5 he had experienced much cross dressing but this was not carried on from about age 5 to age 12. As an adolescent he again cross dressed and began to have fantasies in which he was a girl having sex with a man. He was married in his early twenties and attempted to stop all cross dressing, partially because of his fear that this was a homosexual act. At 29, a family tragedy, and the anxieties and distress associated with this, seemed to lead him back toward spending hours cross dressed, but never in the presence of his wife. She knew nothing of this. He rented an apartment where his women's clothing was kept, joined a TV club, and became highly successful in his professional work. But his marriage was far from happy and when he told his wife of his cross dressing, at about age 41, she reacted by demanding that he give this up entirely and exclude all such activity from his life. Valuing his marriage and his four children, he attempted to do this for 8 rather stormy and unhappy years, and was then divorced.

With unlimited privacy after work, Albert cross dressed "almost daily" and has since felt increasingly that he will ultimately seek sex reassignment. For several years he has taken female hormones under the supervision of a physician, sought psychotherapy, and begun preparations for full time living as a woman. After careful planning, he sought extensive dental and facial surgery in preparation for his transition into the female role. He began doing so immediately upon becoming eligible for retirement. The following narrative was written about 5 months before his retirement. He has since then lived full time as Agatha.

> Living full time as a woman is more important than ever to me because I must find myself . . . I've always been playing a role . . . I've had to be two individuals and I don't want to have to play a role ever again." He expresses a feeling of "high internal ambivalence" while "forced" to live in the masculine role. But the delightful expectation of living full time as Agatha is seen as much more than an experiment: "I'll give it a try for 6 months or so, and if I like it I'll continue—if not, nothing has been lost."

When asked to reflect upon his reasons for wanting to make a gender change he offered the following:

> In my very early childhood—at age 3 or 4 perhaps—I noticed that I felt much like a girl. I can still recall the feeling of being like the girl next to me when I lay on the bed at home, sleeping or resting. But no erotic or sexual feelings were ever associated with cross dressing during my preadolescent years. Taking a few items of clothing and putting them on was just a way of feeling good—of feeling more natural. A boy showed me how to masturbate. I wasn't interested but learned from him what this was about. I never used feminine clothing as fetishes and these were never associated with orgasm or masturbation. I met a girl when I was about 13—her name was Agatha. She was a very beautiful girl and she was all that I wanted to be. I couldn't bring myself to talk to her as I was too shy and I didn't know what to say, but she fascinated me. I wanted to *be* Agatha! During the summers, I spent time at the home of a relative, and there were times when I could dress in her clothes. Then I'd masturbate and my fantasy was that a boy was making love to a girl and that the girl was me. My cross dressing has always been a matter of my becoming a girl even if just for a short time. It was never primarily a way to become sexually excited. At present, when I am dressed as Agatha I am able to be my real self, to put aside the male self who has always felt

conflict and discomfort. I can express my authentic, genuine, real self which is that of being a woman. It is natural for me to do this. I am much more comfortable, much happier, and without conflict and tension than I've ever felt as a man.

When I do begin living full time as Agatha, in about 6 months, I'll obtain considerable facial surgery and dental assistance, but no transsexual surgery—not at that time. If my children need me as a man, say, at a wedding or a funeral, or some other family event, I have told them that I will return as their father. But except for that, I plan to be the woman that I have always felt I should be and to make no compromises or excuses to anyone! In the community where I shall live as Agatha, I expect to become known as the 'resident TS'. I won't be trying to pass—just to live as Agatha, the person who I am. Throughout my career, I've always felt like I was up there, high on a trapeze, but I had to keep going on with the act or fall. Now I feel that I've made a decision not to struggle or play a false role. I'll be giving up relationships, my job and all that they have meant to me, but I don't care! I feel I'm moving toward peace and rest and not having to struggle to maintain a level of achievement." Agatha did carry out this plan much as stated above. At the end of the first 6 months as a full-time woman, Agatha reported that all was going even more pleasantly than anticipated.

Comments on the Case of Agatha

Despite Agatha's insistence that she always felt she should have been a girl, Albert's actual history is much different from the profile of the primary transsexual. There was extensive and apparently satisfying functioning as a husband and father, and the marriage was highly valued before it collapsed. From the account, it is clear that much cross dressing with fetishism and masturbation occurred during adolescence. He was highly successful in several typically masculine roles.

The fantasies he describes of female role taking are very common in heterosexual transvestites, and his sexual orientation has been totally heterosexual. All of these characteristics are in harmony with the pattern of secondary transsexualism, not the primary TS pattern. Because some secondary transsexuals are thought to become disenchanted with female role-playing, it remains to be seen if this will be true for Agatha. At present, this is not the case.

Secondary Transsexualism (Homosexual Type)

Less is known about this subgroup than the above categories. The essential diagnostic criteria hinge on a history as a homosexual but without cross dressing, and an absence of long-standing gender dysphoria. As described above, this variation is also believed to be a stress-related response. In fact, however, so little is clearly established at this time concerning this syndrome that we must consider the following description as tentative. The secondary transsexual (homosexual type) is described as follows:

- History of predominantly homosexual erotic preference
- Absence of lifelong gender dysphoria
- Seeks sexual reassignment surgery following stress or major life change
- Lives full-time in cross gender role, with or without sexual reassignment
- No history of fetishistic cross dressing, but other cross dressing may have occurred (e.g., female impersonation on stage; male prostitution)
- Strong features of narcissistic or borderline personality attributes

Summary of Major Attributes of Secondary Transsexualism

The gender dysphoria hypothesis has been highly influential as an explanation of primary transsexualism, and it is frequently invoked as a causal factor in secondary transsexualism as well. But no matter how powerful or appealing this construct may be, it is both elusive and intangible. Confounding the problem of assessing gender dysphoria is the fact that transsexual applicants are typically very much aware of the gender dysphoria thesis and seize upon this as a causal attribution to explain their own behavior (Blanchard et al., 1987). Their proclamations, if accepted at face value without external validation, may constitute key misleading statements in the gender history. It is obvious that the clinician as well as the researcher must be sensitive to this potential distortion. To summarize:

1. In heterosexuals and bisexuals, the basic cause of secondary transsexualism may be based upon an ever-strengthening sexual script founded on a history of fetishistic cross dressing. Hence, cognitive systems mobilize and "drive" this behavior. But as this script evolves, there is a major change from the fetishistic beginning stage. We shall argue in Chapter 8 that it is the management of the developing cross-gender identity which is critical to the transsexual outcome of what began as marginal transvestism.

2. In both the transvestic and homosexual types of secondary transsexualism, there is a strong desire to unload male identity, thereby achieving a sense of identity relief, and to reorganize the sense of self. Such thinking is tinged with magical and instant solutions to reality-based problems. Sex reassignment comes to symbolize rebirth, renewal, and new opportunities. There are exaggerations and unrealistic expecta-

tions concerning the passive-receptive aspects of female role taking in contrast to the uncomfortable demands of male role taking.

3. There is a strong quest for greater security and anxiety management that is assumed, by the future secondary transsexual, to be more available to women. Through cross dressing and adoption of the woman's role, there is the experience of role-relief and reduced anxiety. In place of the earlier fetishism, this behavior becomes a stress management tactic. This is highly reinforcing. Hence, cross dressing and cross-gender living become resistant to extinction.

4. For unknown reasons, cross dressing and female role playing generate intense feelings of pleasure and delight unmatched by other sources of satisfaction. They come to occupy a uniquely powerful and persistent set of expectations.

5. There is a gradual "erosion" of masculine identity, perhaps a weakening of the self-system, as cross-gender behavior is rehearsed and reinforced for many years. This process of self-destruction of the masculine identity is especially worthy of more intensive study. A parallel growth of cross-gender identity occurs.

6. Gender reversals, even for short intervals, are associated with a sense of rebirth, self-renewal, positive change, newness, and increased joy in living.

7. Male gender-role taking is associated with decreasing satisfaction and declining sexual pleasure.

8. The sexual script involving gender change is elaborated and refined, always changing in the direction of how superior it would be to live as a woman, to actually *be* a woman. Although not delusional, this thinking involves great simplifications, misjudgments, and masking of real-life difficulties. Reality testing is diminished where cross-gender identity is concerned.

9. Intense anxiety and conflict is associated with continued functioning in the male role. This may be exacerbated, in the transvestite type, by rejection by a wife who can no longer tolerate a husband who wants to be a woman. With a life in partial disarray, the attraction of sexual reassignment takes on even greater meaning as a kind of cure-all.

10. The insistence upon gender transformation is believed to be transient in the secondary transsexual with stress factors playing a part in the timing of the gender-change demands. It is said that when a 2-year test period of living in the opposite gender role is required, as called for in the standards of the Harry Benjamin International Gender Dysphoria Association (1985), many of these men will abandon their belief that such a change is imperative (Steiner, 1985b).

The nationally publicized case of René Richards, who became a transsexual after achieving distinction as an eye surgeon and a tennis champion, has been reported in autobiographic form (Richards & Ames,1983). Richards describes a history of fetishistic cross dressing and of strongly ambivalent feelings about having a sex-reassignment operation which was ultimately carried out. Applying the criteria discussed here, this case would fall within the boundaries of secondary transsexualism.

For the case of a distinguished scholar who underwent transsexual surgery at the age of 56, see Latham and Grenadier (1982). In another case, a former Navy commander and successful business entrepreneur, who was happily married until widowed when he was 61, became the oldest example of surgical reassignment; he was 74 (Docter, 1985). Both of these cases seem to have been secondary transsexuals. Postoperatively, each described herself as entirely satisfied with the decision to undergo reassignment surgery. Although gender professionals have generally proclaimed that the prognosis for the reassigned secondary transsexual is worse than for the primary transsexual, we know only of anecdotal case reports to back up this belief and there appear to be many cases of secondary transsexualism without subsequent regret. The test of living in the opposite gender for an extended period of time is widely accepted as the only useful screening procedure. It would appear very unwise to facilitate major surgical intervention without the completion of such a test which, we believe, should extend for at least 2 years. One of the key findings of such a test would be the capacity to function occupationally and interpersonally in the new gender role.

Drag Queens and Female Impersonators

Drag Queens

The term "drag queen" is a slang designation for cross dressed males who function as prostitutes. The term is used very loosely, and is frequently applied, by police for example, as indicative of any cross dressed male. There is much variation in the extent to which actual impersonation of a female is attempted or accomplished by cross dressed male prostitutes. Many of these men have transsexual interests but lack both the resources and the motivation to proceed with transsexual reassignment. A valuable fieldwork report of this transsexually inclined group has been provided by Driscoll (1960) who lived among these working prostitutes in San Francisco for several weeks and obtained in-depth histories. A similar group has been described by Cohen (1980) who identified about 100 male, cross dressed prostitutes in New York City. The men in Cohen's group presented a very flashy appear-

ance and operated on the less desirable fringe area of female prostitution. Eighty-three percent were black and most had obtained breast
implants or used female hormones.

A slightly different subgroup, sometimes called "she-males," is distinguished by flamboyant feminine attire, makeup and hairstyling,
while signalling an unmistakable male body beneath the costume. The
usual motivation is solicitation of prostitution with men. The unusual
and dramatic appearance which is presented is said to serve as helpful
advertising to potential dates and also to serve as a way to feel more
attractive. Although so-called drag queens and she-males are observable
in many larger cities as part of the prostitution scene, they have not been
systematically studied other than as a part of that social network. While
many of these men use female hormones or seek body feminization
through surgery, especially breast enhancement, few appear to become
candidates for full transsexual surgery.

So-called drag queens are a street-oriented and far more socially
deviant group of cross dressers compared to the heterosexual transvestite club members who have been subjects in the studies we will
report in Chapter 6. Among the dozen or so drag queens we have
interviewed it is very common to find serious drug dependency and
strong indications of narcissistic and borderline personality features.
Vice police in the Los Angeles area frequently look upon the drag
queens or she-males as dangerous, not primarily because of prostitution
activities, but because of their knowledge that some of these people do
engage in robbery, assault, and even murder. From a factual standpoint,
it is not clear to what extent this group is dangerous or whether it is any
more dangerous than other nonconforming individuals who are affiliated with the prostitution subculture. So far as gender deviance is concerned, there may be as much mythology among vice officers as there is
among psychologists and psychiatrists.

Female Impersonators

Newton (1972) developed rapport with a small number of female
impersonators who were followed over a period of months. She described them as a stigmatized subgroup within the homosexual community. They varied considerably in terms of personal adjustment, personality, and interpersonal relationships. Newton approaches this topic
from the perspective of sociology and social anthropology, examining
group memberships, roles, status, and intergroup tensions. It would
appear these men are the subject of much misinformation and little is
known about them based on adequate sampling. Roger Baker (1968) has

provided a history of female impersonation on the (British) stage, but this tells us nothing of the personalities of the men involved.

From our own experience based on interviews with 10 female impersonators, the only summary we can offer is that these individuals were invariably homosexual, nearly all had enjoyed cross dressing for many years, some lived full time as women although this is not typical, and transsexual reassignment was not an objective in any of this sample. For these 10, cross dressing was clearly more than a way to earn a living on the periphery of show business. Most of them said they felt more comfortable when in the feminine role, and often they elected to adopt this role long after their impersonations shows had ended. Within the female impersonator group there is much variation in personal adjustment and maladaptive behavior. Some consistently avoid lawbreaking while others have a considerable history of involvements with drugs, stealing, prostitution, and other sociopathic conduct.

Outcomes of Transvestite and Transsexual Careers

As Brierley (1979) has noted in his review of variations of transvestism, each of the diagnostic categories or patterns of behavior can be considered "areas" of adjustment within a life span. They may be stable and virtually unchanging, they may evolve slowly, or they may be highly unstable with swift escalation from transvestism to transsexualism. In very rare cases, transsexualism is abandoned after an experimental period in favor of transvestism or transgenderism. Occasionally, long periods of abstention of cross dressing is seen in fetishistic transvestites, but total cessation is thought to be rare. Where cross dressing is abandoned, substitutive behavior closely related to cross dressing is usually seen (e.g., photographing TVs and TSs, dating cross dressers, attending bars and social events with cross dressers).

The aging transvestite (Wise & Meyer, 1980), or secondary transsexual, is said to experience an ever stronger gender discordance. In his later years, at times of crisis, he is thought to seek sexual reassignment as a transsexual. His gender dysphoric feelings, however, are believed to be both transient and stress-induced. If encouraged to try living full time in the feminine role he may abandon his transsexual demands. Although these generalizations no doubt fit some cases, it is not clear how accurately they describe most secondary transsexuals. Much remains to be learned concerning possible reasons for progression from one transvestic stage to another or from tranvestism to transsexualism. We shall be considering this in the multistage theory of transvestism presented in Chapter 8.

Clearly, the clinical management of individuals who seek sexual reassignment is far more difficult today than when Christine Jorgensen became a transsexual in the early 1950s. Today, hormones are obtainable through illicit sales, even by mail-order, and transsexual surgery can be arranged both within the United States and elsewhere with modest evidence of screening. The transsexual-to-be who has sufficient money can take control of his or her own gender destiny despite the standards and procedures advocated by professionals. Whether this circumvention of professionals is actually in the best interest of persons having gender difficulties remains to be seen. For a discussion of the clinical management of transsexuals, see Steiner (1985b). Another practice for avoidance of professionals by transsexual applicants for gender reassignment is through virtually complete reliance upon other transsexuals as counselors. No one has evaluated whether transsexuals having extensive experience with gender-concerned individuals counsel any better or worse than the mental health professional, but two things are clear: First, most of the transsexual counselors we know have taken on the role of the gender counselor without training even roughly equivalent to licensed mental health personnel. Neither do most of them meet the training standards advocated by the Harry Benjamin Gender Dysphoria Association (1985). Second, by presenting a role model of the successful, well-functioning transsexual to the transsexual applicant, a critical element of bias may be introduced into the counseling relationship. Although there are clear standards recommended for selection of transsexual applicants, it would appear possible to arrange for such surgery in the United States virtually in the absence of any licensed professionals. As Stoller (1985c) has stated so clearly, there are many dimensions of lapsed responsibilities resulting in a professionally unacceptable "mess" in the field of sex reassignment.

We move now from issues of classification and assessment to a consideration of the knowledge base for transvestism and transsexualism. Our goal will be to pull together the scientific literature on these topics, integrate the common themes, highlight the differences and inconsistencies, and emphasize what appear to be the most promising theories and supporting hypothetical constructs.

Summary

The spectrum of cross dressing encompasses nine behavior patterns, some of which have much in common and some of which are quite unique. The five heterosexual variations are: fetishism, fetishistic transvestism, marginal transvestism, transgenderism, and secondary transsexualism (TV type). The four homosexual variations are: primary transsexualism, secondary transsexualism (homosexual type), drag queens, and female impersonators.

Fetishistic and marginal transvestism are believed to develop from erotic and sexual beginnings, usually in adolescence or earlier. The developmental process of transvestism typically extends over several years, gradually involving social presentations of the pseudowoman. There are several distinguishing features between fetishistic transvestism and the more intense, marginal transvestism. One of the most important differences seems to be the strength of the cross-gender identity which is experienced in connection with cross dressing. In transgenderism, there are longer-term cycles of functioning in both genders, with oscillation from one to the other. This may be prodromal to secondary transsexualism (TV type).

The etiology of primary transsexualism is unknown. It is believed to be based on very early, perhaps fetal, deflection of gender identity, but why this occurs is not understood. Such cases are said to be rare. The current belief is that most transsexualism is of the secondary variety with its two variations: a transvestic type and a homosexual type. These earlier careers as transvestites or as homosexual males are thought to be the primary modes of personal adjustment; the desire to live full-time in the cross-gender mode and to obtain sex reassignment typically comes late in life. While both drag queens and female impersonators cross dress, the psychodynamics and sexual orientation of such individuals are believed to differ significantly from all other categories along the spectrum of cross dressing.

Chapter 3

A Review of the Literature on Transvestism and Transsexualism

Transvestism and transsexualism have existed throughout history (Bullough, 1974, 1976a,b, 1987; Green, 1969) in all parts of the world despite the clear-cut gender distinctions most cultures require. Transsexualism occurs in both men and women, perhaps at a ratio of about three to two in favor of men (Steiner, Blanchard, & Zucker, 1985).

There is no register or census for transsexuals in our society, and no definitive data exist to clarify the base rate. But if transsexualism is defined as involving full sexual-reassignment surgery, it is estimated (Stoller, 1985c) there may be from 6,000 to 10,000 transsexuals in the United States. The basis for this estimate is not clear. There are probably many times this number who live continuously in the cross-gender role without full reassignment. The essence of this gender deviance is that it involves a permanent gender role reversal. From a social and behavioral perspective, it makes little difference whether such individuals have had transsexual surgery, take hormones, or simply function in the opposite gender without these interventions.

In contrast, transvestites do not live continuously in the cross-gender role; their cross dressing is periodic and fetishistic. For reasons incompletely understood, transvestism, unlike transsexualism, appears to occur almost exclusively in men. Very few convincing cases involving women have ever been reported (Stoller, 1982, 1985c). Although women in our culture wear many articles of clothing which might be called "men's clothing," their motive is not to imitate a man or take the social role of a male; such clothing is worn for the same reasons as any other clothing—for comfort, convenience, style, or protection. There is no issue of cross-gender role behavior whatever. Nor is there any sense in saying that the reason transvestism is not seen in women is because our culture "allows" them to wear men's clothing. Unlike the women we are discussing, when a transvestite dresses as a woman and presents himself in public as a woman he is usually not much concerned with the comfort, convenience, or protection afforded by his feminine wrappings. What he wants most is to be successful in appearing (temporarily and periodically) to be a member of the feminine gender and to experience whatever subjective feelings accompany the reported pleasure he derives from enacting his cross-gender identity fantasy. But despite the apparent clarity of the term transvestism, a satisfactory operational definition has not emerged. The word continues to have several meanings. Like the term gender dysphoria, we have to depend upon an individual's history and subjective feelings to spell out what we mean by transvestism.

It is far from clear what motivates men to dress as women and in many cases to seek to pass in public. The scientific study of this behavior remains at a very elementary stage. What is clear, however, is that virtually all articles and books which have appeared on this subject over the past 75 years emphasize the sexual arousal and sexual reinforcements that somehow come to be intimately connected with this behavior. It will surprise no one, therefore, that we shall also report data which support this well-established finding. But the trouble is that transvestism almost certainly involves other motives and reinforcers as well as the sexual. With the passage of years, not only are there major differences in the cross dressing behavior of the transvestite, there are also changes in the motivation for doing this and in the reinforcements obtained. The understanding of such phenomena has been overshadowed by the all too easy conclusion that sex explains all. We shall present some data in Chapter 6 which will go beyond the sexual factors, although sexuality may, for most transvestites, be primary at least at the beginning of cross dressing. A key point that we shall often emphasize is that the understanding of transvestism necessitates a process or developmental view of this behavior rather than a time-bound or "slice of life" portrait. Just as the description of personality formation has profited from a developmental perspective, so, too, must we take such a view in order to properly describe and assess both the fetishistic and the cross-gender components of transvestism.

Early Research and Clinical Description of Transvestism

Hirschfeld (1910) outlined the general features of transvestic behavior in a seminal paper that for the first time pointed up the heterosexual features of erotic cross dressing. He left no doubt that he considered sexual excitation to be important in heterosexual cross dressing. For example, the subtitle of his 1910 work is *"An Investigation into the Erotic Impulse of Disguise."*

Despite the term transvestism, which some thought gave too much importance to the clothing alone—rather than including so-called feminine identity factors (Ellis, 1936)—Hirschfeld was aware of the fetishistic aspects of cross dressing and of the common history of masturbation as a correlate in these cases. Using case histories, he described 10 different patterns of cross dressing behavior. He emphasized the heterosexual orientations of most of these men. This was a major departure from the prevailing conception of cross dressing as a variation of homosexual behavior. Some of the cases presented by Hirschfeld would now be called either transgenderism or transsexualism, but the central theme of his work focused upon fetishistic cross dressing. As we shall see in the types of transvestism listed below, Hirschfeld described not only heterosexual cross dressing but bisexual and homosexual variations as well. These variations have been studied even less than the heterosexual transvestite, but there is no dispute that such variations exist.

Here are the 10 varieties of transvestism Hirschfeld identified, derived from the translation and description given by Lukianowicz (1959) to whom we are much indebted for his scholarship:

1. The complete transvestite. This was seen as cross dressing with the desire for sexual-reassignment surgery and corresponds to the presently used term transsexualism.
2. The partial transvestite. This individual was said to be satisfied with cross dressing and had no desire for surgery. This pattern is what we now refer to as transvestism.
3. The constant transvestite. Hirschfeld described this pattern as very similar to what we now call transgenderism.
4. The periodic transvestite. This category is similar to what we now recognize as transvestism; the fetishistic aspect of this behavior was recognized. Periodicity is presently viewed as one of the key differences between transvestism and transsexualism.
5. Transvestite in name. It is now apparent that the adoption of a feminine name is a common step in the transvestic career, and a separate category for this step in the transvestic career is not necessary. Adoption of a name usually follows many years of practice in cross dressing. We shall present data on this later.
6. The narcissistic transvestite. While narcissistic personality features are believed characteristic of some transvestites, this is no longer considered a subtype.
7. The homosexual transvestite. It is likely that many of Hirschfeld's homosexual transvestites would today fall within the

bounds of a transsexual classification. He reported that about one-third of his "transvestites" were homosexual, but he was almost certainly describing transsexuals, not transvestites. Non-transsexual homosexuals who cross dress have not been systematically studied, although such cases are not rare in our experience. The DSM-III-R criteria for transvestism exclude homosexuals who are not sexually aroused, past or present, by cross dressing.

8. The bisexual transvestite. As with the homosexual cross dresser, this is a sexual pattern which has not been adequately explored. There may be substantially greater bisexuality among so-called heterosexual transvestites than has been thought.

9. The metatropic transvestite. The cross dresser who seeks the love of a mannish woman was placed in this category by Hirschfeld. This has not proven to be a useful classification.

10. The automonosexual transvestite. This category included sexually isolated individuals whose entire sex life became directed toward the image of their transvestic self—the "beautiful woman in the mirror." This has not proven to be a useful category although this sexual pattern is common in cross dressers.

Hirschfeld created the word *transvestiten* to encompass all variations of cross dressing including transsexualism. It was not until the 1950s, especially through the work of Benjamin (1953), that transsexualism and transvestism were split into separate diagnostic categories. Except for this division and for the refinement of the descriptions given first by Hirschfeld, there has been only modest progress in the scientific understanding of transvestism since 1910. We shall consider these promising new areas of research as we proceed. Let us conclude this introduction to early research by summing up Hirschfeld's major points:

1. Fetishistic transvestism and transsexualism were combined into the single grouping: transvestiten.
2. This classification was clearly separated from other sexual syndromes for the first time.
3. The significance of sexual factors in fetishistic cross dressing was identified and, to some extent, separated from transsexual behavior.
4. The predominance of heterosexual erotic preference in fetishistic transvestism was correctly emphasized.
5. Several major personality and sexual deviations were said to be associated with fetishistic cross dressing, such as: narcissistic features, exhibitionistic features, and exclusive reliance upon autoerotic practices.

6. The periodic occurrence of cross dressing was emphasized in fetishistic transvestism.

Randell (1959) attempted to sort out a mixed group of TVs and TSs who were patients in a clinical setting. The sample consisted of 37 males and 13 females, many of whom were referred in connection with an expressed interest in sex reassignment surgery. He classified his subjects as transvestites or transsexuals, but in each group he found many complex examples of fetishistic behavior. He also thought many showed an exhibitionistic tendency through their desire to appear in public in female garb, and he noted some masochistic behavior. Randell ultimately divided his patients into the following two categories, which appear to represent a transsexual group and a transvestite group:

The transsexual group. This included both males and females. Strong homosexual preferences were seen.

The obsessive-compulsive (or transvestite) group. In these patients, strongly obsessional personality characteristics were seen. Sex preference was primarily heterosexual. Their behavior was often part of the quest for sexual gratification. "A characteristic attitude was the self-conscious assumption of idealized and wish-fulfilling concepts of masculinity or femininity, the subsequent use of this assumption to justify the practices, and the demand for surgical intervention, which is seldom, if ever, justified" (p. 1451). No evidence supported the older idea that these fetishistic and, apparently, gender dysphoric patients had anatomical characteristics of both sexes or of the sex opposite their anatomical sex; in fact, no such evidence has ever been produced. Randell's observations were largely in harmony with the earlier descriptions of Hirschfeld (1910) and Benjamin (1953, 1954), and also with contemporary distinctions made between transvestites and transsexuals (Blanchard, 1985a,b,c; Blanchard et al., 1987; Freund et al., 1982; Buhrich & McConaghy, 1977a).

In an exceptionally important paper, Ovesey and Person (1976) examined transvestism as a disorder of the self, drawing upon histories and clinical interviews with 22 transvestite men. They considered fantasy and dream material, the social enactment of cross dressing, "closet" and vicarious transvestism, the social-support and commercial network which connects many transvestites, the various tactics for relating to wives, passing in public, relationships with women and with prostitutes, and problems of treating cross dressers. Judging from the descriptions they give of their subjects and their motives for seeing these psychiatrists, we would assume that the "marginal transvestites" may be overrepresented in their sample because many of their patients had been referred from other mental health agencies. As Prince and Bentler

(1972) have reported from their sample of 504 TVs, consultation with mental health professionals is uncommon in transvestites. In any case, Ovesey and Person have compiled a rich combination of clinical impressions, hypotheses, and theoretical initiatives. Their view of the transvestite is anchored by self theory and they see the "full-blown syndrome" as involving two different personalities—one male and one female. "The female personality may be perceived as 'fighting' with the male personality and crowding it out" (p. 228). Money (1974) also expressed this division-of-self view and it is central to the "feminine self" or second self which has been so extensively described in the writings of Prince (1976). But an important point is their emphasis on the fighting and tension between the two competing self systems. As will be developed in Chapter 8, we believe it is the dynamics of this competition and the outcome of this struggle for integration of the self which is the principal cause of the changes in the transvestic career. Returning to Ovesey and Person, they note that the transvestite is " . . . trying to validate two realities which are ultimately mutually incompatible, two realities which are predicated on a split in the ego and consequently in the sense of self" (p. 228). Some of their patients interpreted this duality as an asset in which they enjoy a "richer personality" having components of both gender identities. Prince (1976) and Talamini (1982) would agree.

Concerning human relationships, Ovesey and Person found that " . . . transvestites relate relatively well to women and avoid intimacy with men except for other transvestites" (1976, p. 229). They reason this may stem from a "holding on" to the mother throughout life because she was perceived as positive and nurturing. They also discuss the mechanism of introjective identification in which certain valued attributes of another person (such as feminine components) are especially valued and then internalized or "taken within" and experienced as one's own. There are many reports of how this can complicate the transvestite's marital experience. Although he may see marriage as a way to consolidate his masculine gender identity he may also face the difficulty of wanting to incorporate symbols of his wife's femininity (clothing, makeup) into his previously established transvestic fantasies or enactments of such fantasies.

Ovesey and Person point out that many similarities exist in the personality structures of transvestites and borderline personalities. For example, they see each of these groups as having failed to adequately separate the self from others—both projective and introjective identification are said to "contaminate" these relationships. The result is an impairment in the capacity to relate to others in satisfying ways.

"Transvestites, as a group, are invariably anhedonic and experience feelings of loneliness and emptiness . . . " (1976, p. 231), according to Ovesey and Person. With very limited range in pleasure getting and impoverished relationships, "They find relief through preoccupation with fantasies and through their enactment" (p. 231). Periods of acting out their fantasies are punctuated by intervals of renunciation, guilt, and negative self-evaluations—but the predominant sources of pleasure soon return. "In fact, the fantasies are a major source of pleasure, ease, and sometimes a prerequisite for orgastic release. As such, they present a constant temptation to withdraw from reality pursuits" (p. 231). While these fantasies are not ego-alien, they result in intense motivation for enactment when stress is increased, according to these authors. The defenses of the transvestite are seen as "unstable and easily over-whelmed" by threats to masculinity, vocational stressors, losses, and other major life changes. They believe the TV's personality is "inte-grated on an obsessive-paranoid axis and that typically he is irritable, hyperaggressive, and hypercompetitive" (p. 233).

Taken as a whole, we are much impressed with these clinical in-sights but Ovesey and Person's descriptions may or may not be gener-alized beyond their marginal transvestite. The facts of this matter remain unclear. Their descriptions seem more pathological than most views of the nonmarginal or fetishistic TV group (Brierley, 1979; Buhrich & Mc-Conaghy, 1977b; Bullough, Bullough, & Smith, 1983; Feinbloom, 1976; Talamini, 1982). These transvestites are said to show greater ego-integra-tion and self-efficacy (Bandura 1977, 1982) than the 22 patients Ovesey and Person saw in a clinical setting. Let us now turn to these more typical heterosexual transvestites.

Contemporary Studies of Heterosexual Transvestites

The behavior of transvestite members of cross dressing clubs has been extensively described on three continents. Most of this sample appear to be fetishistic (at least in the history), heterosexual TVs. Data derived from these samples offer a look at the cross dresser which may be significantly different from case studies and other research materials derived from applicants at gender identity clinics or from a counseling or psychiatric facility. It is virtually certain, for example, that only a very small percentage of the members of transvestite clubs ever live full-time or even for extended intervals as women. In contrast, cross dressers seeking sexual reassignment or prescription of hormones are far more likely to be seen in major gender identity services since it is there that their needs may or may not be met.

Studies in the United States

What may have been the first national convention of transvestites in the United States was described by Beigel (1969), who noted some of the unrealistic self-perceptions of these men. Prior to about 1960 there seems to have been very little social organization among cross dressers, although I have been told of small groups meeting, very secretly, long before then. The beginning of *Transvestia* magazine in 1960 also marked the origin of the first national "sorority" for transvestites under the guidance of Virginia Prince. A history of this magazine and of the ups and downs of what ultimately became Tri Ess (The Society for the Second Self) is given by Prince (1980) in the 100th volume under her editorship.

There have been several analyses of the common themes found in transvestic fiction (Beigel & Feldman, 1963; Buhrich, 1976; Talamini, 1982). Such themes include fantasies of forced cross dressing, being transformed into a full-time woman, having all sorts of requirements which justify becoming a beautiful young lady or a seductive woman, and engaging in both lesbian and "heterosexual" relationships. So far as individual cases of transvestism are concerned, these general themes are of no help in sorting out the motives or the psychodynamics of a person's cross dressing. What the fantasy literature does offer is a very general insight into what some transvestites find most pleasurable and erotic; that is, these stories offer a glimpse into the generalized transvestic sexual script.

Prince and Bentler (1972) surveyed 504 transvestites during the period 1962 through 1972 and their report has been extensively quoted in textbooks describing cross dressing. Eighty-nine percent of their sample described themselves as heterosexual, with 28% acknowledging some history of homosexual experience. Seventy-eight percent were currently married or had been married. Five percent reported taking female hormones and 50% said they would like to do so. Fourteen percent said they would like to have a sex change operation if this were financially and legally feasible. Twenty percent of the wives were unaware of their husband's cross dressing. The men surveyed represented a wide range of occupations, educational backgrounds, and socioeconomic levels. The subjects were recruited from cross dressing clubs and from subscribers to *Transvestia* magazine. Prince and Bentler note that these clubs and *Transvestia* magazine cater to heterosexual men, and that therefore, despite the exceptionally large size of the sample, these men may not be representative of all TVs.

Prince (1976) provided extensive information about cross dressing clubs and their members throughout her 20-year stint as the publisher-editor of *Transvestia* (Prince, 1980), and developed an alternate-identity model to explain cross dressing. Prince's theory is founded on the hypothesis that innate gender-role motives are somehow a part of the person. She postulates a "girl within" which is ultimately expressed through transvestic behavior and feminine role playing (Prince, 1976). Throughout her years as publisher-editor of *Transvestia*, Prince discussed many other explanations, possible motives, and reinforcers pertaining to cross dressing which seem plausible and original. For example, deriving pleasure, achieving role relief, gaining attention and respect, the enhancement of self-esteem, and the enactment of erotically toned fantasies. Prince accorded sexual factors a minor role in transvestism. Her central explanation is based on the idea that a feminine self demands expression. Other than the massive survey by Prince and Bentler (1972), Prince's work is generally not data-based. There are unresolved questions inherent in Prince's formulation, including these brief examples: Why do some men become TVs and most do not? Why do some, as exemplified by Prince's own history, function as fetishistic heterosexual transvestites for decades and then commence living full-time as women? What is the basis of the apparent persistence of transvestism? Although Prince wrote of the changing stages and patterns of cross dressing in many of her articles and editorials, this has not been organized into a theoretical statement. Taken as a whole, however, no one has provided a more extensive or in-depth view of the heterosexual transvestite than has Virginia Prince.

Feinbloom (1976) followed a Boston group of about 12 transvestites for several months and described the members as likeable and adequately functioning individuals bearing no resemblance to psychiatric cases. Transvestism was interpreted within a sociological frame of reference with heavy reliance on social deviance and role theory, but little explanatory theory was attempted.

Talamini (1982) surveyed 50 TVs and their wives mainly drawn from east coast and New England cross dressing clubs. He described the functioning of these groups and the problems reported by the wives as well as some of their adaptive efforts. Using a sociological orientation, he interprets transvestism as an expression of social deviance much as did Feinbloom. While the TV is engaging in a life-style which includes some taboo behavior, he is not seen as manifesting any major psychopathology. He noted four motivational factors in heterosexual cross dressing: (p. 23)

1. *Relaxation.* The TV is motivated and reinforced by being able to break from his daily role routines and role demands. In his femi-

nine role he is more able to express " . . . emotionality, sensitivity, playfulness, gracefulness and similar qualities. . . ."

2. *Role-playing.* "A transvestite who goes out in public and passes as a woman gains a huge sense of achievement in enacting the role."

3. *Eroticism.* Sexual pleasure is derived from cross dressing and they " . . . feel sexy and attracted to themselves."

4. *Adornment.* Women's clothes are said to be more attractive than men's and to fulfill a " . . . need for adornment."

Talamini turned away from total reliance upon sexual arousal as an explanation of cross dressing. He attempted to analyze this expression of deviant behavior through sociological analysis. Many examples of social and interpersonal factors associated with transvestism are cited, and he also provides data pertaining to the attitudes and coping tactics of the wives of TVs. We shall take up his data concerning the gender identity of the transvestite derived from the Bem Sex-Role Inventory when our Bem data are discussed in Chapter 6.

Croughan, Saghir, Cohen, and Robins (1981) interviewed 70 male members of cross dressing clubs about half of whom had been in some kind of mental health treatment situation related to their cross dressing at least once, with the other half never having been involved in such treatment. They compared these groups across many reported dimensions and found that the only variables on which the treated group differed significantly from the untreated were these: The treatment group reported more

- fantasizing of themselves as females while masturbating [cross dressed]
- having engaged in heterosexual intercourse while cross dressed
- current preference for both heterosexual intercourse and homosexual behavior while cross dressed
- experiences of adverse consequences from cross dressing (pp. 520–521)

They described a chronic course of cross dressing, beginning for all subjects by "middle adolescence." Occasional evidence of remission was seen for periods of from a few months to several years. They agree with many others that transvestism almost invariably is associated with sexual arousal, often with masturbation, during the early years of cross dressing. Greater heterosexual intercourse while cross dressed with a drop-off in masturbation is reported as subjects approach "middle age." There is a "trend toward a more asexual nature to the cross-dressing during late adult life. Cross-dressing is infrequently associated with sadomasochism and not at all with exhibitionism" (p. 515). Again, these researchers clearly favor the view that highly significant changes are taking place both in cross dressing behavior and in the motives and reinforcers experienced by the transvestite across the life span.

These investigators report that the two groups do not differ in the frequency of cross dressing for various periods of their lives; there is a trend toward greater frequency with age and experience, and we shall take this up at greater length when our own data on this is presented in Chapter 6. No clear-cut indicators of precipitating external stimuli are reported by their subjects.

Nonsexual psychiatric diagnoses were acknowledged in their subjects with " . . . frequencies of unipolar depression and alcoholism [found to be] elevated" compared to the general population. There were less clear suggestions of some sociopathic behavior, obsessional neuroses and even schizophrenia in their subjects. However, their data "appear to be consistent with prior reports in that there does not appear to be any obvious relationship between cross-dressing and other nonsexual psychiatric diagnoses" (p. 527). They did not, for example, find supporting evidence of the alleged link between transvestism and an obsessive-compulsive personality type. This has been a much favored hypothesis.

Studies in England

Brierley (1979) concluded that transvestism is neither a psychiatric illness nor a perversion of the sexual motive. Rather, he believes this behavior stems from "a choice to obtain pleasure while alternating between the role of a man and a woman." Like virtually all who preceded him, he believes the TV begins with fetishistic learning experiences and that this is the first stage of an extensive process. An even more important second stage involves experiencing the gender identity of a woman periodically and on a temporary basis. This is necessary, he reasons, to overcome unpleasant or gender dysphoric feelings associated with functioning in the masculine role. Hence, cross dressing becomes an example of role relief and escape from the pressures of being male.

The transvestite's difficulties are seen as primarily "social and interpersonal" rather than primarily biological or sexual. He agrees that transvestism is a heterosexual male phenomenon and that: "It is a condition which may involve no other person and almost never concerns people outside the transvestite's own family and friends. He is not, in his transvestism, a person who seeks or demands notice but rather looks for an unremarkable acceptance in his cross-gender role. The practice has rewards and pleasures for the individual and he usually cannot understand his causing distress to others . . . " (pp. 241–242).

Brierley concentrated upon three categories of cross dressers: (1) The fetishist—who dresses without wanting to appear or "feel" like a complete woman; (2) the heterosexual transvestite—who wants to dress and pass as a woman, feel like a woman, and take the social role of a woman periodically (while erotic arousal is not the primary goal, some fetishistic arousal may be experienced); and (3) the transsexual— wherein the essential feature is a continuing and intense desire for sex reassignment surgery. He does not present these as absolute categories but rather as "areas" or "regions of adjustment" having some recognizable stability, yet also having the possibility of development, change, and variation.

He also noted the absence of knowledge concerning the changes and developments that are seen in the life histories of transvestites: "Questions of the stability and predictive validity of the heterosexual transvestite pattern are crucial" (p. 227). As we have emphasized above, the question of what kinds of developmental paths may be seen in the lives of transvestites has never been adequately researched. For example, Brierley questions whether the practices of transvestism " . . . are likely to displace the gender identity further or [whether] . . . transvestism itself . . . may promote even further gender identity displacement toward transsexualism. That is to say, does transvestism set up its own reward systems and prove self-reinforcing?" (p. 229). Brierley has here brought out a major research issue which deserves far more satisfactory study than it has thus far received.

The only comparative study contrasting heterosexual transvestites, rubber and leather fetishists, and sadomasochists was reported by Gosslein and Wilson (1980). The TV sample consisted of 269 members of Great Britain's Beaumont Society, which is patterned after Tri Ess, an American organization of heterosexual TVs. Their research is based upon self-report data using the Sex Fantasy Questionnaire (Gosslein and Wilson, 1980) and other measures that have not been widely applied, but which are quite interesting. Their goal was to obtain deeper insight into the fantasy scripts of several sexual variations such as transvestism, several forms of fetishism, and sadomasochism. Concerning the sexual fantasies of transvestites, Gosselin and Wilson found this group quite similar to a control group except for the fact that the transvestites, as expected, place cross dressing first on their list of preferred fantasies. Beyond this level, the transvestites report an array of fantasy material much like controls and quite unlike the fantasy preferences of other sexually variant groups (sadomasochists, rubberites, and leatherites).

One of the conclusions reached by Gosselin and Wilson was that a script built upon fetishistic themes was a common element in all three of the sexual variations. Additionally, they found 35% of each of the three groups (heterosexual transvestites, fetishists, and sadomasochists) shared " . . . all three predilictions" (1980, p. 167). Clearly, there is considerable overlap of sexual behavior across the three groups. They surmise that both transvestism and sadomasochism are based on fetishes learned early in life, and that the formation of a sexual script to organize this fetishism is therefore central to the sexual variations they studied.

Studies in Australia and New Zealand

Working in Australia and New Zealand, psychiatrists Neil Buhrich and Neil McConaghy have contributed extensively to the study of transvestism. They have described the operation of a TV club (Buhrich, 1976) in Australia, analyzed the fictional themes of TV stories (Buhrich & McConaghy, 1976), identified the major syndromes of fetishistic transvestism (1977b) and compared TVs and transsexuals (1977a). Their work also includes assessment of clearly fetishistic components of the cross dressing of many transsexuals (1977c) who we can only assume would be called secondary transsexuals using our present classification terminology. Buhrich (1981) also reported on the psychological adjustment of TVs and TSs. Buhrich and McConaghy (1985) described the emergence of preadult feminine behaviors seen in some cross dressers. Buhrich and Beaumont (1981) compared the members of TV clubs in Australia and the United States and found them to be "remarkably similar."

The distinctions they make between two syndromes of fetishistic transvestites (1977b) are in harmony with the observations of many other researchers (Benjamin, 1954; Bentler, 1976). Here are the characteristics of their two groups:

Group 1: The Nuclear Transvestite. This group is said to be predominantly heterosexual. They do not desire sex-reassignment surgery nor do they typically take female hormones. Developmentally, they have had more satisfactory heterosexual experiences than Group 2 men. There is less of a subjective feeling of wanting to become a woman or of wanting to appear as a woman in public compared to Group 2. First cross dressing was at a later age than in Group 2. There is the same intensity of fetishistic arousal to feminine clothing as seen in the other group. Fetishistic arousal diminishes with age but less than in Group 2. A stronger feminine identity does not grow with aging. This group is higher socioeconomically than is Group 2.

Group 2: The Marginal Transvestite. These transvestites fantasized having sex with a man more than did those of Group 1. They were predominantly heterosexual but somewhat less so than the other group. They were more likely to go out in public cross dressed, began cross dressing at an earlier age, and had a more intense feminine gender identity than the above group. As they aged, they showed a greater drop-off of fetishistic cross dressing than did Group 1. They were less socially and vocationally successful and were more likely to seek hormonal or surgical treatment.

Concerning the preadult feminine behaviors reported by these two groups, Buhrich and McConaghy (1985) found the TVs in Group 2 (marginal transvestites) reported significantly more childhood feminine behaviors than did the men in Group 1. Both groups reported more early feminine behaviors than did non-TV control subjects, but these differences between the two TV groups are not attributable to early fetishism to women's clothing as the groups did not differ on this variable. The preadult feminine behaviors which seemed best to discriminate between the two groups were these: preferring the company of boys *vs.* girls, participation in rough-and-tumble play, girlish interests and hobby preferences, and being called a sissy (all more evident in Group 2). The research carried out by Buhrich and McConaghy is one of the rare examples of a series of project-oriented studies carried out over several years with a carefully defined group of cross dressers, most of whom were not initally seen as applicants for any mental health or sex reassignment service.

Treatment of Transvestism

Efforts to change the cross dressing behavior of transvestites is generally thought to be highly unsuccessful with insight therapies, although we know of no systematic research concerned with this. On the other hand, there are many reports of encouraging results based on behavior-modification approaches (Bancroft, 1974; Dupont, 1968; Fischer & Gochros, 1977; Lambley, 1974; Marks, Gelder, & Bancroft, 1970; Marquis, 1970; Rekers, 1977; Rosen & Rehm, 1977). These procedures have been applied with male adults and with children who cross dress or show other gender deviant behavior. These reports indicate that transvestism can be reduced or even eliminated with sustained satisfactory results over a period of several years. For the most part, behavioral methods seem to have worked best. But most of these studies are based on very few cases, and while some include follow-up reports, most do not or give very little information. It is important that the subjects in many of these studies are atypical compared to the club-member heterosexual transvestites who have so often been described. Most transvestites who affiliate with cross dressing groups do not want psychotherapy or behavior modification to assist them in stopping an activity they have found to be highly satisfying and pleasurable. The men who are most motivated to eliminate transvestism from their lives are usually under pressure to do so, often from their wives as a condition of continuing the marriage. Another source of pressure would be when transvestism is interpreted by an employer to justify dismissal, or for discharge from the military or revocation of a security clearance.

The most frequent presenting concern of transvestites may not pertain to giving up this practice, but rather, finding solutions to troubles within the marriage. Here, the practical realities of short-term, goal-directed counseling may be more helpful than the in-depth quest for insight. As discussed in Chapter 7, which deals with the concerns of wives of TVs, where there is a mutual commitment to problem solving and a willingness to negotiate issues, couples can usually find ways to alleviate their most distressing concerns. The management of these counseling relationships goes beyond our topic here, but there is nothing about the problems and frustrations of the transvestite that is much different from those of other high functioning individuals. As with transsexuals, the act of cross dressing or not cross dressing does not, in itself, change other personality problems.

Personality Characteristics of Transvestites

Certain personality characteristics of cross dressers have been studied by Bentler and Prince (1969, 1970) and by Bentler, Sherman and Prince (1970). In their first report (Bentler, Sherman & Prince, 1970), the Holtzman Ink Blot Test (Holtzman, Thorpe, Swartz, & Herron, 1961) was given to 25 transvestites who were not in psychotherapy; they were mostly members of cross dressing clubs in the Los Angeles area. Test performance of the TVs was compared to norms for the "general adult population." TVs showed " . . . generally organized and intellectually adequate thought processes . . . ," but also showed " . . . anxiety, hostility, and pathognomic verbalizations" (p. 290). Some possible rigid and compulsive features were suggested. Except for some greater bodily preoccupations which were seen, the TVs did not differ much from norms on this inkblot measure. Using an experimental version of an MMPI-type inventory, Bentler and Prince (1970) obtained data by mail from 180 transvestites and 76 control subjects. They concluded " . . . no gross differences [were] detectable between the transvestites and controls on neurotic or psychotic scales" (p. 435). In their third paper

(Bentler & Prince, 1969), 181 TVs were compared with 62 control subjects on 20 variables of the Personality Research Form, a Cattell 16 PF-type test. They found " . . . the transvestites presented themselves as more controlled in impulse expression, more inhibited in interpersonal relations, less involved with other individuals, and more independent" (p. 140). It seems fair to say that across the three studies the main thing which stood out was the tendency for TVs to describe themselves as somewhat more inhibited in emotional expression compared to control subjects and norms. There is nothing in these personality studies to suggest that TVs are much different than non-TVs across most personality variables. But there is another point of view about the personality of transvestites. For example, Sperber (1973) viewed these men as having well-established features of what is now called the borderline personality (e.g., marked changes in mood, depression, identity problems, difficulties with impulse control, bizarre and peculiar behavior).

Using the Eysenck Personality Questionnaire, Gosselin and Wilson (1980) reported that 269 transvestite club members appeared to show " . . . clear evidence of introversion and high neuroticism compared with normal males" (p. 104). This conclusion is similar to Brierley's (1979) findings that were also derived from members of cross dressing clubs in England.

Although there are substantial differences among the conclusions presented by those who have reported on the personality characteristics and the personal adjustment of transvestites, there seems to be agreement that this group is to some extent higher in anxiety and perhaps more introverted and neurotic than non-cross-dressing males, but the facts are far from clear.

Childhood Origins of Transvestism

Developmental psychologists have given extensive research attention to the formation of sex-role behavior in children and young adults (Maccoby & Jacklin, 1974; Mussen, 1983). There is also a long-standing research interest in the development and organization of the self (Harter, 1983). Many aspects of this research have implications for the shaping of fetishistic sexual interests and for the emergence of gender identity. For a comprehensive conception of gender identity theory as related to transvestism, transsexualism, and homosexuality, see Bancroft (1972). Researchers interested in what may predict later homosexual preferences have contributed extensively to the literature on erotic orientation (e.g., see Storms, 1981). Rekers and Jurich (1983) have provided a superb review of the scientific study of problems of pubertal development and sex-role development in adolescents. One of their major conclusions is that where serious difficulties in sex-role development have occurred, such deviations " . . . are strongly predictive of transsexualism, transvestism, and homosexuality in adulthood" (p.797). They cite many references to back up this conclusion. A second major point is that although " . . . biological abnormalities may theoretically serve as potential contributing factors . . . social learning variables have been considered to be the main source of sex-role deviance in childhood and adolescence . . . " (p. 797). There is some evidence that a history of effeminate behavior is retrospectively reported by at least some transvestites (Green, 1974; Prince & Bentler, 1972; Rekers, 1977), although most heterosexual TVs are described as unremarkably masculine except when cross dressed (Stoller, 1968a). Very extensive documentation exists to show that cross dressing often begins in early boyhood and persists into the adolescent years for the majority of adult transsexuals and transvestites (Green, 1974; Money & Primrose, 1968; Prince & Bentler, 1972; Walinder, 1967; Zuger, 1966, 1978).

Zuger (1978) followed a small group of gender-disturbed boys for 20 years and found 65% were homosexual, 6% were transsexual, 6% were transvestite, and 12% were heterosexual. Taking many studies into consideration, Rekers and Jurich (1983) summarize as follows: "Considering all the available literature, therefore, the best scientific prediction is that a sex-role disturbed boy will progress into adolescence with a high risk for transsexualism, transvestism, or homosexuality as contrasted to normal heterosexual development" (p. 798). Concerning transvestites alone, it important to keep in mind that most seem not to have emerged from a background of deviant sex-role development or confused gender identity, although as we have seen, such beginnings are certainly possible.

Freund et al. (1982) advance the thesis that cross-gender identity is experienced by transvestites, and this presumably is a product of childhood learning experiences. The idea here is that the TV does experience a temporary cross-gender identity, but only when cross dressed. Freund et al. do not ignore the fetishistic component which is typically seen in TVs; the temporary cross-gender identity reversal is simply another motive or reinforcer associated with cross dressing. Aside from the retrospective reports of TVs, many of whom acknowledge such cross-gender identity changes, there is little known about the subjective experience of temporary gender-reversal ideation. Such changes would seem to fit into a theory of transvestism which emphasized an identity disorder or a disorder of the self along lines developed by Ovesey and Person (1976) and others.

Beitel (1985) has developed a conceptual model of gender identity disturbances based on self-theory and object-relations theory. The core idea involves a splitting of the developing ego, which may be reinforced by the mother's nonacceptance of the male gender qualities of her child. "The split-off ego serves as a compensatory internal structure . . . and the child becomes, in this symptomatic way, his own 'self object'" (p. 198). The amount of difficulty attributable to this split-off ego may be due to several variables, such as the cohesiveness of the entire ego system, according to Beitel's formulation. This line of theory supports those who think of transvestism as an expression of a "second self" (Prince, 1976). Jucovy (1979) has also discussed early childhood personality characteristics in transvestites.

Bradley (1985) presents a formulation of gender disorders in childhood which has many implications for theories of transvestism. The vulnerable, gender-disturbed child is seen as having an " . . . increased sensitivity and poor anxiety tolerance perhaps because of major inadequacies in family relationships" (p. 181). The mothers of the transvestite are said, by Bradley, to be often " . . . outstanding in the degree to which they overtly reject their children" (p. 180).

Bradley (1985) also presents several interesting hypotheses concerning the learning of transvestic behavior. For example, in considering the adolescent transvestite, she reasons that when such youths feel rejected by the mother they may respond with strongly felt anger—a view widely associated with the consequences of separation or loss of a significant other. Cross dressing and masturbation, then, may have an immediate reinforcing value as an anxiety management tactic and serve a "self-soothing" function. "The use of maternal garments may act as a fantasized protector against fear of loss of the mother at these times" (p. 185). Given a propensity for anxiety in sexual–interpersonal situations, this youth may fall back upon his transvestic experiences to obtain anxiety reduction. Buckner's (1970) view of this learning process is also pertinent here; he discusses many alternative developmental difficulties that may contribute to the career path of the youthful transvestite. We shall rely heavily upon his multistage approach to explaining transvestism when we consider a theoretical scheme in Chapter 8.

Bak (1968) has described the psychoanalytic conception of the "phallic woman" said to be a prototype for paraphilic behavior, including transvestism. Concerning transvestites, Stoller (1968a, 1974, 1985c) also believes a common experience among heterosexual TVs is the trauma and damage to one's sense of masculinity which occurs when the youthful boy is humiliated by being dressed as a girl. But little evidence other than Stoller's own cases can be cited to back this up. A history of traumatic early cross dressing, with or without another person taking the lead, is not commonly found in heterosexual transvestites. Stoller also believes that major, very early trauma interferes with the emergence of a sense of maleness and in sustaining male gender identity, and that this may be rooted in mother–child relationship difficulties. Again, there is little if any hard evidence that either the mothers or fathers of transvestites or the particular interpersonal dynamics of the family unit are causal in transvestism. To be fair, we should add that there is no proof that such variables do not play a major role in transvestism. Later, we shall report some data from our survey of transvestites bearing on how they describe certain family relationships.

Primary and Secondary Transsexualism

Primary Transsexualism

Primary transsexualism is defined by a history of lifelong gender dysphoria, a homosexual orientation rather than a predominantly heterosexual preference, and by an unremitting quest to live in the cross-gender role (Benjamin, 1966; Bentler, 1976; Buhrich & McConaghy, 1977a; Money & Ehrhardt, 1972; Person & Ovesey, 1974a; Steiner,1985a; Stoller, 1968a, 1974, 1985c; Wise & Meyer, 1980). All students of transsexual phenomena, beginning with the earliest medically based work in the 1920s, through the recent comprehensive report of Steiner (1985a), have agreed that the etiology of transsexualism is unknown.

Secondary Transsexualism

The transvestic and homosexual variations of secondary transsexualism as formulated by Person and Ovesey (1974a,b) have been discussed in Chapter 2. Others have reported similar behavior patterns although using different terms to characterize this. For example, the secondary transsexual is conceptualized by Wise and Meyer (1980) as an aging transvestite with a fetishistic cross dressing history. However, this individual is believed to show massive regression and loss of defenses following a major life crisis. The result is not a spontaneous occurrence of transsexualism, but rather, a request for sex reassignment based on late-developing feelings of gender dysphoria. Considerable overlap is postulated spanning the developmental personality features and the gender identity of fetishistic transvestites and transsexuals, both primary and secondary. Wise and Meyer (1980) reason that their aging transvestites (secondary transsexuals in our terminology) are a group which "bridges" the fetishistic cross dressers and the primary transsexuals. These transvestites typically had a strong masculine-role history despite long-held ruminations concerning transsexualism. Of the 20 cases they report, all had strong fetishistic histories and none had a homosexual background. This is not inconsistent with Person and Ovesey (1974b) who saw the homosexual transsexual applicants as yet another distinctive group. Wise and Meyer give emphasis to the role of major life changes and stressors as causal factors in the emergence of these late-occurring transsexual applicants. A report generally supporting the distinctions necessitated by differences in sexual orientation, fetishism, and gender identity has been provided by Freund *et al.* (1982).

It is not rare for preoperative transsexuals to abandon their quest for reassignment; it is not well-established that such cases are more likely to involve secondary transsexuals, but this is what we would predict. Shore (1984) reports the case of a young man who was positive he wanted sexual reassignment, was favorably evaluated for surgery, and was on his way to the hospital when he learned the hospital had changed their policy and now prohibited sex reassignment surgery. This man, soon thereafter, changed his entire life-style and reportedly gave up his sex reassignment plans.

Studies Differentiating Transvestites and Transsexuals

In 1953, Benjamin published his initial effort to draw a clear distinction between transvestism and transsexualism. He later summed up his ideas and clinical insights in book form (Benjamin, 1966). His work was highly influential and played at least some role in the later formation of gender identity clinics and sexual reassignment programs throughout the world. His view of transsexuals was this:

1. The transsexual has experienced a life-long gender dysphoria. He or she has felt cast into the "wrong body."
2. This gender dysphoria is the keystone of a major disruption of identity development resulting in massive personal adjustment problems all due to the underlying sense of gender incongruity.
3. The "true" transsexual carries out an unrelenting campaign to obtain sex reassignment assistance through various procedures, including hormonal and surgical interventions, and demands to live full-time in the opposite gender role.
4. "Cross-dressing exists (with few exceptions) in practically all transsexuals, while transsexual desires are not evident (although possibly latent) in most transvestites" (Benjamin, 1966, p. 26).
5. All cross dressing—from mild transvestism through the most persistent transsexualism—was conceptualized as part of a spec-

trum of "sex and gender role disorientation . . . " (Benjamin, 1966, p. 31).

6. The differences between transvestism and transsexualism were reflected in the balance among these variables as experienced by a given cross dresser: (a) TVs are fetishistic; the TS is not fetishistic. (b) TVs are predominantly heterosexual in sex object choice; TSs may be "autoerotic," "passively homosexual," or, in high intensity cases they may strongly "desire relations with a normal male" while the TS is in the female sex role.

Several other investigators have reported quite similar distinctions between transvestites and transsexuals (Bentler, 1976; Buhrich & McConaghy, 1977a; Bullough *et al.*, 1983; Feinbloom, 1976; Freund *et al.*, 1982; Green & Money, 1969; Ovesey & Person, 1973; Prince, 1976; Steiner, 1985a; Stoller, 1968a,b, 1974, 1985c; Wise & Meyer, 1980).

Although such distinguishing criteria seem objective enough, there are several serious problems that may be noted. For example, some TVs are not fetishistic or are very slightly fetishistic; some TSs have a history of substantial fetishism associated with cross dressing (Buhrich & McConaghy, 1977c). Some TVs do not have a history of predominant heterosexuality, although most apparently do. Some TVs progressively become less fetishistic in their cross dressing while developing various intensities of cross-gender identity. In unusual cases this may lead to secondary transsexualism.

These examples of transvestism which do not fit the traditional mold were partially anticipated by Benjamin who described them with much insight. It is such cases that have led to the present view that more than one kind of transsexual process needs to be recognized (Person & Ovesey, 1974a,b; Wise & Meyer, 1980).

Bullough *et al.* (1983) surveyed 65 heterosexual transvestites, 33 transsexuals (most of whom were not surgically reassigned), 57 homosexual men, and 61 control subjects. They were especially concerned with childhood family relationships, interest in sports and boyish activities, erotic orientation, gender identity, and motivation for sexual reassignment. Summing up what they found:

- TSs were more likely to have been unhappy as children and to have had less success in school.
- As adults, TSs held lower-status jobs (often those typically held by women).
- The absent father theory for TVs and TSs " . . . simply did not hold up . . . " (p. 255).

- TVs were more interested in sports and in cross dressing than were the other groups.
- Homosexual men rarely cross dressed in childhood or as adults.
- Family relationships were not different across the groups.

Bullough *et al.* speculated that " . . . transvestites might well be distinguished from transsexuals in their life goal orientation and their motivation toward material satisfaction and occupational prestige" (1983, p. 255). This may be true, but it is also fair to point out that neither this study nor any other has, as yet, identified the critical causal factors in transvestism, transsexualism, or homosexuality.

Steiner, Sanders and Langevin (1985) compared 18 heterosexual transvestites seen as patients at a major gender identity clinic with 31 homosexual transsexuals. Of interest was their relative performance on the MMPI, the Cattell 16 PF Test, the Clarke Sex History Questionnaire (Paitich, Langevin, Freeman, Mann & Handy, 1977) and the Clarke Parent Child Relations Questionnaire (Paitich & Langevin, 1976), parent–child relationships, erotic preferences, aggression, and criminal activity.

The two groups showed few clinical differences in personality except for greater introversion in the transvestites. Keep in mind these subjects were patients in a medical setting and may not be typical heterosexual transvestites. Very possibly, many of the Steiner, Sanders, and Langevin (1985) sample of TVs would meet at least some of the criteria for the marginal transvestite discussed above. Steiner and her colleagues also found these transvestites had engaged in a variety of sexually anomalous behavior including exhibitionism (17%), voyeurism (33%), toucheurism (22%), frottage (28%), rape (6%), and obscene telephone calls (6%). These authors then ask if the characterization of transvestism as merely heterosexual fetishism may not be simplistic. We consider such a characterization misleading and incomplete, but not just because of these statistics based on a small, clinically derived sample. There are many other reasons why the fetishistic explanation of transvestism is simplistic and misleading. Continuing with the report of Steiner *et al.*, both the TV and TS groups had 55% of their membership reporting depressive symptoms and marked femininity was self-described by 78% of the transvestites and 97% of the transsexuals. There can be little doubt that for some transvestites not only is their personal adjustment uncertain, but the range of unusual sexual behaviors they find attractive is considerable. Only much more research will reveal if this can be generalized to the population of known transvestites.

From this brief review of studies which were based on quite different samples it is clear that sampling variations have played an enormous part in how different researchers have described and come to conclusions about similar, but often very different subject matter. There is a deceptive similarity among all of those who have been called transsexuals or transvestites. A more definitive classification system which breaks down various subcategories of these syndromes is much needed. The fact that we are still lumping all transsexuals into what amounts to two large groupings (primary and secondary) is indicative of the rather primitive status of assessment research in the gender deviance field. In order to gain the benefits which have historically derived from studying tightly defined samples of a particular syndrome, we shall have to develop far better ways to do this for both transsexualism and transvestism.

Etiology of Transsexualism

Biological Correlates of Transsexualism

The first medically sponsored transsexual reassignment surgery was predicated upon the assumption that biological development had somehow produced a man who was partially female; hence, medical intervention was justified (Hoyer, 1933). Supporting evidence was not found. And today, although a few biological indicators have been shown to be strongly correlated with transsexualism, evidence is not yet available to link any particular set of determinants to the cause of this condition. Fortunately, a superb review encompassing this area of research has been provided by Hoenig (1985). We shall rely upon his authoritative summary for much of the brief summation that follows. Let us begin where Hoenig ends—that is, with his conclusions:

1. The claim that " . . . psychological factors determine gender identity—be they by learning, conditioning, or imprinting—cannot be regarded as established . . . " (p. 66).
2. At the least, biological forces must contribute to the formation of transsexualism.
3. "The search for . . . constitutional factors has brought to light some interesting findings, but can at best be regarded as 'promising.' It is certainly in no sense conclusive" (p. 66).

Hoenig follows the lead of Benjamin (1966) and many others who ultimately depend upon a biological force or forces to account for transsexualism. The search for supporting evidence has turned up many important leads. These include studies of specific brain structures, such as the temporal lobes that have been associated with the regulation of sexuality since the reports of Kluver and Bucy (1939). It is a short step, taken by many, to speculate that transsexualism may have its roots in limbic system abnormalities, possibly occurring in the earliest stages of brain development. Hoenig (1985) should be consulted for his review of this work which encompasses many studies involving the central nervous system and transsexualism. Concerning temporal lobe matters he concludes: "It is possible that the concurrence of temporal lobe abnormalities and transsexualism is merely fortuitous and that they are not causally connected" (p. 43), but he goes on to note that perhaps transsexualism occurs in many forms and that our present ability to classify these is inadequate. This could be an important explanation of the fact that most biological correlates of transsexualism fall well short of applying to even a minority of transsexualism cases in any given study.

An extensive literature exists linking EEG abnormalities to transsexualism which is reviewed by Hoenig (1985) and by Hoenig and Kenna (1979). From several studies of transsexuals there is a considerable range in findings of "definite" EEG abnormalities; the percentages are from about 13% to 48% of the transsexual samples assessed. Such percentages are certainly high enough to capture the interest of future researchers, but as Hoenig concludes "The significance of the abnormal EEGs in a high proportion of transsexuals remains elusive. Nevertheless, the incidence is too high to be ignored . . . " (p. 46).

Hoenig (1985) points to the review by Meyer-Bahlburg (1977, 1979) concerning hormonal factors that may be unique in homosexual and transsexual men and women. In this area " . . . the final conclusion on the presence or absence of hormonal abnormalities will have to be postponed until further well-controlled investigations have been carried out" (p. 51). Others have supported the same conclusion (Kupperman, 1967).

Careful attention should be given to Hoenig's conclusions concerning the reports of Imperato-McGinley and her colleagues (Imperato-McGinley, Peterson, Gautier, & Sturla, 1979; Imperato-McGinley, Peterson, Stoller, & Goodwin, 1979). These reports have been interpreted in some quarters as contradicting the social-learning model of gender identity as presented by Money and Ehrhardt (1972). Imperato-McGinley *et al.*, in their two widely cited 1979 studies, described boys erroneously reared as girls due to pre- and postnatal hormonal deficiencies. At puberty, testosterone changes triggered the development of the secondary sex characteristics and these pseudogirls threw off their feminine gender identities and began living as young men. On the surface, it would seem impossible to account for this following the model of gender identity development favored by Money and Ehrhardt (1972). Hoenig explains the Imperato-McGinley evidence in this way: " . . . one would have to assume that the brain in these subjects had been adequately masculinized during fetal life . . . and that the gender malassignment and rearing temporarily overlaid this. The pubertal flooding with testosterone, however, activated the brain and restored the masculine gender identity and eroticism" (Hoenig, 1985, p. 52). Notice here that Hoenig implicitly assumes the formation of some kind of gender system within the brain that is fundamental to ultimate gender identity and gender-role development, a premise that is strongly espoused by Diamond (1965, 1977). Money (1987) has published an impressive alternative explanation of the Imperato-McGinley reports. Citing additional factual material, he believes that social factors probably played a critical role in the gender development of the subjects in the two Imperato-McGinley *et al.* reports. For example, the rearing practices of the parents of these unfortunate youth may have been influenced by family awareness of how these genetic males were likely to develop. This knowledge may have been passed along from one generation to the next, as all of the subjects are from a genetically related group who maintain communication ties with one another.

The exceptionally strong link between presence or absence of the H-Y antigen and male/female transsexualism is also reviewed by Hoenig (1985). This antigen is believed to be very powerful as a kind of genetic triggering agent in the differentiation of cells very early in development into either testes or ovaries. It must be present for fetal male development according to some authorities, but it does not seem vital to subsequent development of masculine and feminine biological attributes. The important point is that one group of researchers found 93% of their sample of transsexuals showed an abnormal H-Y antigen response in a group of about 100 transsexuals. They worked with both male and female transsexuals. Another group reported an abnormal response in 65% of their cases and this figure would probably be higher if identical testing procedures had been used by each group. The H-Y antigen is a genetically potent biological determinant of sex-related attributes, and we therefore must follow this line of research with care. (Refer to Hoenig for his comprehensive description of this research.)

Twin studies of transsexuals and familial incidence reports have also been thoroughly reviewed by Hoenig (1985). There have been many family incidence studies of transsexualism. Similarly, there are numerous twin studies and sibling reports showing concordance for transsexualism. But these studies are far from decisive since even in identical twins, when transsexualism occurs in one it is far from certain that it will occur in the other. The most that can be made of this is that some kind of biological factor may operate to facilitate transsexualism but these reports do not provide many clues concerning what factors may be involved.

The Gender Dysphoria Theory of Transsexualism

Prior to the Christine Jorgensen case, all cross dressing had been referred to as "transvestism" with no distinction made concerning transsexualism or other motivation. Benjamin clarified the descriptive terminology (1953) and wrote the first account of transsexualism that had wide circulation (1966). He was the first to describe a continuum of cross-gender behavior ranging from transvestism through transsexualism. We have described this continuum in Chapter 2. For Benjamin, the transsexual end of this spectrum consisted of three intensities of gender dysphoria described as follows:

1. *The nonsurgical transsexual.* Dresses and lives as a woman as often as possible. He/she fluctuates between masculine and feminine identity. Dressing gives insufficient relief of gender discomfort. Asexual, bisexual, or autoerotic orientation is seen. These men may have been married and fathered children. Hormonal treatment is recommended for comfort and emotional balance.

2. *The true transsexual, moderate intensity.* This individual lives and works as a woman, if possible. Insufficient relief is developed from cross dressing alone. Sexual motivation is low. Asexual, autoerotic or passive homosexual activity is seen. As above, this individual may have been married with children. Usually, female hormones are requested which may substitute for surgery or be preliminary to surgery. This person hopes for reassignment surgery and feels trapped in a male body.

3. *The true transsexual, high intensity.* This individual lives and works as a woman, if possible. Intense gender discomfort is not relieved by cross dressing alone. He strongly desires sexual relations with normal males as a 'female' if young. In later years there is little sexual interest. He may have been married with children. This person insists upon reassignment surgery. Female hormones are usually required for partial relief of tension. He despises his male sex organs. There is a danger of suicide or self-mutilation if too long frustrated.

Benjamin (1966) presented cases of preoperative transsexuals who were intensely frustrated by their inability to obtain reassignment surgery. He also commented on the problems faced by wives of transvestites and preoperative transsexuals, noting that " . . . many marriages fail, some work out an adjustment, and in a few 'rare examples' . . . the wife actually was more homo [sexual] than heterosexual and liked her husband better as a woman than as a man" (p. 53) Benjamin's theory of transsexualism stresses several lines of development but never departs far from the concept of "gender-role dis-orientation," as he called it. He saw unknown biological factors at the core of the transsexual phenomenon with learning processes determining the "final shape."

He was among the first to encourage his transsexual applicants to cross dress as a outlet for their intense gender dysphoric feelings. Twenty years after their initial publication, Benjamin's descriptions seem generally up-to-date and reflect a remarkable insight into the spectrum of cross dressing and gender discordance, except for the fact that no distinction was made between primary and secondary transsexualism.

Richard Green, in his discussion and review of transsexual theory (Green & Money, 1969), generally endorsed the gender dysphoria thesis. He agreed with the concept of a gender discordance continuum, a precept now widely accepted, but concluded that "the exact etiology of transsexualism must be considered unknown" (p. 51).

Green reviewed research which involved the possible linkage of female biological features, if such existed at all, in males who became transsexuals or transvestites. He concluded: " . . . there is now a large body of information which demonstrates agreement between the genetic and anatomical variables in cases of transsexualism and transvestism" (p. 51) . That is, such men are not literally "women" trapped in the bodies of men, despite this overused and simplistic description. We know of nothing in the more recent literature that would contradict Green in this matter.

Money and Ehrhardt (1972) pioneered the study of gender formation as this relates to the gender disorders and their work is among the seminal research efforts in this field. Central to their theories are the concepts of gender identity and gender role although they recognize the possibility of underlying biological factors that may contribute to the transsexual process.

Gender identity is defined as: "The sameness, unity, and persistence of one's individuality as male, female or ambivalent, in greater or lesser degree, especially as it is experienced in self-awareness and behavior; gender identity is the private experience of gender role, and gender role is the public expression of gender identity" (Money & Ehrhardt, 1972, p. 4).

To enlarge on this a bit, we may think of gender identity as the organized perceptions of oneself as masculine or feminine. A sense of gender identity is therefore a totally subjective-experiential matter. What counts is how one perceives oneself and this is a phenomenological matter. Although gender identity may be inferred from behavior, to some extent, this is not always the case. It is useful to think of gender identity as multidimensional—as encompassing potential feelings and evaluations having both masculine and feminine qualities rather than as a point along a gender continuum.

Money and Ehrhardt (1972) view transsexualism as the product of gender identity. Their reasoning is in harmony with the thinking of

Benjamin (1966). Both see gender discordance as a motivating force resulting in the desire to function with the identity and the role opposite
that of anatomical sex. Money (1984), like Benjamin, also sees a continuum of discordance running from transvestism through transsexualism. This theory of gender discordance or gender dysphoria is the most
widely-accepted explanation of transsexualism today, yet most authorities strongly urge that we consider the full etiology of this behavior
to be largely unknown. It appears likely that, for some, transsexualism
may be a final common path with many alternative beginnings, as suggested by Person and Ovesey (1974a,b).

The Psychoanalytic Model of Transsexualism

Modern psychoanalysts tend to emphasize early separation anxiety
(Bowlby, 1969, 1973) as a major factor in the development of transsexualism, although they may differ on how this takes place. An even greater
challenge would be to explain why early separation-individuation difficulties would produce transsexualism rather than some other expression
of psychopathology. For example, various neurotic disorders, the major
personality disorders, and various psychotic disorders have been attributed to trauma associated with the separation-individuation period.
Although these issues cannot be resolved at this time, it is nevertheless
useful to consider several psychoanalytic interpretations of transsexualism. From an historical perspective, Fenichel (1930) presented a classical
psychoanalytic study of transvestism and transsexualism when both of
these behaviors were simply called transvestism.

Stoller (1968a, 1974, 1985c) believes that an overclose affiliation with
the mother may be causal. This symbiosis is said to be much too intense,
too intimate, for healthy personality development. As a result of the
symbiotic fusion with the mother, a feminine core gender identity develops during the first 3 years of life. This core gender identity is conceptualized as the earliest and most enduring sense of being masculine or
feminine. Stoller also postulates family-based social learning processes
that demasculinize the young boy and reinforce both a feminine gender
identity and feminine role playing.

A closely related view is given by psychoanalysts Person and
Ovesey (1974a,b) although they differ from Stoller in some important
ways. Most importantly, they do not accept the claim that the transsexual necessarily experiences a cross-gender identity throughout life, and
they question whether the male transsexual actually manifests a feminine core gender identity as proposed by Stoller.

Person and Ovesey (1974a) believe transsexualism is founded upon a "repairative fantasy of symbiotic fusion with the mother" (p. 5)—a striving to repair losses experienced during the first 3 years of life. This is clearly very much in tune with Stoller's view, so that we have agreement concerning the early years of development. It is then that the differences are seen between the two theories. Person and Ovesey advance the thesis that an ambiguous gender identity is present throughout development in the transsexual; he feels neither clearly male or female. This is a major departure from Stoller's (1968a) theory of opposite core gender identity. This ambivalence may be due, they reason, to pre-oedipal fixation or to a damaged capacity for healthy gender-role development. They see the transsexual as suffering from significant and pervasive personality problems and associated symptoms. For example, they cite symptoms of being emotionally withdrawn, having asexual feelings, having few childhood companions, experiencing discomfort in expected boys' play, and showing an obsessive personality style. Further, they report TSs have low psychological insight, hate their penis, and typically have cross dressed in childhood but not fetishistically. They view this early cross dressing as a form of anxiety management. They see the transsexual as a variation of the borderline personality syndrome (Grinker, Werble, & Drye, 1968): " . . . primary transsexuals are schizoid-obsessive, socially withdrawn, asexual, unassertive, and out of touch with anger. Underlying this personality they have a typical borderline syndrome characterized by separation anxiety, empty depression, sense of void, oral dependency, defective self-identity, and impaired object-relations with absence of trust and fear of intimacy" (Person & Ovesey, 1974a, p. 19). Unlike other borderline personalities, however, the transsexuals are said to also show " . . . severe impairment of both core gender identity and of gender role identity from earliest childhood" (p. 19). For the case of a transsexual who sought relief for a host of serious personal adjustment difficulties through sexual reassignment, then ultimately suicided, see Levine (1984) and Levine and Shumaker (1983).

Person and Ovesey (1974b) have contributed much toward clarifying the difference between primary and secondary transsexualism, a separation we consider imperative. They do not believe primary transsexualism occurs in females. Such cases, they reason, are invariably based on a history of homosexuality and the transsexualism is said to be secondary to this process. Whether they are correct on this matter remains to be seen.

An object-relations model of how major distortions in the development of the self might lead to transsexualism has been presented by Beitel (1985). Taking a single case which manifested virtually the entire spectrum of gender symptoms—from fetishistic cross dressing through transsexual motivation—Beitel presents a theoretical model to explain these changes. The central hypotheses revolve about major difficulties in the formation of the self, identification processes focused on the mother, failure to articulate and distinguish elements of the good-self and bad-self and of the good-object and bad-object during the separation-individuation phase.

Follow-Up Studies of Sex Reassignment

The existing data-base of follow-up research concerning sex reassignment is so incomplete and methodologically flawed that few broad conclusions are warranted. Blanchard (1985c) and Stoller (1985c) present summaries of the evaluation literature. There seems never to have been an adequate commitment to reassignment follow-up research, and so we have at best, scattered reports using all kinds of transsexual subjects (males, females, primary and secondary types), various preoperative and postoperative measures, all kinds of outcome criteria, and a virtual absence of adequate control subjects. This is not to say that any such follow-up could be easily done; a host of problems must be addressed in order to deal with the question of whether reassignment is effective. At once, we must face the question of what we mean by "effective." How much weight should be given to the subjective, postoperative report by a transsexual that he or she feels better than before, enjoys life more in general, and considers the surgery the most valued step ever taken? Should these more or less self-serving and highly subjective evaluations be accepted as critical criteria for success? If so, transsexual surgery could be said to be quite successful, as one of the few things that seems to shine through clearly from the available data is the finding that most transsexuals report feeling better off, feeling happier, and valuing their reassignment (Hunt & Hampson, 1980; Meyer & Reter, 1979). But if the test of "effectiveness" or "success" or "usefulness" of reassignment is taken to be some combination of occupational achievement, marital stability, educational advancement, or social rehabilitation (whatever that means), the data are supposedly far less convincing according to Meyer and Reter. Let us consider their study in greater detail.

Based at Johns Hopkins University—a major center for gender studies, and a pioneering medical center which facilitated sex-reassignment surgery—the Meyer and Reter report (1979) was apparently the major factor in the termination of the sex-reassignment program at Johns Hopkins. They assessed 15 transsexuals who *had* been surgically reassigned and compared them to a group of 35 nonreassigned applicants for a "sex change." The use of this comparison group of 35 men leaves much to be desired. For example, it is reported that of this number, 14 went on to receive reassignment surgery and the remaining 21 all said they intended to do so. Since the 15 subjects who first received reassignment were not randomly selected from the pool of applicants selected for reassignment, we need to know, but we are not told precisely, why these 15 were reassigned and the others were not. In any case, Meyer and Reter compared the operative and nonoperative subjects 5 years following surgery for the following variables: residential stability and change, psychiatric status and contacts, legal involvements, occupational level achieved, and the gender appropriateness of live-in partners. The operated group did not show "clear objective superiority" (1979, p. 1014) over the nonoperated group. Hence, although the reassigned subjects said they were happier and better adjusted, they did not differ from the control group on the main criterion measures used by Meyer and Reter. The study has been reviewed critically by Hunt and Hampson (1980), Fleming, Steinman, and Bocknek (1980), and Stoller (1985c). The most serious criticism targets the inadequacies of the Meyer and Reter outcome criteria and the methods they used to assess these criteria.

Reporting on 17 cases of transsexual reassignment, Hunt and Hampson (1980) found no changes in the amount of psychopathology before and after surgery. This was measured by using records of criminal activity, drug use, and psychiatric symptomatology. All 17 were satisfied that their reassignment was the correct choice; none regretted the decision. Their "strongest positive gains" involved sexual adjustment and family relationships. Unfortunately, these variables were not reported by Meyer and Reter.

Blanchard (1985c), Lothstein (1980, 1982), and Stoller (1985c), in their reviews of follow-up research, have concluded essentially the same thing: Very little is factually known about the social or psychological effects of sexual reassignment, although it seems well-established from many reports that most individuals indicate they are happier and more comfortable in the cross-gender role. There is no agreement concerning the ultimate criteria of successful reassignment. For some evaluators, the resolution of a long-standing gender dysphoria seems highly significant and justifies the surgical intervention. For others, however, such as Meyer and Reter (1979), the ultimate criteria of success require various improvements in social functioning (e.g., occupational status, marital status, criminality. As might be expected, the reassignment procedure, taken alone, does not seem to have much impact on whatever psychopathology may be present, other than gender dysphoric feelings. Some of the things we would most like to know, such as which kinds of applicants may benefit most and which may regret this procedure, have not been adequately treated as research issues. The data base for decision making is not in place, and so far as we know, there is no suitable project of national scope to provide such a data base. Stoller (1985c) provides a much needed discussion of the ,value judgments, and the moral and ethical concerns which permeate decision making on this topic.

Summary

Transvestism and transsexualism have existed in nearly all cultures for centuries but virtually no scientific approach to these topics began until 1910 with the work of Hirschfeld. He used the term *transvestiten* to apply to both transvestism and what we now call transsexualism. An essential component of transvestism is sexual excitement produced by cross dressing, at least in the history of the individual. It is generally agreed that the erotic aspect of this cross dressing diminishes with years of practice, although it is described by transvestites of all ages as a highly pleasurable, mood-altering experience. For many, there is said to be the growth of a cross-gender identity which is experienced only when the person is cross dressed. Transvestism is thought, by some, to be an expression of an alternate identity, a second self, or a subsystem of the self. There is increasing support for the view that transvestism should be conceptualized more as a "disorder of the self" than as a sexual alternative or merely as complex fetishistic behavior. This is predominantly a heterosexual, male phenomenon, although bisexual and homosexual men also cross dress but, it is believed, for different reasons. No adequate theory has emerged to explain transvestism.

Primary transsexualism is seen as a major identity or self disorder based in the earliest mother–child relationship. It may be a product of some sort of biologically set effeminacy whereby the "core gender identity" propels the child toward a strongly held cross-gender identification. This diagnosis must be restricted to individuals who have manifested cross-gender behavior and identity from the earliest years, have a profound and extensive history of gender dysphoria, and do not occupy social roles which are gender appropriate relative to their anatomical sex, and who insist upon sex-reassignment procedures. Primary transsexualism occurs in both men and women. Its causes are unknown.

Secondary transsexualism also involves the self-report of gender dysphoric feelings and the desire for sexual reassignment, but the history is quite different. These individuals must lack the long history of gender dysphoria and they must, at some time, have functioned in gender appropriate roles compared to their anatomic sex. Further, they must have had a prior career as either a transvestite or a homosexual—hence, the late-in-life insistence upon sex reassignment is said to be "secondary" to this earlier career. This is believed to occur only in men and often in response to major life reorganization demands following the loss of loved ones, retirement, and other stressful changes. Although the facts are not well-established, some consider secondary transsexualism to be much more common than primary transsexualism.

The main theoretical approaches to both transvestism and transsexualism have involved an interactional model consisting of biological variables, gender identity and self system variables, and psychoanalytic conceptions of personality development.

Follow-up studies of the effects of sex reassignment indicate that the recipients say they feel happier and few reportedly regret their decision. There may be a positive change following reassignment, in sexual relations and in family relationships, although this is not well established. Neither the case in favor nor the case against these radical procedures is well documented and there is a great need for systematic, long-term, controlled studies in sex reassignment.

Chapter 4

Self and Identity

There is a very close link between the constructs of identity and gender identity and the more broadly defined construct of self. In this chapter we shall review the concept of self because it is the self-system that seems most critically associated with both transvestism and transsexualism. Our focus will be upon how the self has been conceptualized, what changes and developments in self theory seem provocative and useful for our purposes, and especially, how the idea of alternate and subordinate subsystems of the self can be accounted for. In a moment, we will turn to some definitions and see that there is no problem fitting the concept of identity into a formulation of self theory. But before we do, a word about self theory and transvestism.

Transvestites often attribute their behavior, at least in large part, to the existence of a feminine self or a second self. As we have previously noted, these terms have been extensively communicated as explanatory theories since about 1960 when Virginia Prince began the publication of *Transvestia* magazine (Prince, 1980). But there is considerable agreement among researchers that most transvestites do not experience anything akin to the gender dysphoria of the transsexual (Benjamin, 1966; Brierley, 1979; Buhrich & McConaghy, 1977b; Ovesey & Person, 1976; Stoller, 1968a, 1974, 1985c). As described in the preceeding chapters, transvestites are seen as typically heterosexual, masculine in gender identity and gender role, and whatever feelings of cross-gender identity they may have (which has not been adequately established) is said to relate to the time when they are cross dressed (Freund *et al.*, 1982). Or is it the other way around? Does the TV cross dress because of motives somehow set in action (or intensified) by feelings of cross-gender identity? The facts are not clear. But what seems certain from the self-reports of many TVs is that they do experience some kind of duality of self or a sense of a shared self—which they identify as a feminine self. To the extent that this attribution is valid—that is, there really exists some kind of feminine self—then we have the interesting questions of where this came from, when, what kinds of variations in intensity may be recognized, and whether the very long process of transvestism sustains or even fosters the strengthening of this component of the self system.

Primary and secondary transsexualism have been conceptualized as gender identity disorders and the differences between these two categories have been considered in Chapter 2. Both behavior patterns are said to be characterized by intense gender dysphoric feelings, the wish to live in the cross-gender role, and, very often, the wish for some kind of body feminization, ranging from taking female hormones to full sexual reassignment surgery (Benjamin, 1966; Person & Ovesey, 1974a,b; Steiner, Blanchard, and Zucker, 1985; Stoller, 1968a, 1974, 1985c). There is said to be an incompatible difference between anatomical sex and the subjective sense of masculinity or femininity—that is, one's gender identity. In the most direct sense, the entire phenomenon of transsexualism, then, comes down to the matter of gender identity—and to the dysphoric feelings associated with this identity. But both transvestism and transsexualism almost certainly involve many other kinds of feelings, self-perceptions, and sex role expectations rather than feelings about gender identity alone (Docter, 1985).

Gender identity is a hypothetical construct; it cannot be assessed without recourse to highly subjective information. Usually, we must ask people how they feel about themselves in relation to masculinity and/or femininity, or have them take tests, or be observed in a standard situation. What we would ideally like to have is an independent measurement system for gender identity—free from subjective appraisals by either the subject or the person making the measurements—so that we might better understand this construct. We could then assess the emergence of gender identity problems, their ebb and flow, various outcomes over time, and it would surely be much easier to formulate the subdivisions of transsexualism. Alas, no such objective measurement scheme has yet been invented. For our purposes we must rely upon two main ways to assess the transvestite and the transsexual: (1) We can ask questions and interpret the responses, using interview and test procedures; and (2) we can observe and assess behavior in "real-life" situations, thereby overcoming some of the artificiality of the clinical or research environment. In both clinical practice and research work, both procedures may be necessary and desirable but each has serious difficulties involving not only the bias of the interviewer or observer, but the propensity for transsexuals to give a history which supports their self-diagnosis. Many have commented on the difficulty of getting an objective personal history from an individual who is strongly motivated to "sell" himself as a transsexual. And so we have the same kind of problem faced by any personality theorist, for basically we are concerned with the experiential world of a person and that is not something we can measure with physical precision.

There is another difficulty with leaning too heavily on gender identity and gender dysphoria: too much is being asked of these constructs. The construct of gender dysphoria, for example, is a massive generalization; it is not, as the name suggests, a simple dimension of affective experience. Rather, both gender identity and gender dysphoria are ideas which necessarily are linked to a complex network of affective experience and cognitive stimulus processing. Quite obviously, the fact that an individual states he experiences intense unhappiness because of gender dysphoria does not prove that that is the case.

We are also impressed with the possibility that there may be far greater situational determination of gender identity than has historically been thought—at least in the populations of transvestites and transsexuals with whom we have worked. For example, we have observed several cases wherein men who had considered themselves heterosexual and fetishistic transvestites developed a "mentor" relationship (often in counseling) with a transsexual. In these cases, the impact of the social role-modeling presented by the transsexual mentor seemed to be paralleled by major reversals in gender identity and by demands for sex reassignment. We suggest that to attribute major changes (as with transsexualism) in self-perception, social-role expectancies, and goal setting to gender dysphoria or gender identity disturbance is stretching the explanatory power of these constructs too far. The massive reorganization of an individual's view of himself, as seen in secondary transsexualism, seems to us to involve many dimensions of personality and not exclusively gender-related cognitions or affects. Hence, cross-gender behavior (transsexualism) involves the expression of all types of cognitive and affective experience, and not merely gender-related ideas and feelings.

There is nothing wrong with inventing constructs about gender to account for transsexualism, but as in all scientific endeavor, there is a responsibility to attempt to clarify the meanings of constructs, to determine their validity, their relationships to other variables, their relationships to pertinent areas of theory, and in short, to refine and advance knowledge by moving from vague conceptualizations to testable theories. Bentler and Abramson (1981) have identified the major scientific issues which need to be addressed in sexual and gender research. In the next section we define some terms and see how the concept of self fits into present-day behavioral theory.

The Concept of Self

Unless otherwise stated, the terms self, self-concept, and concept of self will be used synonymously. From a behavioristic standpoint, the serious objection to all of these words is that they have no tangible or operationally definable anchors which have proven satisfactory. But as we shall see, the status of the self as a major explanatory variable in psychology has gained strength as never before with the emergence of cognitive psychological theory. Cognitive precepts currently enjoy high status in many areas of the behavioral sciences, and especially in child development, clinical psychology, social psychology, and motivational theory.

An historical review of the landmarks of self theory has been provided by Epstein (1973), together with his conceptualization of the self to be discussed below. Harter (1983) has written a very extensive review of the self from the perspective of a developmental psychologist. The importance of self-esteem as a factor in deviant behavior has been extensively studied by Kaplan (1980). Kaplan (1986) has also considered the social antecedents of four components of the self system: self-conceiving, self-evaluating, self-feeling, and self-protection/self-enhancement. For a somewhat different overview of self theory, see Sarbin (1952). Let us begin our discussion of self theory by noting some major conceptual landmarks.

William James was one of the first psychologists to use self theory to explain behavior (1910). He distinguished between the self as knower — a kind of executive manager within the mind—and the self as the object of knowledge—that is, something you can look upon as belonging to yourself and as a knowledge resource. The self as knower, James dispatched to philosophers. The self as object, according to James, was comprised of three component parts: (a) a material self, (b) a social self, and (c) a spiritual self. The material self was seen as containing one's own body, his family and possessions. The social self included the views others hold toward an individual. The spiritual self included a person's emotions and desires. All components of the self were said to be capable of contributing to either increases or decrements in self-esteem and well-being.

Cooley (1902) presented what became a classic in his description of the looking-glass self. His idea was that we build up views of ourself through our interpretations of the reflected appraisals of others. That is, through social interactions, we use the responses of other people as a looking glass which reflects back to us their appraisals of our conduct. We interpret this, and the self is thereby developed. As simple as it sounds, the idea is central to all conceptions of the self which take as the starting point the idea that we use social interactions to learn about ourselves and others, to evaluate, to discriminate, and to thereby construct a sense of self.

The same theme was further developed by George Mead (1934), who also emphasized our use of social data about ourselves in the development of the self. He proposed the view that we assemble from our experiences a "generalized other" consisting of our expectations and understandings concerning what others think about various behaviors, attitudes, and beliefs. By referring to this "generalized other" as a standard, we develop a self-based regulatory mechanism. Mead believed we have as many "selves" as we have social roles and that these vary greatly in terms of their significance for our total personality.

Carl Rogers (1951) defined the self as " . . . an organized, fluid, but consistent conceptual pattern of perceptions of characteristics and relationships of the 'I' or the 'me,' together with values attached to these concepts." Rogers believed the self-concept included only those characteristics of the person that he or she is aware of and over which control is maintained. He assumed a basic need exists to maintain and enhance the self and that threats to the self result in anxiety. Threats which cannot be defended against were said to lead to major disorganization.

After noting that the work of Lecky (1945), Snygg and Combs (1949), Sarbin, (1952), and Allport (1955) refine and sharpen the ideas presented above, Epstein (1973) summarized the main characteristics associated with the self which are as follows:

1. It is a subsystem of internally consistent, hierarchically organized concepts contained within a broader conceptual system.
2. It contains different empirical selves, such as a body self, a spiritual self, and a social self.
3. It is a dynamic organization that changes with experience . . . manifesting something like a growth principle . . . .
4. It develops out of experience, particularly social interaction with significant others.
5. It is essential for the functioning of the individual that the organization of the self-concept be maintained . . . .
6. There is a basic need for self-esteem which relates to all aspects of the self-system . . . .
7. The self-concept has at least two basic functions. First, it organizes the data of experience, particularly experience involving social interactions, into predictable sequences of action and reaction. Second, the self-concept facilitates attempts to fulfill needs while avoiding disapproval and anxiety. (Epstein, 1973, p. 407)

The Self-as-a-Theory

Kelly's (1955) theory of how we use personal constructs to make sense of the world, to understand ourselves and others, and to guide behavior comes down to this: He believed we build up an organized set of "personal constructs" —hypothetical concepts, explanations, attributions, beliefs—and that we apply this theory of how the world works to our everyday experience. The product is our ongoing behavior. We apply our theories, rearrange hypotheses and ideas as experience requires, and develop new theories or minitheories to fit our new experiences. This, quite obviously, is a cognitive view of what governs personality and behavior in general. It gives weight to what we think we know, the predictions and forecasts we make, our expectancies, and to our flexibility in reorganizing our personal constructs in accordance with actual experience. We do not have to erect a new theory for every new situation we meet; we can apply a theory already available from our reservoir of personal constructs.

Epstein (1973) builds upon Kelly's ideas and adds a very important emphasis: For Epstein, " . . . emotion occupies a position of central importance" (p. 408) within the self theory. Going beyond knowledge, data, judgments, information processing, hypotheses, beliefs, memories—all the stuff of cognitive processes—Epstein points up the critically significant additional dimensions of emotion, of pleasure getting, of pain-avoidance and of self-esteem building—all as components in a new conception of the self as a *self-theory*. This has become a theory . . . *that the individual has unwittingly constructed about himself as an experiencing, functioning individual, and it is part of a broader theory which he holds with respect to his entire range of significant experience*" [italics added]. We examine this next in more detail.

Epstein (1973) postulates three main parts of this cognitive system: One is concerned with the "nature of the world" (the body self). "By the body self, I mean the individual's biological self, his possessions, and those individuals he identifies with" (p. 412). A second major "postulate system" is concerned with the "nature of the self" (the inferred inner self). This " . . . refers to all aspects of the individual's psychological self, or personality. It includes the individual's cognitions, conscious and unconscious, that relate to his abilities, traits, wishes, fears, and other motivational and emotional dispositions" (p. 412); this represents the bulk of the self theory. A third major part of the self theory is concerned with the interaction between the other two (the moral self). This unit " . . . contains the self-evaluative reactions of the individual, including an overall appraisal of himself as a worthwhile human being as well as evaluative reactions to individual aspects of himself" (p. 412). We may think of these as three major domains of the self-theory. For example, whereas gender identity may fall mainly within the "inferred inner self" postulate system, one's view of one's own gender has many implications for his or her self-perceived body self and human relationships.

Hence, we must keep in mind that all three subsystems are involved in the determination of behavior.

The functions of this system of theory about one's self—the self theory—are said to be closely interrelated. Epstein sees them as follows: The most important function is to " . . . optimize the pleasure/pain balance . . . over the course of a lifetime"; the second is " . . . to facilitate the maintenance of self-esteem"; and finally " . . . to organize the data of experience in a manner that can be coped with effectively" (p. 407).

Epstein reasons very persuasively that by reconceptualization of the self into a self theory we gain far more than an exchange of terms. The point is, we can now examine one's self theory and evaluate this theory as we would any other theory—something that could not be done with the older view of self. For example, a good self theory should be characterized by its ability to explain a wide variety of experiences using the least complicated ideas possible. There should be an internal consistency across the main hypotheses and postulates comprising the theory, and the constructs employed should be testable. But most of all, the theory must have practical utility—it must help to achieve pleasure and the avoidance of pain, the gaining of self-esteem, and the assimilation of new data from life experiences.

Alternative Selves, Divided Consciousness, and Cross-Gender Identity

We are interested in understanding cross-gender identity because this is thought to be at the heart of transsexualism and it also seems to be experienced, to some degree and under some conditions, by transvestites. This is handled within Epstein's (1973) theory by his conceptualization of a *master self*—a so-called "generic self"—that maintains relationships and communications with the "different empirical selves. . . ." These subordinate self systems " . . . retain a degree of independence despite being influenced by, as well as influencing, the generic self-system" (p. 412). It is very straightforward to assume that one such subsystem could be organized around hypotheses, attributions, values, self-esteem building, pleasure, and pain-avoidance directly associated with cross-gender identity. Figure 2 shows how various components of the self system might be organized. Connecting lines are intended to show two-way paths for communications and control.

Hilgard (1977) presents a very similar model based on his studies of hypnotic and dissociative behavior. In his model of executive and subordinate cognitive control systems, a little adjustment of terminology is required. Hilgard sees the "executive ego" as a central control structure

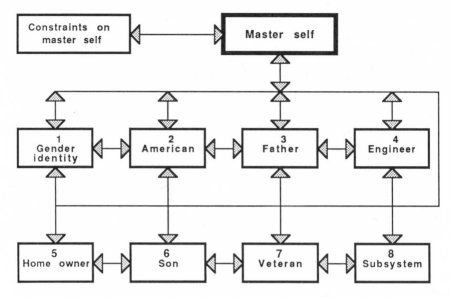

Figure 2. Schematic representation of the self system (derived from Hilgard, 1977). A master self serves as the manager, maintaining two-way communications and control ties with many subsystems. Constraints limit and regulate the self-system. Subsystems consist of major roles and all subidentities, including gender identity and cross-gender identity. In a harmoniously operating self system, these many subsystems are integrated into the self and support one's sense of unity and clarity of self, or identity. Secondary transsexualism may be conceptualized as an "overthrow" of the self system by the cross-gender identity (one of the subsystems), thereby producing a new identity and a new self system, with the cross-gender identity elevated to the master self.

which monitors and carries out necessary ego functions (perceiving, managing, adapting, responding, and integrating competitive inputs). There is said to be a subordinate control system for each of the roles we play—an idea akin to Mead's view of our multiple selves. Beliefs, attitudes, reality factors, and other major constraints interact with the executive ego, holding it in line, helping it to function effectively. The many subordinate cognitive control systems (one can call them subsystems) have interactive communications and control ties with the executive ego, and additionally, the subsystems have their own capability for receiving various inputs and emitting various cognitive outputs. The subsystems are said to be comprised, for example, of habits, interests, values, attitudes, abilities, prejudices, and roles. We would add gender identity and cross-gender identity, for our view of these constructs is that they occupy precisely the functions, the status, and the power of subordinate cognitive control systems. As we see it, then, much can be gained by conceptualizing gender identity and cross-gender identity as subordinate cognitive control systems.

When the self system is working effectively, the executive ego is able to turn on and off the subsystems selectively and in accordance with all constraints and controls which are operational (Epstein would say: in accordance with the logic and operations of the self theory—so as to derive pleasure, gain self-esteem, etc.).

But very importantly, Hilgard (1977) notes that problems can occur which are roughly analogous to a minor insurrection within the self system. Once a subsystem is activated and begins to take control or share control (as through hypnosis or extreme stress) it " . . . *continues with a measure of autonomy; the conscious representation of the control system may recede, leading to some degree of automatization.*" [italics added] Although there is much variation across subjects, both transvestites and transsexuals report the experiencing of a feminine self akin to the autonomous subsystem postulated by Hilgard. Transvestites, for example, often report feeling temporarily "taken over" by feminine feelings and subsequently behaving differently than when not cross dressed. Transsexuals report feeling despondent over their gender status and urgently seek to live in the opposite gender role.

Epstein's (1973) body self and inferred inner self would appear to occupy status and power similar to that of Hilgard's executive ego; the moral self would be a closely affiliated subsystem of the inferred inner self. But why should an inner self or an executive ego—whatever the inner hypothetical structure is called—conceive beliefs and direct behaviors that are inconsistent with reality? More directly, why would a chromosomal male come to believe that, at all cost, he must become a transsexual female? Epstein provides an example of how the healthy growth of the inner self can be stunted or shut off.

> Under certain circumstances, an inferred inner self might be a detriment to the individual as it could contribute to an unfavorable pleasure/pain balance. Consider the case of a child who is unconsciously, if not consciously, hated and who, if he were to internalize the values of significant others, would hate himself. Consider, further, that the only attention he could hope to obtain would be when he failed in something. We are considering a situation in which the self-system, were it to develop, would have to be turned against the welfare of the individual, contributing to low self-esteem and to an unfavorable pleasure/pain balance. It is hypothesized that under such circumstances, if extreme enough, a self-system would not develop at all, while under less extreme circumstances, the development of a restricted or distorted self-system would occur. (p. 414)

Transforming this example into gender identity terms, the most obvious parallel is that if a male predicts, for whatever reason, that he will be likely to fail in roles requiring masculine-gender competencies and skills—then either the formation of that subsystem would be weakened (or stopped), or a feminine gender identity will develop, thereby facilitating pleasure and self-esteem. This is the model of a more extreme recasting of gender identity that appears to operate in transsexuals. In transvestites, the less overbearing feminine self or cross-gender identity is said to be brought forth by the act of cross dressing (Freund *et al.*, 1982) and, we argue, it is thereafter progressively strengthened through two processes: First, through the social interactions of this pseudo-woman who is publicly presented in the cross-gender role and therein finds some measure of acceptance (or tolerance, at least). Second, through the enhancement of self-esteem (e.g., "I am the beautiful woman I've always wanted to love"), pleasure, and sexual reinforcement—mostly in the form of foreplay-like arousal—derived from cross-gender presentations of self.

Identity and Gender Identity

The concept of identity will be defined exactly as we have defined the inferred inner self (above). It is a summation of one's theories about himself or herself, both conscious and unconscious, of one's self-perceived personality characteristics, and of motivations and emotions as experienced. It is simplistic to ask, merely, "Who am I?" in attempting to define identity, for the answer to that question encompasses only a part of the broader concept of identity. A major subsystem of one's identity is gender identity.

Gender identity refers to those theories of ourselves that reflect masculine or feminine characteristics as judged within a given cultural framework. The most important aspect of gender identity is not overt behavior, but the inner, private, self-perception and self theory an individual maintains pertaining to his or her masculinity or femininity. If all goes smoothly during the early years of development, it is likely that one's sense of gender will be harmonious with biological sex. However, for reasons largely unknown, the process of gender identity development may swing far from the more typical path. Primary transsexuals, for example, are defined as having sustained a life-long self-perception of gender identity which is at variance with their biological sex. For an especially lucid exposition of the process of identity (self) formation, see Breger (1974).

The simplicity of a two-category model of gender (that is, we are either masculine or feminine, not androgenous) fits the traditional view in our culture—that one's identity and behavior should be either masculine if you are a male, or feminine if you are a female. A reappraisal of such categorical thinking has been underway for some time. But we should not confuse issues here. It is one thing to encourage the loosening of rigid sex-role stereotypes—as in assignment of women to certain traditional vocational fields and men to others—and it is another matter to mix gender identity. The proponents of greater androgeny in sex roles do not necessarily link this objective with the goal of either weakening an individual's gender identity or of encouraging some sort of shared masculine-feminine gender identity. Notice the difficulty of considering this kind of question without invoking one's very strongly established cultural values relating to gender and biological congruence; men should be masculine, we are all taught, and women should be feminine. When this is not the case, as with boys who are highly feminine, such individuals are said to be at risk relative to future "gender problems." There is some good longitudinal research in this area as reviewed in Chapter 3. The main point comes down to agreement that highly effeminate boys are more at risk relative to homosexuality, transvestism, and transsexualism than their more masculine male peers (Green, 1974, 1985; Rekers & Jurich, 1983; Zuger, 1966, 1978). But this is not proposed by anyone as the exclusive, or even the most probable, pathway for either transvestism or transsexualism—it is simply one starting point.

Assessment of Gender Identity

Gender identity has been studied in children using various interview, parent rating, behavioral observation, and psychological testing procedures, many of which are described by Green (1974, 1987). However, for the most part these procedures are not designed for use with adults. Promising self-report measures incorporating gender identity questions are now being developed by Blanchard (1985a,b,c) and his colleagues at the Clarke Institute of Psychiatry in Toronto. In Chapter 6 we shall describe an experimental self-description inventory of cross dressing behaviors and attitudes that we believe has promise as a measure of gender identity and cross-gender identity.

Green (1974) has listed the major criteria that may be taken as starting points for the assessment of gender identity, but how this may be accomplished in the most reliable and psychometrically defensible manner is unclear. In adults, these questions are usually assessed either in a clinical interview format or they are more extensively examined as part of psychotherapy, as exemplified best by the work of Stoller (1968a, 1974, 1985c). Green (1974) urges attendance to:

- Childhood behavior and fantasies
- Adult body imagery
- Masturbatory fantasies and sexual relations
- Social behavior
- Evidence of gender conflict as a child
- Adequacy in various aspects of the male sex role
- Presence/absence of sexual arousal while imagining self as male
- Sexual excitement to cross dressing
- Self-view as man or woman when dressed in men's or women's clothing
- Expressive body movements connoting femininity (in men)

Money's Social Learning/Critical Period Model of Gender Identity Formation

Money and Ehrhardt (1972) and Money (1977) have described developmental studies tracing the gender identity formation of human pseudohermaphrodites (newborns with ambiguous sexual anatomy). In carefully conducted research using these subjects, they studied the emergence of gender identity, its stability over time, and the marked resistance to change in gender identity once this was well in place by about the age of 3. These researchers did not assert that social learning processes were the exclusive cause of gender development and they did not claim that a possible underlying biological substrate should be discounted or ruled out.

Money and Ehrhardt (1972) consistently recognize that during the fetal development period, central nervous system changes might take place that could exert some kind of influence upon subsequent gender identity development. Certainly, we can see many examples in animals of clear, sex-specific differences, especially in reproductive behavior, even when learning cannot possibly account for such behavior.

In humans, there also is some evidence that a gender bias or tendency toward masculinization or feminization may be developed *in utero* (Diamond, 1977, 1979; Imperato-McGinley, Peterson, Gautier, & Sturla, 1979; Money, 1987). We must therefore keep an open mind concerning this impressive biological theory. But we must also be objective in looking at the evidence for what appears to be the powerful impact of social learning upon gender identity during the first 2 to 3 years of life. As Money has shown (1977), there appears to be a critical period, akin to imprinting, from birth to about the age of $2\frac{1}{2}$ years. The social assignment or socialization as a boy or a girl during that period seems to be a particularly significant gender learning experience. Such social learning

has been shown by Money and Ehrhardt (1972) to be sufficiently powerful to override whatever biological determinants of gender identity may
be formed *in utero*—at least in their pseudohermaphrodites. For them,
once gender identity becomes firmly established without ambiguity during the first 30 months of life, that identity appears highly resistant to
change. And therefore, if a chromosomal female is erroneously thought
to be a boy at birth due to masculine appearing genitalia, and if this child
is socialized as a boy, then he will strongly resist evidence to the contrary. This holds true even when adolescence brings about major bodily
changes that would only be interpretable as evidence of female mor-
phology. While the work of Money and Ehrhardt has not been embraced
by all gender researchers, their studies offer an impressive array of
applicable data pointing up the significance of very early gender identity
learning. The main point comes down to the significance of the first 2½
years as critical to gender development, and to the overwhelming impact of social learning processes impinging upon the young child during
that time.

Psychoanalytic Theory and Gender Identity Development

Within the psychoanalytic model, the processes of identification
and internalization are believed to have a central role in the creation of
both identity and gender identity. Additionally, the idea of gender envy
is very much tied in with a psychodynamic view of personality formation, and we shall repeatedly return to the importance of this belief. The
concept of castration anxiety and the elaborate theory of oedipal conflicts and their resolution is also a key part of the psychoanalytic theory
of personality. These developmental problems have been invoked by
psychoanalysts to account for virtually all kinds of unusual behavior—
from neuroses, through the character disorders, and certainly, the sexual disorders. While a literal reading of the oedipal theory of transvestism or transsexualism may not be very convincing, the central theme,
which relates to strong conflict with the same-sex parent, is believed by
many theorists to be of great significance. And so we shall find components of the psychoanalytic model running throughout this book
whenever we touch upon such concepts as identity, gender formation,
dissociative processes, identification processes, and unconscious motivation. While the psychoanalytic model may not be successful as a scientific method, the hypotheses derived from long-term clinical observations are fully worthy of our attention.

Stoller (1968a, 1974, 1985c) distinguishes between core-gender identity and gender identity. Core-gender identity is seen as a kind of "pri-

mordial" part of character structure and it is defined as " . . . a conviction that the assignment of one's sex was anatomically, and ultimately psychologically, correct" (1985c, p. 11). He postulates the basis of this underlying gender predisposition to be, most basically, "a biologic force" acting upon the fetal brain with later influences of sex assignment at birth, socialization, parental attitudes, and possibly some sort of "subliminal or unconscious" communication from the mother during the earliest symbiosis. It remains to be seen whether the idea of core-gender identity as a foundation for later gender identity development will prove correct or theoretically useful. It is not a precept which has been widely adopted, although the idea of a biological gender system of some sort is widely held.

Social and Cognitive Learning Theory and Gender Identity Development

From social-learning theory we derive the richness and power of imitation and modeling as key elements in the formation of identity and gender identity. Were it not possible for the newborn child to be aware of gender behavior during his or her earliest years, it is unlikely that the behaviors which we call masculine or feminine would emerge as they typically do. Direct reinforcement is not required in connection with learning through imitation and modeling. The child is increasingly aware of gender differences and searches the environment for examples to confirm his growing sense of the abstract ideas of masculinity and femininity. Usually, such evidence is readily available and these abstractions emerge as clear concepts during very early childhood.

Gender learning is an example of cognitive development, as the idea of gender is very much based in knowledge, meanings, and memories. With each year of development, there are great gains in the capacity to process complex ideas, and some of these ideas relate to gender. Gradually, the child comes to learn, first, of his or her own gender. Then, a far more complex kind of generalization takes place in which the child learns that gender is a constant (Kohlberg, 1966). It is not a human characteristic which comes and goes. It does not change with renewal of clothing or when hairstyles are altered. It is a constant attribute. We can refer to this as the concept of *gender constancy*. Such learning is basic to a clear understanding that specific rules govern the roles taken by each gender. These rules are highly explicit in our culture and apply especially to boys who are expected to refrain from any gender deviation. Cross-cultural comparisons of gender role training in boys has been reviewed by Green (1974). Conformity to these gender rules are very strongly demanded of male youth. Deviations from these socially defined role expectations will be punished, especially in boys, and the punishment becomes greater with advancing age. In early play, the preschool boy may dress like a girl, but the high school age boy who does so may be considered most unusual unless this is done within the context of some socially acceptable role deviation, such as playing a female-impersonation part in a play. There are many examples of such acceptable outlets for gender deviance, such as mock weddings, cross dressing on Halloween, and turn-about costume parties. Such events carry with them an understanding on the part of all participants that permission has been given for the presentation of oneself in public in some sort of gender violation expressly because all know in advance that such permission for deviance has been granted. The main point here is that we learn through social learning processes both the elements of our gender identity and also the complex role differences governing both masculine and feminine behavior. In addition, there is progressive learning of abstractions and generalizations about gender, such as gender constancy and gender-appropriate behaviors. We must also keep in mind that gender is not formed once and for all during a 30-month period. We are adding, refining, modifying, and consolidating our gender identity throughout childhood, adolescence, and across the entire life span. Perhaps the years through adolescence carry the greatest weight of all, for once this developmental period has been completed, the overall structure of gender identity seems resistant to change.

Gender Identity in Transvestism and Transsexualism

Is gender identity a causal variable in transvestism? Most heterosexual transvestites are said to have an unambiguous sense of who they are, both in terms of their overall identity or self-system, and in terms of gender identity (e.g., see Stoller, 1968a, 1974, 1985c). For now, let us set aside those unusual examples wherein this seems not to be the case—wherein some TVs may behave as typical heterosexual cross dressers for many years and then proceed through a transgenderism stage and on to secondary transsexualism. We have discussed these exceptional cases in Chapter 2. Unlike these atypical individuals, for most TVs there is reported to be little unpleasant affect pertaining to gender identity. Were this not the case, that is, if there were substantial gender dysphoria, it would be appropriate to view such a case in terms of possible transsexual features. As many have noted, cross dressing for the TV is a highly pleasurable activity and we know of no evidence that this pleasure is derived from overcoming gender-discordant feelings. We suggest two things are involved in what the TV considers the expression of feminine feelings. First, cross dressing appears to produce various pleasurable feelings—changes in affective status—which are highly reinforcing; this appears no different from many other kinds of pleasure-getting; there is no reason to assume that reduction of gender discomfort is somehow involved. Second, cross dressing appears to facilitate social reinforcement, enhancement of self-esteem, and temporary escape or avoidance of stress or boredom.

But are we saying here that no feelings of cross-gender identity exist in the heterosexual transvestite? Certainly not. We shall present evidence in Chapter 6 from our experimental Cross Dressing Inventory that such a temporary excursion into the realm of a cross-gender identity is described by TVs as an important dimension of the cross dressing experience.

These men commonly describe a strong identification with women. Similarly, feelings of gender envy—an intense longing to be like women—are often reported by TVs. The fantasies and fictional stories (Beigel & Feldman, 1963; Buhrich & McConaghy, 1976) favored by transvestites also suggest intense identification with women. But envy and identification are not the equivalent of gender identity. Such identity is not switched on and off as easily as clothing can be changed. We believe transvestites do experience marked cognitive changes when cross dressed but we are inclined to be skeptical that such changes represent actual gender identity transformations. Our preference would be to reserve such terminology for long-term processes of change in gender identity.

Transvestites do not speak of having a "cross-gender identity" when cross dressed; this is a research-based construct (Freund et al., 1982). The TV simply states that he experiences his "feminine self"—or that a second self is being expressed. It is easy to see why a man who presents himself as a woman, even quite temporarily and often with at least the unspoken approval of others, might prefer such an attribution. There is a face validity to the idea of a feminine self or an alternate self. But whatever this remarkable cross-gender identity be named, the important point for now is that cognitive and affective changes associated with cross dressing clearly call for some sort of indication that a feminine self is experienced. We prefer to consider this a subordinate cognitive control system, as discussed above. Let us now consider how deviations in masculine gender identity development is thought to influence behavior.

Stoller (1985c) believes that at the heart of most paraphilic behavior is a shaky, uncertain, threatened sense of masculine gender identity. The sexual acting out which defines the paraphilic pattern is seen as a defensive struggle representing an attempt to overcome the humiliation of this threatened masculinity and an attempt to convert the trauma of the past into an expression of erotically tinged mastery (Stoller, 1968a, 1974, 1975, 1976, 1985b, 1985c). Stoller places great emphasis on the high intensity of the mother–infant symbiosis in the months immediately following birth said to be observed in individuals with gender disorders who later manifest some additional form of paraphilic behavior. Stoller reasons that this intense emotional linkage may result in a later " . . . conflict between the urge to return to the peace of the symbiosis and the opposing urge to separate out as an individual, as a male, as masculine" (1985c, p. 18). Such a person must struggle against showing any feminine attributes, thereby showing masculinity—even hypermasculinity—to oneself and others. Transvestism, and other paraphilic behavior, then, stem from feeling " . . . pressure from envy and anger toward women" (p. 18) who have contributed to this damaged sense of masculinity.

Stoller (1968a) makes an excellent point about transvestism and masculine sexuality. The transvestite, he argues, cross dresses as a kind of "detour" maneuver in an effort to express his sexual feelings which are based on a masculine gender identity. We should not be misled, according to Stoller, just because the TV enacts the feminine role as a device to feel himself a more masculine person—that is, a more sexually fulfilled person. Another Stoller hypothesis (1968a, 1985c) that we find most worthwhile is his minitheory of how the perennial, but poorly supported, theory of the "distant father" may play a part in the motivation for transvestic cross dressing. The transvestite, in this view, longs to regain or gain closeness to this partially lost significant other; the TV assumes the father is distant because of the dynamics of the father–son competition, and he thinks to himself: "If I were a girl, you'd love me; so I'll be one even if I am also, and will always be, a male" (1985c, p. 133).

In primary transsexualism almost all authorities agree that gender dysphoria is at the heart of the difficulty, although the definition and measurement of this concept remain vague. It is believed that a life-long and intense mismatch has existed wherein the individual believes he or she is in the wrong body. Such feelings are said to invariably surface in early childhood so far as the primary TS syndrome is concerned. It is not known why such extreme identity incongruity originates or what sustains such feelings if, in fact, the gender dysphoria thesis proves correct.

There appears to be a growing acceptance of the view that most transsexuals do not meet the criteria for primary transsexualism and that secondary transsexualism is far more typical, although hard data are lacking. For example, Stoller notes that " . . . hermaphrodites and primary transsexuals make up only a handful of those who want 'sex change'. The rest—secondary transsexuals—though they have severe disturbances in masculinity and femininity, strike me as having a pretty intact maleness or femaleness" (1985c, p. 161).

In secondary transsexualism the theory is that a major defensive or adaptive process, either homosexuality or transvestism, precede the quest for sexual reassignment surgery (Person & Ovesey, 1974b). This motivation is said to be crisis-related and therefore, the secondary transsexual is expected to surrender his insistence upon surgery when the crisis has past. The facts in support of this scenario have not, thus far, been well established although such cases are frequently reported in clinical settings.

Summary

We are interested in the self system because both transvestism and transsexualism have been described as disorders of the self. The main functions of the self are believed to involve achievement and maintenance of self-esteem, maintenance of a favorable pleasure/pain balance, and the management of coping with change. For most transvestites, there appears to be a temporary exchange of gender identity associated with the cross dressing experience. This change is ego-syntonic and pleasurable. There is said to be a feminine self or an alternate self. If this is a valid attribution then a duality of the self would appear to exist during the cross dressed period. But the idea of having a feminine self may be a misattribution, in which the erotic excitement of cross dressing, together with other controlling stimuli and reinforcers, are incorrectly attributed to the hypothetical "girl within."

The secondary transsexual describes feelings of gender dysphoria, believed indicative of intense cross-gender identity strivings. But can we accept these descriptions at face value, or do we have here another example of misattribution? Many have noted that the sex reassignment applicant may overstate gender dysphoric feelings based on his assumption that such symptoms will facilitate sex reassignment. Another difficulty is that the idea of gender dysphoria sounds like a simple, straightforward concept, but it is not. As presently used, the construct of gender dysphoria is much too broad. It is an oversimplification of multiple feelings, affects, self-evaluations and expectations—not a unidimensional indicator of self-perceived gender.

A cognitive model of the self system was presented, based on the work of Epstein (1973). Here, the self is seen as comprised of various theories that an individual holds about himself or herself. The structure of the self is thought to consist of a master self with executive responsibilities, various constraints upon the self, and subsystems which maintain two-way communication and control ties with the primary self. Hilgard's model of divided consciousness (1977) is described, and its possible application to transvestite and transsexual self-perceptions is discussed. The self system strives for internal consistency and the resolution of cognitive dissonance. But in unusual circumstances, there may be an "overthrow" of the self system and an the establishment of a new primary or master self. This line of reasoning is applied to secondary transsexualism.

Different models of gender identity development have been described, spanning the social-learning position and the biological view. All authorities agree that each of these lines of influence may play a part in the formation of gender identity. Only in primary transsexualism would gender identity seem deflected mainly by biological factors, and even here, the evidence is far from clear.

Chapter 5

Sexual Excitement, Fetishism, and Pleasure

Across the phylogenetic spectrum, from single-celled organisms to man, no abilities vary more dramatically than our ability to think, to reason, to remember, and to process information. This is fundamental to the management of our most unique capability, the system of language, which makes possible both abstract concept manipulations and interpersonal communications. Thinking as we do—with language concepts—allows us to know, to understand, to study, to reason, and to anticipate future events with complexities far more effectively than any other organism.

When psychologists refer to cognitive processes they are speaking of the total system of information management basic to thought and information processing. Memories are drawn upon, new ideas are added or old ideas are reinterpreted; judgment, the extraction of meanings, and the emotional or motivational significance of certain thoughts all play a part. The end product is our mental life, our thinking processes. In our study of transvestism and transsexualism, we shall find powerful explanatory significance in one particular set of cognitive operations—the sexual script.

Sexual Script Theory

The sexual script is comprised of plans, expectations, and guidelines for action, but for the typical transvestite, nothing surpasses the fantasy components of his sexual script. Consider this example:

> I like to think of myself as a realist—a male I was born and a male I'll die, but I must admit I'd trade places temporarily with a female for the experience. In all honesty, I've never really psychoanalyzed why I love cross dressing, but [I] simply love to do it every time.

This individual's sexual script incorporates a cross-gender identity theme which is very common in heterosexual transvestites. We shall have more to say about this in the chapters to come, but for now, the main point is that the sexual script provides an organizing set of ideas around which transvestic behavior is organized. Our cognitive capabilities underlie our capacity for the development of sexually excitatory mental stimuli and for the appreciation of what comes to be seen as erotic imagery. Such cognitions and imagery play a central part in both the formative organization or shaping of transvestic behavior and in sustaining this behavior, often throughout life.

Virtually without exception, all students of human sexuality have in one way or another recognized the importance of well-organized erotic ideation as central to both the sexual stimulation and the sexual responding of individuals. Such cognitive activity and recurrent fantasies are critically important in the the organization, control, and direction of behavior. These are not transient daydreams or unstructured, pleasant thoughts; they are among the most powerful and persistent forces basic to sexual behavior. Once set in place through learning and practice, sexual scripts often maintain the same general character for a lifetime, despite refinements and elaborations on familiar themes. The general outline of these cognitive structures, at least for most, is thought to be more or less permanent, but little of an empirical nature has been reported.

A valuable theoretical statement about the role of cognitive factors as mediators in sexual arousal and responding has been provided by Rook and Hammen (1977). They see cognitive processes as greatly influencing sexual arousal through such mechanisms as these: perception of both internal and external cues associated with arousal and the linkage of erotic meaning to these percepts; cognitive monitoring of the arousal processes and judging of the intensity of arousal based on expectations; giving attention to and evaluating the status of the self; perception of intra- or interpersonal expressive behavior; and finally, the initiation of behaviors in response to these cognitive signals. Both conscious and unconscious thought processes are said to be involved. Geer and Fuhr (1976) and Przybyla and Bryne (1984) take a similar approach in their consideration of cognitive factors in sexual arousal.

Cognitive interpretations of behavior have achieved considerable status in psychology during the past several decades (Neisser, 1967). The theoretical foundations of this approach are very old, but a resurgence of interest followed the publication of the classic work of Miller, Galanter, and Pribram (1960) concerning what they called the plans and structure of behavior. More recently, the Mandlers have independently discussed cognitive theory in ways having many implications for the construction of sexual scripts (G. Mandler, 1975; J. Mandler, 1984). For example, G. Mandler (1975) postulates "releaser" stimuli of environmental origin, which have two effects: first, releasers trigger overt behavior; second, they may result in emotional arousal that potentiates this overt behavior. He sees this sequence as applicable, for example, to sexual and aggressive behavior as well as other emotional responses. Mandler makes the important distinction between physiological responses as patterns of action which are mainly response processes, and physiological patterns that act as "controlling stimuli" for emotional behavior. He conceives of cognitive processes as both learned and innate "action structures," intermediate between sensory inputs and overt behavior. In Mandler's view, sexual fantasies may be founded on innate motivational urges; the child responds to these motives by gradually building what amounts to a sexual script.

Sociologists John Gagnon (1973) and William Simon (Gagnon & Simon, 1973; Simon, 1973; Simon & Gagnon, 1986), have given considerable attention to sexual script theory. Gagnon defined a sexual script as " . . . an organized, time-bound sequence of conduct through which persons both envisage future behavior and check on the quality of ongoing behavior" (1973, p. 29). He discusses scripts as examples of cognitive behavior and the functions of scripts are said to include the following: "Such scripts name the actors, describe their qualities, indicate the motives for the behavior of the participants, and set the sequence for appropriate activities, both verbal and nonverbal . . . " (p. 29).

Simon and Gagnon (1986) postulate that scripts are formed through the interaction of cultural factors, biological determinants, and individual learning experiences. Scripts, therefore, structure the culturally set expectations and determine the framework for a sexual encounter. They emphasize the changing qualities of sexual scripts with a continuing reordering and revision process going on throughout life. Although noting this flexibility and propensity for change in scripts, they may somewhat understate the so-called "locked-on" or rigid script characteristics commonly seen in persons with sexual difficulties. Three levels of scripting are described: first, "cultural scenarios" which involve the learning of common meanings; second, "interpersonal scripts" which involve a combination of cultural scenarios and the meanings these hold for a specific individual in a specific context; and third, "intrapsychic scripts" which involve the management of desires by a particular individual. These scripts are seen as regulating and ordering sexual behavior.

In order to understand both the power of sexual scripts and the

diverse significance which they have in directing behavior, we next
review the 10 defining characteristics and attributes that we propose are
most important.

The Defining Characteristics of Sexual Scripts

These defining characteristics may be set forth in 10 major areas:
1. *Stimulus attributes*. Sexual scripts provide an organizing focus for
erotic ideation and action. They feed information to other parts of the
brain. They stimulate activation and arousal systems of the brain, participate in the release of hormones, and alter the emotional life of the
individual. Sexual scripts are highly complex and involve both purely
mental activity, as in daydreams, as well as combinations of mental
activity and subsequent action. The interaction of erotic mental activity
and environmental stimulation is interwoven and mutually dependent.
Hence, the same stimulus (a sexually arousing event) may be highly
stimulating in one situation and not at all stimulating under other circumstances because of differences in the expectancies of an individual.
2. *Response attributes*. Sexual scripts involve ideational responses
and interpretations of mental activity. These responses are powerful
motivators of action. They involve expectancies and predictions of how
future behavior may or may not be reinforcing, and whether such behavior will lead to positive or negative consequences. These responses
may be thought of as conditioned emotional responses set off by mental
activity. That is, the total response array which comes from energizing a
sexual script does not end with mental activity, but with more complex
behavior which is part of the human sexual response pattern.
3. *Affective attributes*. Sexual scripts carry an affective message. This
may range from highly pleasurable to highly displeasurable. They participate in the modification of arousal level and typically involve erotic
yearnings, fantasies, and expectancies. Highly rehearsed scripts may
take on a "life of their own" by becoming substitutes for interpersonal
erotic experiences. This is seen in some solitary fetishistic behavior
which comes to take the place of person-to-person sexual responding.
Paradoxical pleasure may be derived from sexual scripts which call for
real or imagined pain, suffering, humiliation, or subordination. Why
such "painful" activity is pleasurable for a person can only be understood through knowledge of the details of one's sexual script and its
origin.
4. *Persistence attributes*. Sexual scripts are highly persistent although
they evolve and diversify throughout life. Little detailed knowledge

exists concerning the factors contributing to such changes, the amount of redirection or initiation of new themes, or the relationship between life experiences and the modification of scripts. Most sex researchers have commented upon the persistence of scripts. Such lifelong significance may be related to connections between these cognitive systems (memories, knowledge, plans, expectancies, feelings) and the instinctual motives of humans. We refer here to such basic needs as security, love and affection, and interpersonal trust.

5. *Intrusive attributes.* Sexual scripts take an active role in motivating humans; they are not weak or passive. They are intrusive, persistent, emotionally significant, and highly motivating. For a given individual, they may take on obsessional characteristics, but not in the sense of being unwanted; rather, they are intrusive in their redirection of attention. Through maintenance of tightly focused concentration, scripts may facilitate feelings of relaxation. At other times their intrusive power may disrupt other task-centered attention.

6. *Motivational attributes.* Sexual scripts organize and motivate complex behavior. They are a network of both reality-based and fantasy ideation mixed with emotionally significant and sexually colored thoughts, often including hopes, fears, and uncertain expectations of failure and mastery. The product contributes to organized, goal-directed, motivated behaviors, all of which are key elements in the human sexual response pattern.

7. *Need-fulfilling attributes; gaining mastery and control.* Sexual scripts are highly structured and organized into need-fulfilling themes. These may be so disguised as to keep the central meaning of the theme out of consciousness, displaying instead, symbols, meanings, and conflicts through patterns which are incompletely understood by the individual. Many developmental psychologists believe the play of childhood may, in part, incorporate strivings to overcome the hurts and conflicts children endure. Through acting out these frustrations and anxiety-producing events, a sense of mastery and control is developed. Hence, the powerless child can become all powerful, the master of his fate rather than the victim. This thesis is supported when a child repeatedly enacts a similar theme, as in awarding himself or herself the role of the adult or the teacher and subsequently disciplining other children. More erotic play can involve the familiar body exploration games, such as playing doctor and nurse. Humans seem well constructed to use their imaginative abilities to strive to overcome emotional hurts. The energy which drives and shapes childhood experiences into well-organized sexual scripts may stem from this need to overcome adversity, to avoid anxiety, and to replace pain and sadness with pleasure and delight.

Early childhood is inevitably filled with frustrations for most children and the response to this includes mastery strivings. The goal is to overcome these frustrations. Just as Freud viewed dreams as the "royal road to the unconscious," sexual scripts offer a kind of royal road to the understanding of conflicts central to childhood development. It seems likely that a careful study of the daydreams and sexual fantasies of a person should yield rich insights into the earlier conflicts and frustrations which gave rise to these themes. Surely, for example, there must be personality differences among men who find satisfaction in such diverse cross dressing behavior as dressing up as an infant, as a prostitute, a grande dame, or a sexy teenager. But it is not implied that a man who wants to dress up as a prostitute, for example, necessarily wants to be a prostitute. It is the symbolic meaning of such imaginal role taking that is important.

Satisfying personal adjustment seems to require a feeling of control and potential mastery—a capacity to cope and deal with the problems of life. It is unpleasant and anxiety producing to feel a childlike impotence or weakness. People seem to function best when they feel they are effective and potentially successful. Through building sexual scripts, an individual uses one of the potential tools for achieving a sense of mastery and control. At least his own sexual impulses and fantasies can be organized and mentally manipulated under self-control. Sexual scripts eventually tell a person what to do, or what to strive to do, when to do it, where, with whom, and in what way. The script is, therefore, a guide for action, offering a way to feel in control and to have a definite plan.

8. *Scripts as an outlet for feelings.* Sexual scripts provide a much needed outlet for feelings. In our culture, men in particular are taught that it is inappropriate to display emotion and feelings except in certain situations. This is supposed to be weak and effeminate. Little boys are supposed to learn to "show backbone" and to take punishment "like a man." Girls are allowed far greater range of emotional expression. Whereas the experience of a daydream-like sexual script may be very pleasant or sexually arousing, it is the actual enactment of such mental imaginings that generates the greatest emotional satisfaction. Given the right circumstances, a fetishist can arrange his stimuli, his interpersonal dynamics, and his erotic arousal to maximize the emotional impact of the entire scene. Imagine the exhilaration of the sexually fearful person who is able to enact (and thereby master and overcome) scenes of kidnaping, imprisonment, torture; or sexual attack, weakness, or effeminacy—and to experience conquest and control over any of these.

Another example of this quest for mastery is the behavior of the adult heterosexual transvestite who urgently wants to appear in public as a woman and to pass. Most TVs harbor a long-standing fantasy of doing this and most ultimately do so. They report a sense of fear, excitement, and thrilling danger mixed with triumphant victory. The delightful arousal changes associated with this risk taking do not dissipate. They may endure as permanent components of self-regulated pleasure getting; a kind of nondrug "quick fix." If there is a lessening of arousal with practice, the sexual script can be upgraded to incorporate greater risk. And so the pattern of elaboration and development is without limit. And so far as the expression and experience of strong emotional feeling is concerned, all of this is accomplished without much real risk. Even the danger of public exposure and ridicule is a controllable and bearable risk because, in reality, actual horror stories of severe rejection are seldom encountered. One exception, however, would be transvestites in the military services who are frequently removed from sensitive jobs, demoted, or discharged when their cross dressing behavior is discovered or admitted.

9. *Scripts as positively reinforcing events.* Sexual scripts are positively reinforcing events. They have been repeatedly linked with pleasurable sexual arousal and with orgasm and, thereafter, acquire ever stronger significance as both stimuli and responses. They come to take on a quality of autonomy and importance apart from direct sexual behavior. Scripts become a source not only of sexual stimulation but of joy, escapism, and erotically colored pleasure. This is the energy that keeps the sexual script in place and resists erosion or extinction. By providing one key to opening strong feelings of pleasure, a sexual script guarantees itself a long life.

10. *Scripts as focused expectancies.* Scripts offer an organized format for expectations which have powerful motivating significance. In humans, our sexual feelings are not primarily founded upon hormonal regulation, but rather, upon our mental experience—our expectations. By having a sexual script which can, at least in part, be enacted, a person develops a self-regulated mechanism for sexual arousal. The script, while in the form of a daydream or transient fantasy, promotes both momentary pleasure and the excitement of anticipating far greater pleasures to come. These mental expectancies have profound motivational significance and direct behavior into action. When so aroused by his own thoughts, the fetishist or cross dresser may begin to make specific plans to bring together the elements essential to script enactment. Anything which then blocks this goal-directed behavior is likely to arouse irritability, discomfort, and anger. There is a strong inner motive which seems to call for erotically toned action. These focused expectancies of pleasure which are so central to the sexual script are what keep this action plan on course despite frustrations and barriers.

Innate Affective Systems and Script Formation

Innate affective systems are believed to underlie the learning of sexual scripts. In particular, we refer to the basic needs of human organisms for physical and emotional security. This basic requirement applies to very young children and has been studied in humans by Bowlby (1969, 1973) and in animals by Harlow (1958) and his associates. It is now clear that a process of infant–mother attachment and bonding takes place during the early months of life, and that if something interrupts or terminates this early developmental process the consequences for personality development are expected to be very adverse. We also refer here to those brain systems which support pleasure-getting and the quest for relief of anxiety. Similarly, we are concerned with the growing child's progressive knowledge about the manipulation of his or her own arousal level; this self-induced alteration of activation level and sensation seeking is highly significant in sexual research and it has thus far not been adequately studied.

Attributes of Innate Affective Systems

For the past 30 years, brain researchers throughout the world have developed a strong factual basis for understanding the roles of the reticular-activating system, the limbic system including the autonomic nervous system, and very possibly, parts of the frontal lobes as key components in the regulation of our emotional lives. We shall not delve into brain research here, but instead, our focus will be upon what appear to be the central attributes of innate affectional systems. The reader should keep in mind that we are reviewing this topic because it seems to be central to the formation of sexual scripts, and such scripts appear to exist at the heart of sexual behavior.

High Conditionability.   Our innate affective systems are highly responsive to conditioning through a variety of processes and without the conscious awareness of the individual being conditioned. The very early learning which underlies formation of favored sexual stimuli and the self-awareness of what ultimately comes to be regarded as pleasurable, as in falling in love, need not be learned through conscious awareness. Why one stimulus is ultimately valued more than another—one scene is perceived as highly exciting and another as dull—is not known. The best we can do now is to attribute such differences to individual learning experiences. But the important point is that we are well-constructed to facilitate this very kind of highly individualistic learning experience. Basic to such learning are the flexible, highly conditionable, innate affective systems of the brain.

Permanent Linkage to Sexual Scripts. Once a network of ideation—a sexual script—is formed and linked to innate affective systems, this regulatory ideation remains largely in place throughout life. There may be extensive experimentation, both mentally, through fantasies, and through actual behavior, but in the final analysis the preferences of youth often reflect the most powerful sexual themes running through a person's life. Very possibly, this permanence is less mysterious than it appears. It may be that through intermittent positive reinforcement, high rates of similar sexual behavior are sustained much as is seen in other modes of behavior. Given the reality that preferred sexual scripts will be enacted throughout life, it is little wonder that we see their continuity across the life span.

Elaboration and Stimulus Generalization. Whereas the brain mechanisms which are basic to innate affectional systems may not be altered through experience—an issue which remains unresolved—it seems clear that extensive elaboration and stimulus generalization do occur within a sexual script. In humans, there appears to be a need for sexual variation, for enrichment, and for novelty in sexual responding if pleasure is to be at a maximum. Perhaps this is basic to the extensive elaboration and development of sexual scripts that feed into the innate affective systems. But there is another way of looking at this. Very possibly, our arousal and emotional experiences are more satisfying when there is a fluctuation and change experienced; we appear to be built to need a variety of stimulus inputs. We are highly discontented in stimulus isolation chambers. Hence, the most basic motive for variation of the sexual script may originate in this innate quest for stimulus variation and novelty of stimulus input (Fiske & Maddi, 1961). Humans are stimulus-seeking organisms, searching like radar antennae for new signals, new thrills, new combinations of old stimuli, and variations on tested sexual themes. Given such basic needs, it is to be expected that some variation and development of the sexual script is observed despite its basic continuity and stable thematic structure.

Learned Environmental Control of Affective Responses. Learning to value a fetish is an example of how we can develop external stimuli that are powerful in turning on our affective brain systems. This is extremely important in the understanding of fetishism and erotically toned cross dressing. The commonly observed resistance of transvestites to change of their behavior despite heroic efforts to bring about such change may be due, at least in part, to the impact of conditioned (fetishistic) stimulus–response connections that tie the innate affective systems to both environmental stimuli and to sexual scripts.

We turn now to a discussion of contemporary thinking about sexual excitement. If we are to understand fetishistic behavior and transvestism we must study sexual excitement, sexual scripts, and pleasure—topics that have been more extensively treated in the literature of poetry than in science. As we review these critically important topics, our goal will be to clarify the constructs believed most useful, and to propose those attributes which we believe are most basic to each of these constructs.

Sexual Excitement

For the most part, sexual excitement has been defined in terms of the subjective self-report of individuals. No rigorous behavioral definition has come into general use, although in laboratory settings measurements of changes in penis volume have become well-accepted as objective indices of sexual excitement (Freund, 1971; Freund, Sedlacek, & Knob, 1965; Freund, Langevin, & Barlow, 1974; Geer, 1980; Jovanovic, 1971; Zuckerman, 1971).

Some define sexual excitement (Masters & Johnson, 1966) as a preliminary stage of the human sexual response pattern—and that is the definition we shall use. Sometimes the terms sexual excitement and human sexual response are used synonymously. In order to be explicit about what we mean by sexual excitement let us identify seven attributes of this behavior pattern. Thereafter, we will review Stoller's psychoanalytically based view of sexual excitement and the work of Masters and Johnson.

Seven Attributes of Sexual Excitement

1. *Physiological responses.* The bodily changes representing the emotional and motivational processes basic to the human sexual response pattern have been studied by Masters and Johnson (1966). These are the basic building blocks of sexual excitement. Changes in muscle tension, autonomic and central nervous system arousal, and adjustments of the cardiovascular system and elsewhere in the body are imperative to sexual excitement, but they are not the essence of this excitatory process. As we shall see, the unique and most essential component is in how the individual interprets these bodily processes. *Fundamentally, sexual excitement is a set of cognitive responses—meanings, knowledge, judgments, and*

interpretations of what stimulation means. These cognitive processes are accompanied by physiological changes which reinforce and support responding throughout the sexual response cycle.

I have requested many heterosexual transvestites to take their pulse under various conditions before, during, and after cross dressing. Most report marked increases in pulse rate associated with preparation for cross dressing and throughout a transvestite episode. Here is the report of one long-practicing cross dresser:

> I did take my pulse at rest—before—during—and after dressing, as you requested, and have done so a number of times. At rest my pulse is around 82. During dressing it rises to between 92 and 100. While out in public it can sometimes go to 120, especially in situations where I am sure I am being 'read' by someone. While changing back to my male dress it drops again to the mid-90s and usually takes an hour or so to return to normal.

2. *Multidetermined emotional behavior.* Sexual excitement is a combination of cognitive and physiological changes. The interplay between these physiological processes and mental activity is complex and poorly understood. For example, although sexual feelings may be clearly recognizable and highly goal directed they are sometimes concealed even from oneself, or expressed "nonsexually"—as in the sublimation of sexual motives. Psychoanalysis offers many examples of these deflections of sexual motivation. But our concern is with sexual excitement as actually experienced, and when we use the term we shall assume that the subjective experience of sexual meaning is recognized by an individual.

3. *Drive reduction motives and incentive motives.* Sexual excitement encompasses both drive reduction motivation ("push motives") and incentive or expectancy motivation ("pull motives"). Within the same person, these two quite different kinds of motivation may be experienced in a different manner at different times. For example, at one time there may be intense motivation to reduce perceived sexual tension, and at another time there may be intense motivation to enhance or supplement perceived sexual tension with the ultimate aim of having this reduced. We see, then, a good example of how tension or sensation seeking can be pleasurable, as in foreplay or any other sexually preparatory behavior. Many contemporary books about the enjoyment of sexuality discuss tactics for generating and sustaining sexual tensions. Cross dressing behavior involves sexual script enactment that is largely arousal and tension inducing rather than based on sex drive reduction. The point is that such sensation-seeking behavior is interpreted as highly pleasurable.

4. *Pleasurable or displeasurable affective experience.* The subjective experience of sexual excitement may be either pleasurable or displeasurable.

The particular environment in which a person experiences such feelings may be a principal determinant of how he or she feels. Of great importance is the expectation of sexual tension reduction. Very often, transvestites behave so as to maintain mild sexual excitement over many hours.

5. *Memory systems and sexual excitement.* In humans, sexual excitement is highly dependent upon the formation of memories. These organized cognitive structures make possible the retention of preferences we sustain about sexual feelings and expectancies. They shape the assumptions we make about the conversion of sexual motivation into sexual pleasure. We strive to reduce unpleasant tension and to sustain a sense of control and mastery; our tactics for dealing with sexual motives reflect this objective. Memory systems, then, are basic to the construction of one's unique sexual script.

6. *Innate reinforcers.* The arousal of sexual excitement generates responses which are innately reinforcing, not only at the time of culmination of the sexual response pattern in orgasm, but importantly, through the preliminary responding and expectancy responses as seen in foreplay. These preorgasm behaviors may be considered learned or secondary reinforcers. They play a major role in sustaining the complete sexual response pattern and they have a vital part in both the formulation of the sexual script and in reinforcing the continuity of this cognitive scenario.

7. *Subjective mental experience.* The most critical component of human sexual excitement is the perceived probability or desire to engage in actual sexual responding. This is mental experience—a subjective interpretation which is the product of many learning experiences. It is the feeling of being "horny," "sexually alive," "turned-on," "hot," "on-the-make," or simply, of wanting to have sex. As subjective as this is, such self-report remains the most powerful information about an individual's sexual status. But whereas self-report may be a very sensitive indicator of sexual excitement, it lacks the objectivity we would prefer.

Stoller's Theory of Sexual Excitement

There are important differences in the definition of sexual excitement. Masters and Johnson (1966), for example, use this term to describe the entire process of physiological changes leading up to and resulting in orgasm. Stoller (1975, 1976), in contrast, defines sexual excitement as the anticipatory and expectation components of a sexual episode: " . . . 'excitement' implies anticipation in which one alternates with extreme rapidity between expectation of danger and just about equal expectation of avoidance of danger, and in some case, such as in eroticism, of replacing danger with pleasure" (Stoller, 1975, p. 4).

Stoller describes sexual excitement as a mental state which is the product of fantasy—a past experience "reinvented to serve a need" (1975, p. 4). He reasons that while different patterns of unusual sexual behavior, such as transvestism, exhibitionism or voyeurism " . . . all show sexual excitement at times . . . ," that these states of excitement differ from each other both physiologically and in the fantasy content they involve. So far as physiological patterns are concerned, this assertion is not adequately supported by experimental findings. The physiology of different emotional states have proven to be remarkably similar despite differences in our subjective emotional state, and this very possibly holds true for the sexually related behavior to which Stoller is referring.

In attempting to conceptualize the origins of sexual excitement, Stoller sticks strictly to mental factors—our cognitions of all kinds—and says little about possible physiological or neurological correlates of sexual motivation. He believes that the central factor in sexual excitement is " . . . hostility . . . the desire, overt or hidden, to harm another person . . . " (1975, p. 6). It is this hostile foundation, he believes, which enhances intense sexual feelings. Stoller does not use the word "hostility" in its common usage, but what he means by it instead is a more general interpersonal power over another person. In a developmental sense, these are said to be "old" feelings of anger and hostility and their connection with the need to assert personal power is seen as relating directly to the trauma–conflict–mastery model of symptom formation. This, of course, is in harmony with Stoller's psychoanalytic approach to personality development. He put it this way: "The hostility of eroticism is an attempt, repeated over and over, to undo childhood trauma and frustration that threatened the development of one's masculinity or femininity" (p. 6).

Masters and Johnson: The Human Sexual Response

For over 11 years, obstetrician William Masters and psychologist Virginia Johnson studied human sexual responding under laboratory conditions thereby acquiring more and better information about this than had ever been previously recorded. They used both physiological and self-report measures. Their subjects were 382 women and 312 men ranging in age from 18 to 78 for the women and from 21 to 89 for the men. Fearing that ordinary citizens would not come forward to participate as subjects in their laboratory work, they began in the mid-1950s with a group of 118 female prostitutes and 27 male prostitutes who were paid for their services. After interviewing these individuals, eight women and three men were selected for anatomic and physiological studies involving sexual arousal and orgasm.

As their work proceeded, their subjects, increasingly, were volunteers recruited " . . . from and sustained by the academic community associated with a large university complex" (1966, p. 11). Their research on sexual responding was, and is, an integral part of research concerned with contraception, sexual inadequacy, geriatric sexuality, and other clinical problems.

It is important to give these sex research pioneers credit for the thoroughness with which they measured components of the human sexual response. But without implying criticism, we must also keep in mind that they were mainly interested in physiological responses. At the outset they were not much concerned with sexual fantasies or expectancies which are important aspects of the overall human sexual response pattern. It is remarkable that their work was the first thorough investigation of this topic ever undertaken in humans. The basic format of the work involved having each subject use some form of stimulation to arouse physiological changes culminating in orgasm. Throughout this process, several physiological measures were acquired, such as changes in the cardiovascular system, the distribution of blood through the body, muscle tension, and so forth. Additionally, they measured unique bodily responses preparatory to orgasm, such as sweat-like lubrication of the walls of the vagina in women, and muscular and circulatory changes supporting erection of the penis in men.

Now we shall proceed from this review of sexual script theory and sexual excitement research to the more narrowly focused topic of fetishism—a term now used so loosely that it has nearly lost meaning.

Fetishistic Behavior

The word *fetish* was first used to describe an object believed to have protective or religious significance similar to a powerful good luck charm; more recently it has been used to identify certain aspects of sexual arousal. For example, Sigmund Freud gave considerable attention to the concept of fetishism in his classical monograph, *Three Essays on the Theory of Sexuality*. Freud emphasized the unique qualities of strongly preferred or fetishistic stimuli as part of the sexual arousal process. He reasoned that a fetish may replace the "normal sexual object," the human body, thereby becoming the exclusive sexual goal object, and that such objects may be " . . . entirely unsuited to serve the normal sexual aim" (Freud, 1905, p. 19).

A second property of fetishes as discussed by Freud was said to be fixation, or the tendency to become tenaciously focused on certain objects having unusually strong sexual arousal value. Dependence upon fetishes was considered pathological by Freud " . . . when the longing for the fetish passes beyond the point of being merely a necessary condition attached to the sexual object and actually takes the place of the normal aim, and, further, when the fetish . . . becomes the sole sexual object" (Freud, 1905, p. 27). A more contemporary yet classical discussion of fetishism from the psychoanalytic position has been provided by Bak (1953).

Sex researcher Paul Gebhard (1969) proposed that fetishistic stimuli be conceptualized along a continuum of intensities, each having a behavioral definition. He suggested these four levels of fetishism:

- *Level 1* A *slight preference* exists for certain kinds of sex partners, sexual stimuli, or sexual activity. (The term fetish should not be used at this level.)
- *Level 2* A *strong preference* exists for certain kinds of sex partners, sexual stimuli, or sexual activity. (Lowest intensity of fetishism.)
- *Level 3* Specific stimuli are *necessary* for sexual arousal and sexual performance. (Moderate intensity of fetishism.)
- *Level 4* Specific stimuli *take the place* of a sex partner. (High level of fetishism.)

Gebhard believes that fetishistic behavior occurs in both men and women but that it is less common in women and the intensity is often less than in men. He points to the adolescent years as most critical for the formation and consolidation of fetishistic preferences. It has long been recognized that fetishes are highly resistant to extinction. Given the strong reinforcement properties of sexual arousal, such resistance would be predicted.

Examples of Common Fetishes in Our Culture

While it is theoretically possible for any stimulus to acquire fetishistic significance through a conditioning process, some stimuli are far more likely to become fetishes than others. Here are some of the more common fetishes in our culture:

Intimate apparel of women. The most common fetishes for men seem to be items of women's intimate apparel, such as underwear, hosiery, shoes, and lingerie. Wigs and cosmetics may also be valued. It has long been recognized that for transvestites the cross dressing process usually begins with one or two of these articles of clothing and progresses toward complete cross dressing. In contrast, some cross dressers never move beyond their preference for a certain item of clothing or a combination of similar items. It is these individuals who are properly designated as fetishists.

Objects related to sexual practices. For some, there is highly fetishistic significance associated with objects symbolizing, for example, bondage, submission, dominance, masochism, sadism, humiliation, or infantilism. Fetish materials may include whips, rope, chain, locks, belts, masks, handcuffs, or diapers. Such equipment becomes part of the sexual scenario of an individual.

Apparel made of specific materials. Particular materials may also become strongly preferred fetishes. For example, plastic-like cloth, rubber, leather, latex, nylon, wool, or fur. Many other kinds of materials may also come to have fetishistic value based on the learning experiences of an individual.

Experimental Studies of Sexual Excitement and Fetishistic Stimuli

The most extensive research relating known stimuli to sexual arousal has come from phallometric studies (e.g., Geer, 1980; Jovanovic, 1971) of pornographic materials. Psychologist Donn Bryne (1977) has provided a review of his studies in this area in his chapter, "The Imagery of Sex," which appears in the *Handbook of Sexology* (Money & Musaph, 1977). The usual procedure in this kind of research is to show pictorial stimuli, such as slides, photos, drawings, or motion pictures—or to present auditory material to experimental subjects. Such stimuli can be arranged according to the purposes of the experiment so as to focus upon heterosexuality, gay encounters, scenes with or without implied violence, and so forth.

The typical response measures which are recorded usually include both self-report information (subjective reports of how various stimuli affected feelings of sexual arousal), and also a number of physiological indicators of emotion. These often include changes in the cardiovascular system (heart rate, blood pressure, vasodilation, etc.), skin resistance, and changes in muscular tension. More recently, for males, it has become common to record changes in penis size or temperature; comparable measures appropriate for women subjects have also been developed.

It is important to recognize that specific indicators of pure sexual arousal do not exist. Bryne, for example, concludes that while many physiological and self-report measures vary with presentation of different sexual stimuli, such measures also change due to nonsexual factors. These may include feelings of shame, disgust, anger, or fear. This conclusion is consistent with the more general finding that no physiological indicators are uniqely tuned as markers for specific emotional states. Zuckerman (1971) has strongly supported this point, noting that many emotions may be associated with feelings of sexual arousal. But despite the absence of specific indicators of sexual arousal, this line of experimentation appears to hold much promise toward understanding the complex interactions among stimulus conditions, personal sexual scenarios, and sexual responding. It has been shown, for example, that in addition to the autonomic and muscular measures discussed above, urinary acid phosphatase increases in males who have been shown sexual materials (Barclay, 1973) and plasma testosterone also increases when sexually stimulating films are presented (Pirke, Kockott, & Dittmar, 1974).

Earlier we reviewed the major findings of Masters and Johnson (1966) concerning the human sexual response; they showed that in males, predictable patterns of change in erectile tissue, autonomic variables, and muscle tension accompany sexual arousal. It is of importance, therefore, to consider the conclusion reached by Bryne (1977) and Bryne *et al.* (Bryne, Fisher, Lamberth, & Mitchell, 1974) that the laboratory measures of physiological changes following presentation of pictorial and auditory sexual stimuli are similar to the changes found by Masters and Johnson using human subjects in actual sexual encounters. Bryne found that "In general . . . the use of physiological measuring devices has shown that erotic stimuli and erotic imaginings bring about bodily changes identical to those observed in actual interactions with a sexual partner" (1977, p. 330).

When Bryne discusses "erotic imaginings" he is referring to a particularly interesting finding from one of his own studies (Bryne & Lamberth, 1971). Rather than use pictures or stories, these researchers asked their subjects to use their imagination and create a sexually arousing mental scene while various physiological measures were being taken. They found that these experimental subjects " . . . were considerably more aroused than other subjects who read stories or viewed slides . . . " that depicted sexual activities. Apparently, by giving the subject the freedom to tune in on his own sexual scenario the most intense patterns of mental stimulation were generated. We are again confronted with the extraordinary power of these erotic memory systems. The following is a summary of Bryne's major findings:

1. Males and females show about " . . . equal levels of arousal in response to erotic stories, photographs, and movies" (1977, p. 330).

2. Erotic stimuli presented in experiments results in patterns of physiological change "identical" to those measured in actual sexual encounters (1977, p. 328).

3. Approximately equal levels of self-reported sexual arousal are produced by words, photographs, and movies (1977, p. 328).

4. Subjects were "considerably more aroused" when asked to imagine a self-selected series of sexual stimuli rather than have other materials presented to them (1977, p. 329).

5. Most autonomic measures are not specific indicators or "markers" of sexual arousal because they are known to vary with many stimulus conditions and under various motivational and emotional conditions.

6. Our most important sex information seems to be obtained through friends of the same age with " . . . pornography as a supplementary source . . . " (1977, p. 334).

7. "Because sexual activity in our species is largely under cognitive control, it follows that we can, to a surprising degree, regulate our sexual behavior by creating erotic fantasies or sharing the fantasies of others. In effect, we can become excited whenever we wish to do so" (1977, p. 334).

8. Erotic imagery may enhance sexual enjoyment which, in turn, may further reinforce such imagery (1977, p. 334).

9. "One advantage of imaginal activities is that they can go beyond the confines of reality in allowing one to engage vicariously in activities which are legally and/or morally condemned, which are physically impossible, or which might be intriguing at the level of fantasy but acutely unpleasant in actual fact" (1977, p. 335).

10. Research findings are not clear concerning the amount of difference, if any, between groups of political liberals and conservatives relative to responses to erotica.

11. "The most general conclusion is that sexual books, movies, and photographs have very little effect on subsequent behavior . . . " (1977, p. 342).

12. "On the basis of present knowledge, one could best conclude, however tentatively, that erotica has not been shown to have negative effects on sexual behavior and, if anything, seems to act as a deterrent to sexual crimes (1977, p. 343). Although not definitively proven, Bryne proposes than sexual fantasies and erotic materials may act as a kind of emotional safety valve thereby reducing antisocial actions.

Studies of Sexual Excitement and Brain Activity

Invasive techniques for measuring brain activity in humans are impossible and unethical except when this can be carried out as part of a required surgical intervention. This leaves the EEG as a favored measurement procedure although it is well-recognized that such recordings are the product of massive, but incompletely understood summated electrical energies. The temporal lobe has been a focus of attention for sex researchers for several decades, beginning perhaps with the studies of Kluver and Bucy (1939). There is considerable variation, both methodologically and in the results reported, of EEG studies attempting to determine if particular cortical areas are uniquely linked to sexual excitement. These studies have been reviewed by Purins and Langevin (1985) whose experiments on this topic are the most satisfactory yet published. Purins and Langevin used a set of photographs as sexually excitatory stimuli, arranging these into four levels of erotic intensity. Sexual responding was measured using penile volume changes. Sixteen pairs of EEG electrodes measured standard sites, and several EMG recordings were acquired to assess muscle artifacts. The experimental design provided for control of order effects and erotic-stimulus intensity differences. Here is what they found:

1. Penile volume measures showed expected changes across four levels of intensity of stimulation, but the measures " . . . were not as potent or discrete from each other . . . " (p. 129) as expected. There was a fatigue effect in penile responding.
2. Using four EEG frequency bands (delta, theta, alpha, beta), the delta alone showed changes across the range of nonerotic to erotic stimuli.
3. The sixteen EEG sites did not show differing responsivity to different levels of sexual excitation. Hence, "There was no support for the hypothesis that the temporal lobes in particular are involved in sexual arousal." (p. 130)
4. Right brain vs. left brain differences were not found to be related to changes in sexual excitation.
5. "It seems a general activation of the cortex was elicited by the stimuli used in this experiment." (p. 129)

Alcohol and Sexual Excitement

At least since the time of Shakespeare, alcohol has been said to increase sexual desire but reduce ejaculation. Although use of alcohol is often said to be a complicating factor in violent and sexual crimes, the experimental study of this issue has barely begun. Langevin, Ben-Aron, Coulthard, *et al.*(1985) review six previous studies that yielded conflicting results. Three of these studies showed that " . . . increasing amounts of alcohol reduce the degree of penile tumescence to erotica" (p. 101). Three other reports showed "no difference" due to alcohol, but that the expectation of receiving alcohol "influenced responsiveness." Using 48 paid college student subjects, Langevin and his associates presented six levels of erotic stimuli under three alcohol conditions: none, .05 mg., and .10 mg. Note that these are low-to-moderate levels of blood alcohol. Note also that none of these subjects had a behavioral history which included violence or sexual criminal activity—hence, the results are not intended to be generalized across such populations. Using an appropriate design that controlled for order effects and blood alcohol levels, Langevin *et al.* found the following:

1. Penile volume changes did, in fact, change as a function of erotic stimulus value.
2. Penile responsiveness was not reduced in either of the alcohol groups, and neither group differed significantly from the control subjects.
3. In both alcohol groups, penile volume was not significantly suppressed by alcohol, but these subjects showed a tendency to "react indiscriminately to erotic materials" (p. 109). That is, less predictability was seen between intensity level of erotic stimulus to penile response, or sexual excitement. Therefore, alcohol-drinking subjects may not show reduced potential for sexual excitement, but may be "turned on" by less intense stimulation.
4. Contrary to popular belief, alcohol " . . . may serve a disinhibiting, facilitative role in sexual arousal" (p. 109).

These procedures exemplify the kinds of studies which will ultimately enrich our understanding of variables influencing sexual excitement and sexual responding.

Fetishism and Sexual Scenarios

When a person thinks about a sexual theme and develops clearly formed images of persons or things there is intense mental activity taking place. A chain of memory processes or schemas becomes progressively organized as certain fetishes become favored. It is the capacity of humans to think, to recall, to elaborate and to promote self-stimulation through mental imagery that is at the heart of every sexual scenario. And when fetishes enliven scenarios they provide a kind of cement that holds this cognitive activity in place and gives it the "locked on" quality that many have noted.

By thinking about a sexual scenario it is possible to trigger other memories, set off emotional responding and stimulate the anticipation of pleasure. These emotional changes become recognizable physiological responses which further signify that specific sexual scenarios are powerful and meaningful. It is the interplay between the mental stimulation of fetishistic imagery and the bodily responses interpreted as desirable feeling-states that results in the perseverance of fetishism. The point is that such mental activity becomes highly reinforcing because it is associated with innate responses somehow interpreted as pleasurable. For some, such thinking can take on obsession-like qualities. For example, a man who has experienced similar fetishistic themes for over 30 years put it this way:

> All of my life I have fantasized situations where I am being punished and used by some type of dominant. In my fantasies I sometimes even get stimulated to the point of orgasm. Not too much in recent years, though. And that's what makes me believe that I have psyched myself into callousness or normalcy, because in general, there is just no desire when the real thing happens.

This individual experiences far stronger sexual arousal following the imagination of fetishistic scenes than when such scenes are actually experienced. He wrote:

> All of my transvestic life I have had fantasies of forced [cross] dressing. My imagination runs wild with plots of bondage, slavery, and the like. Recently I met with a dominant and spanking was the main activity. It wasn't a turn-on for me like I had imagined. But a few days later as I thought about what actually happened, I was turned on.

We may ask: Why might an individual experience stronger sexual arousal to the mental activity surrounding a sexual scenario than the actual enactment of a scene from the scenario? Very possibly, an actual sexual encounter is also laden with fear and other negative feelings that are incompatible with optimal sexual responding. Such a sequence is common in fetishism.

In another case, a strongly fetishistic 50-year-old with extensive technical education described his fetishistic cross dressing as a "prelude to sexual activity" with a woman. He said: "You can come home from work . . . get dressed and go out shopping . . . and get yourself into a different frame of mind. You give total concentration to makeup and dressing, all of which give you a different view of your problems." After describing his collection of about 150 pairs of high heels he asked himself: "How much of this fetishism is like running amok?"

While some fetishists may prefer very narrowly defined sexual stimuli or a narrowly defined class of stimuli, such as high heels only, most of the cross dressing fetishists we have interviewed enjoy a broad array of similar stimulation. Often, they seek variety and change as a necessary ingredient in their cross dressing behavior. As with more conventional sexual relationships, there appears to be a desire for variety and change; the exciting fetishistic stimuli of yesterday become boring after repeated experience. Perhaps the traditional view of fetishism as involving invariant objects stems from the historic early cases described by Freud, Havelock Ellis, and other pioneers in sexual research.

The Learning of Sexual Scenarios and Fetishism

What experiences may be identified to help explain the learning of particular sexual scenarios and fetishistic imagery? Are some particular life experiences common to the development of future cross dressers? At least in a very broad sense, it is likely that some similar learning experiences are shared by such individuals, although the details of each life history are very different. In the next three subsections some hypotheses concerning possible common learning experiences are discussed.

Learning about One's Gender

From birth onward, children are subjected to intense socialization experiences which dictate how they are expected to behave in terms of gender. Our culture is highly conscious of various gender differences and many kinds of pressure are exerted through social relationships to train girls and boys to behave in gender-appropriate ways. We shall not digress here to comment on the virtue of these historic distinctions, other than to note that such gender-specific training can obviously have very harmful consequences for both men and women. In any case, although a given child may have considerable opportunity for individual expression and uniqueness within a category of being masculine or feminine, each is socialized so as to clearly perceive himself or herself as male or female.

No sustained switching from one gender to the other is tolerated except in highly unusual cases where, for their own reasons, a parent may encourage mixed-gender role-playing (Green, 1987). But ordinarily, as children move toward puberty they are increasingly forced into a sex-determined gender role. According to Money and Ehrhardt (1972) the most critical stage of this gender learning takes place roughly in a time sequence parallel with language development—perhaps from birth through age 3 or 4.

Boys are usually encouraged throughout their early childhood to become increasingly autonomous and free of parental supervision and protection. They are expected to become physically more assertive than girls, to fight back when challenged by peers, to defend themselves, and to take progressively greater responsibility as chivalrous "big brothers" toward girls. In most families, feminine behaviors are strongly discouraged in boys.

Girls, on the other hand, are usually encouraged to avoid physical contact sports, to remain closer to the nurturing and protective parent, to imitate mothering behavior toward younger siblings, and to refrain from behaviors which connote masculinity. Much greater dependency is both tolerated and encouraged in girls than in boys.

Learning Gender Envy

The process of growing up as a boy may be very stressful and demanding. Some boys appear to deal with this by developing very strong envy of girls who are seen as having it much easier, and as being more attractive and loveable. Envious feelings and subsequent identification with girls are frequently cited by transvestites as a reason for their initial experimentation with the wearing of women's clothing— usually those of the mother or an older sister. For the boy who comes to believe that girls have it better and are more attractive and who therefore feels intense envy of girls, it may be a short step to actually try on clothing or makeup and thereby be a temporary "girl." Betelheim (1962) has written of the "wounds" suffered by men who develop fear and envy of the femaleness of women.

Women's Clothing as "Forbidden Fruit"

Young boys are typically given strong messages about clothing and gender conformity. Despite the contemporary acceptance of unisex clothes, most male youth are strongly socialized so as to wear only gender-appropriate clothing. For boys, this avoidance of cross-gender appearance is far more strenuously demanded than for girls. In our culture the undergarments of women have sometimes been referred to as "untouchables"—at the least, they are intimate clothing. Subtle barriers are erected to keep these undergarments out of public view. For example, a generation ago a properly set out clothesline would have sheets and towels on the perimeters of the clothesline with undergarments in the interior and out of view.

The subtle rules that govern the privacy of women's underwear may be viewed by some young boys as barriers that guard these "untouchables," thereby giving them a special fascination. This possible fascination with the forbidden may set the stage for attributing to this clothing a special significance with erotic coloration. If so, we can envision a mechanism for the learning of erotic expectations that might well play a part in the formation of fantasy, of sexual scenarios, of fetishism, and ultimately in helping to start the processes of learning which underlie complete cross dressing. Transvestites often report a kind of pleasurable "glow" or excitement when cross dressed beginning with their earliest cross dressing experiences.

In summary, then, we are saying that two main lines of influence may precondition the young boy to want to try on his mother's clothing: first, the development of gender envy which may stem from the uncomfortable aspects of growing up as a boy rather than as the favored girl; second, the expectation that a special titillating excitement may be derived from violating the rule that males must not touch the untouchables of women. We believe this process is a better explanation than the view that clothing experimentation is a matter of chance or random experience, a capricious event, or a mere consequence of curiosity. The critical point is that there must be extensive cognitive preparation and emotional readiness for having a unique, erotic emotional experience in association with these clothes. Probably the fact that a gender rule is being secretly violated adds to the excitement of initial cross dressing experiences.

Sexual Arousal Changes as Reinforcing

There is some experimental evidence that changes in sex drive can be reinforcing in rats, even without ejaculation. This has been shown in two studies (Kagan, 1955; Sheffield, Wulff, & Backer, 1951). Interestingly, Kagan noted that when his rats were blocked from copulation this sometimes resulted in the formation of a habit that inhibited future copulation. In any case both of these studies concluded that changes in sex drive alone, without copulation or ejaculation, had reinforcing properties.

With regard to human studies, McGuire, Carlisle, and Young (1965) developed a conceptualization of sexual deviations as conditioned responses, and we have emphasized the sexually reinforcing attributes of cognitive stimuli into elaborate sexual scenarios, a point underscored by Mandler (1975). This erotic tinge or emotional coloration is sometimes characterized by transvestites as a kind of elation or "high" or "rush" not unlike that described by users of marijuana and similar psychoactive drugs.

By periodically associating sexual orgasm with erotic cognitive stimuli there is provided intermittent reinforcement which is known to result in both high rates of responding and resistance to extinction. These mental stimuli and their correlated expectations of pleasure are thought to persist while showing some adaptations and change. For a discussion of the rewarding and punishing effects of erotic stimuli, see Griffit and Kaiser (1978).

One of the less well-understood patterns of fetishistic behavior is that of wearing certain articles of women's clothing for many hours each day in the absence of any reported sexual feelings or responses. But such feelings may not be accurately reported, especially if an individual feels conflicted about his sexual motives. Hence, the fact that an individual reports that no sexual "turn-on" is experienced does not necessarily mean that no components of the sexual response pattern are operative, despite his own interpretation.

In any case, the experience most often reported by those who wear women's clothing beneath their male clothes for extended periods of time is that of a calming effect. It may be that the experience of relaxation or calmness is a major reinforcer which reduces sexual tensions, thereby becoming reinforcing. The mediating events for such a response pattern are not understood if, in fact, this is what takes place. Another hypothesis would be that the mild sexual arousal that may accompany concealed fetishistic cross dressing is subjectively interpreted as calming despite what may be mild physiological arousal. Here is the way one transvestite—an unmarried college instructor—describes his daily fetishism:

> Each morning, upon arising, I take off my nightgown and bra with silicon-filled prostheses, and I put on my garter belt and hose. I've worn panties, girdle, bra, "all-in-ones" for about five years. On rare occasions when I have to put on male shorts I feel partly undressed. However, I'm not aware of any emotional differences between the times I wear female underwear and male underwear. But after those rare occasions of the male underwear, I'm looking forward to stepping back into the female underwear as soon as possible.

It is evident that some significant reinforcement sustains this regular and highly valued daily feminine dressing. The present hypothesis is that it is not purely erotic and sexual, but although some sexual reinforcement may be operating there may also be reinforcement from a conditioned arousal–relaxation response pattern—that is a calming effect.

Fetishism, Attentional Focus, and Stress Reduction

An important theory concerning stress reduction is that the manipulation of attention and concentration are at the heart of stress-reducing practices, such as meditation. The reasoning is that by having something specific to concentrate upon, the unpleasant or anxiety-laden thoughts, which are derived from our daily experience, are somehow pushed into the distant background. Attention to practiced activities, such as a word or a short phrase that is repeated, is a specific stimulus for the relaxation response. This response is believed to be a set of body adjustments involving the musculature, the autonomic nervous system, and the manipulation of cognitive processes. The affective side of the relaxation response is said to involve feelings of calmness, well-being, and relief of tension and anxiety. We are interested in this phenomenon because fetishistic behavior may also provide a way of manipulating attention and triggering the relaxation response. If this reasoning is correct, then such reinforcement could be an important factor in learning and sustaining fetishistic behavior.

Summary

Cognitive psychology provides the conceptual basis for using sexual script theory as a major explanatory thesis in human sexual behavior, and we believe the cognitive aspects of transvestism and transsexualism are highly important. In addressing these topics in the past, too little attention has been accorded to cognitive factors. The views of Simon and Gagnon (1986) concerning sexual scripts and their role in the direction and control of sexual behavior are developed. They see three levels of scripting: a cultural level, an interpersonal level, and an intrapsychic level, all of which work together. Cognitive theory has been applied by many psychologists to problems in emotion, motivation, and human sexuality. A conceptualization of 10 defining attributes of sexual scripts is presented.

Innate affective systems are believed basic to the development of sexual scripts. Although such feeling states are hard to define operationally, they seem critically important in the determination of sexual arousal and sexual performance in humans. The attributes of such innate affective systems are discussed. Both transvestism and transsexualism are, in part, mood-altering behavioral strategies. They generate pleasurable excitement and a sense of well-being; for some, the practice of cross dressing seems to have calming effects, although the associated physiological changes are clearly excitatory.

Stoller (1976) regards sexual excitement as a mental state, the product of fantasy, and as serving basic motivational requirements. He has studied intense sexual feelings using a psychoanalytic model. Masters and Johnson (1966) studied cognitive, autonomic, and muscular re-

sponses in humans in several experimental situations with sexual responding. They identified sexual response patterns for males and
females.

The topic of fetishism is closely related to transvestism and various
problems in the definition and assessment of fetishism are noted. Using
phallometric measures, there has been considerable research concerning
sexually arousing stimuli. Other research concerns have involved the
central nervous system and sexual excitement and the effects of common substances, such as alcohol, on sexual arousal. Sexual scenarios are
learned behaviors and three examples of this which may apply to transvestism are discussed (learning gender rules, learning gender envy, and
learning clothing fetishism). Erotic cognition, fantasy, and fetishistic
behavior can be viewed as ways of manipulating attentional responses,
thereby reducing perceived stressful stimulation and feeling more relaxed.

Chapter 6

Research Results

In this chapter we present results obtained from several sources of data collection, all representing the self-reports and self-descriptions of heterosexual transvestites. One goal is to describe the stages of transvestism, tracing the beginnings of cross dressing through early childhood into adolescence and young adulthood, and ultimately working our way into the more senior years. These retrospective self-reports enable us to examine the cross dressing career across the life span, something that has not typically been done in the past. We shall be especially concerned, for example, with whether this behavior is strengthened or weakened over time, and whether stages of development can be clarified. We shall provide basic descriptive information concerning the present sample.

We shall also report data concerning the early sexual experience of transvestites, and of the onset of cross dressing behavior. Additionally, we shall report data dealing with the sexual component in cross dressing from transvestites representing different age groups and differing in amount of experience with cross dressing. There is a weakness in factual information here, for although many assertions have been made (e.g., see Brierley, 1979) that sexual factors decrease in significance as years of cross dressing increase, little supporting information has been reported. We do not challenge this clinical impression, but we shall attempt to examine changes in sexual behavior based on what transvestites reported to us.

We shall report on several aspects of early family relationships as perceived by transvestites. As Bullough *et al.* (1983) have noted, TVs do not typically describe such early relationships as involving the trauma and conflict some have assumed must be present (e.g., Stoller, 1985c).

Transvestites have seldom been asked in a systematic way to offer their own explanations of why they cross dress. In order to learn how these men view their cross dressing motives and reinforcements, we shall describe their responses to 16 different explanations of cross dress-ing. We shall also examine a principal components analysis of these data, representing ratings for the early years of cross dressing and for the present time period.

A previous report opens the question of how transvestites regard themselves relative to sex roles (Talamini, 1982). Our data from the Bem Sex-Role Inventory will be reported for transvestites who completed this schedule under two conditions: cross dressed and not cross dressed.

An experimental Cross Dressing Inventory will be described and the results of a principle components analysis will be reported. This inventory will be proposed as an additional tool for the assessment of cross-gender identity, sexual excitement ("fetishism"), and pleasure and relaxation as related to cross dressing.

The results of our data collection will be presented in the following order:

Part I: Procedures, recruitment of subjects, demographic and mari-tal data, family and developmental variables, sexual development and behavior, history of cross dressing, attitudes concerning wives' views, harms and benefits of cross dressing.

Part II: Explanations data (how the transvestite explains his own motives and reinforcement for the two time periods—early and pres-ent).

Part III: Frequency and stages of cross dressing.

Part IV: Bem Sex-Role Inventory data.

Part V: Assessment of cross-gender identity. Data from an experi-mental Cross Dressing Inventory.

Because there is a considerable range of data to be presented, we will discuss each section following the presentation of the survey or test results. In the first section we describe how subjects were invited to participate, the procedures used, the sampling problems, and the re-sults of the survey.

Part I: Survey Procedures and Results

Our study dealt with transvestites who fit the DSM-III-R definition. We began by describing our project to the members of two transvestite clubs in southern California and most of the membership in these groups eventually completed the research packets they were given. Sev-eral of these men took research packets to national gatherings of TVs and explained the project to members of clubs from other cities. They, in turn, acted as communicators and explained the project to their memberships. This took place in 1980. Soon thereafter, *Tapestry*, one of the nationally distributed cross dressing magazines, printed a brief informational piece about this study and invited those interested to send a letter volunteering their services. Individuals who completed the research materials often wrote to their TV friends elsewhere and urged them to contact us. This "endless chain" approach to sampling has both advantages and also very serious disadvantages. On the positive side, we received the cooperation of transvestites who were enthusiastic about the research and who considered the project worthwhile. On the negative side, personal advocacy, willingness to complete a very long research packet, and to reveal one's personal history in writing must surely involve major selective factors which inevitably bias a sample.

We cannot say precisely what sampling errors may tilt this group of transvestites in one direction or another, but we have some impressions. First, the length of time required to participate suggests that a subject must have had both very high motivation to be involved and also sufficient time to dedicate attention to test taking and responding to survey materials. Perhaps our sample is biased, therefore, relative to time available and privacy available within the home setting, for it appears likely that most completed these materials at home rather than at work. (We shall later discuss, for example, data indicating that a surprising percentage completed at least some of the materials cross dressed although they were not specifically asked to do so.) Second, the bulk of written materials involved and the extensive decision making associated with hundreds of questions suggests that men who completed all of this must have been good readers, perhaps curious about test taking, and comfortable with the assignment. Third, judging from the correspondence which ensued after subjects were sent a follow-up letter which included specific follow-up questions derived from their collective survey responses, many of these men found the research participation to be an enjoyable exercise in self-examination. Judging from the comments of some, the survey appears to have had a mildly cathartic value, as if they had had the opportunity to reveal closely held, even highly secretive personal facts to a nonjudgmental but trustworthy outsider.

Approximately 350 research packets were distributed, mostly by mail, either to post office boxes or residence addresses, together with a letter of introduction, instructions, and all survey and test materials. One hundred and twenty-seven complete sets were mailed back during the period of 1980–1985. Seventeen cases which did not meet the criteria for transvestism in DSM-III-R were excluded from the final data set. Several of these had a predominantly homosexual background, a few were living full time in a transsexual mode, and a few stated they had never experienced sexual excitement in association with cross dressing.

The number of cases meeting the criteria for inclusion was 110. Our return rate of 36% is similar to the rate of about 40% reported by Prince and Bentler (1972) based on their mailings of about 1300 questionnaires to transvestite club members.

As expected from the DSM-III-R criteria for transvestism (American Psychiatric Association, 1987), our subjects describe themselves as heterosexual transvestites who cross dress periodically. Most have been affiliated with cross dressing clubs at some time, although many have never joined. Almost all are employed full time or have retired. And as we shall see, most are family men who have never been divorced. They tend to place a high positive value on the cross dressing side of their lives, although a few state there have been serious interpersonal problems connected with this. But we cannot say this sample is representative of all transvestites. There are at least two major problems: First, we do not know the characteristics of the total population of transvestites in our culture (and in fact, there is no way to learn this because the behavior is semisecret if not entirely secret), and second, our sampling procedures are heavily weighted with self-selection biases that almost certainly tilt this sample in the direction of highly verbal, socioeconomically successful men who have elected to tell a stranger some of their most closely held secrets—in writing. Now let us proceed with the data. Although there are times in our discussions throughout this chapter when we lapse into theoretical speculation, the main development of a theory of transvestism will be given in Chapter 8.

Description of the Sample

Age

The mean age was 44 (*S.D.* 11.65). Median age was 43. The range was 22 to 83 years. The distribution of ages is shown in Table 1.

Table 1. Distribution of Ages of Subjects

Age range	Percentage
20–30	6
31–40	35
41–50	27
51–60	22
61–70	8
71–80	1
81–90	1

Table 2. Distribution of Number of
Marriages

Age range	Percentage
Never	18
1	62
2	15
3	4
4	1

Number of Marriages

All except 18% of our sample had married at least once. The distribution is given in Table 2.

Number of Divorces

Of the 90 men who had married, 60% had never divorced. Among those who did divorce, 81% did so once, 11% twice, and 8% three times. In order to make a proper analysis of whether this divorce rate is higher than would be predicted for a comparable nontransvestite sample, it would be necessary to correct for religious background, a variable we did not acquire. Using these data alone, it would not appear these men are extraordinarily at risk relative to divorce. Some have asserted that transvestites have a high divorce rate in the absence of supporting evidence (e.g., Feinbloom, 1976).

Self-Categorization of Cross Dressing Behavior

A series of statements describing increasing intensity of interest in cross dressing were presented and the participant was asked to describe himself. The categories (descriptive statements) are given here with the number of respondents for each:

- I am a non-cross dresser. (no respondents)
- I am a former cross dresser. (no respondents)
- I am a possible future cross dresser. (no respondents)
- I am a periodic cross dresser. I cross dress from time to time. I do not live as a woman on a regular basis for several days at a time (except at an event such as Fantasia Fair or Dream). ($N = 110$)

Corroboration of both heterosexual preference and history of fetishistic cross dressing was derived from the Cross Dressing Inventory to be described below. Three subjects were included who were bisexual; in these cases there was a strong heterosexual and fetishistic history. We do not assert that the self-described categorization can be proven to be accurate merely from examining another set of statements from the same subject. At best, our Cross Dressing Inventory is simply a second line of self-report statements describing, for example, erotic orientation, various cross dressing-related behaviors, cross-gender identity feelings or preferences.

Education

This is a well-educated group of men. All stated that they graduated from high school and 56% had completed some college work. They reported the followed academic degrees: None, 44%; 2 years of college, 3%; B.A. level, 32%; M.A. level, 13%; Doctoral level, 8%.

Socioeconomic status was determined from self-report of occupation according to the six levels identified by Warner (1949):

- *Level 1:* Professional, self-employed
- *Level 2:* Semiprofessional
- *Level 3:* Managerial
- *Level 4:* White collar (clerical, sales, administrative, services)
- *Level 5:* Blue collar, skilled workers
- *Level 6:* Blue collar, unskilled workers

Mean socioeconomic status for the 110 subjects was 3.5 (*S.D.* .85). This is evidence of the above-average occupational status of this sample. The subjects were asked to describe the occupation of their father and this rating yielded a mean of 3.8 (*S.D.* 1.2) indicating a slightly lower social status. The difference between these means is significant beyond the .005 level, but this is not important for our purposes. What is important is that this sample is comprised of well-educated men who, for the most part, hold good jobs, often at a managerial, supervisory, or ownership level.

Employment status was reported as follows: Employed full time, 83%; part-time, 8%; retired, 7%; unemployed, 1%; student, 1%.

About 30% percent were living in the midwest with an equal number residing on the west coast. The remainder were drawn from all parts of the United States with three living in Canada.

Alcohol, Cigarettes, and Mood-Altering Drugs

Nine percent of the subjects said they did not drink any alcoholic beverages. Of those who did drink, 65% reported consuming one drink per day or less, 23% reported two drinks per day, 8% three drinks per day, and 4% more than three drinks per day.

Sixty-five percent of the subjects said they are nonsmokers. Of those who do smoke, 41% smoke one pack daily or less, 54% smoke about two packs per day, and two subjects use more than two packs daily.

Ninety-one percent of the subjects say they never use marijuana; 9% have done so or continue the use of this substance. These tend to be the younger men. The same statistics apply to taking prescribed tranquilizing medication.

Ninety-one percent of the subjects also report they have never used female hormones (although as we shall see later, most of them would like to experiment with such hormones); 9% had done so or continue to do so.

Summing up, our sample can be described as a somewhat older group of men, well-educated and holding good jobs, likely to be married and never divorced, and unlikely to have any drug-related habits other than light alcohol usage. This is a similar profile to the sample of 504 heterosexual transvestites described by Prince and Bentler (1972), a group of 50 described by Talamini (1982), and 65 relatively affluent transvestites studied by Bullough et al. (1983).

Family Constellation, Developmental, and Sexual Variables

In this sample, 80% come from families wherein the parents remained married; they describe themselves as having been raised by both parents. About 6% experienced the death of one parent prior to age 10; 12% experienced the death of the mother before age 20; 18% had lost their father before this age. For over half of the sample, either or both parents were still living at the time of the survey. Of course, this reveals nothing about the qualitative aspects of the parent–child relationship, but we will examine some ratings of this below. We can conclude that catastrophic actual early separation from either parent is very uncommon in this group. This does not imply, however, that at an experiential or emotional level such separation did not occur for some.

In order to estimate the perceived quality of "warmth and support" expressed by parents, we asked our subjects to rate their mothers and fathers along the following 7-point scale and gave these instructions: "Describe how close, or supportive, or warm the relationship was between you and your mother and father." The results are shown in Table 3.

The mean for mothers was 3.37 (S.D. 1.68) indicating greater warmth than for fathers. The mean for fathers was 4.58 (S.D. 1.60). We assume this difference in rated warmth of parents is not unique to trans-

Table 3. Ratings of Emotional Warmth of Parents

	Mother	Father
Exceptionally close, or supportive, or warm	19%	4%
Considerably above average	14	7
Above average	17	10
Average in closeness, or support, or warmth	26	30
Below average	13	22
Considerably below average	7	11
Exceptionally distant, cool, or nonsupportive	4	16

vestites. The two parents are retrospectively perceived as very different on this variable, as shown by the fact that 50% of the ratings of mothers are in the top three categories of "warmth," whereas about the same percentage is in the bottom three categories for fathers. The distant father or absent father is a speculative theme that has frequently been put forth concerning all kinds of personality and human adjustment problems. Bullough *et al.* (1983) were unimpressed with the distant father hypothesis based on their data from transvestites.

Heterosexual Preference

Of this sample, 97% describe themselves as exclusively or predominantly heterosexual. The breakdown is as follows: Exclusively heterosexual, 60%. Predominantly heterosexual with only incidental homosexual activity, 28%. Predominantly heterosexual but with more than incidental homosexual activity, 9%. Three percent said they were bisexual.

Sexual Development

Many individual case studies of transvestites have been reported (e.g., see Grant, 1960) in the psychiatric literature and many of these offer insights into the sexual development of such cases. But aside from these case reports, little is known of the early sexual experiences of transvestites. In our survey we included a series of sexual development questions that offer at least a modest beginning toward data collection on this topic.

Sexual Experiences before Age 12

Subjects were asked to describe themselves on a series of scales shown below. We do not have a nontransvestite comparison group with which to compare these subjects; hence, the data are presented simply

Table 4. Before the Age of 12, How Much
"Sex Play" or Bodily Exploration Did You
Participate In?

None	42%
Once or a few times	25
A few times each year	11
About once a month	10
About once a week or more	12

as a descriptive record of what the men report about themselves. Although our findings could be compared with similar information from Kinsey *et al.* (1948) because we used questions based on some they also asked, the differences across the samples are so great and the time of their study so distant we do not believe such a comparison would be helpful. Table 4 is concerned with sex play, and Table 5 with receipt of sexual information.

Without norms for a control group we cannot determine the comparability of the above responses to nontransvestites. We can only say that these transvestites report a considerable range of early childhood experience, both involving sex play and the amount of sexual information they received.

Table 6 shows the amount of cross dressing reported to have occurred prior to age 12. It is not known what the base rates for male children may be in response to this question, but with 78% of our transvestites acknowledging some cross dressing activity prior to age 12, we can conclude that such early experience is very common in heterosexual transvestites. Bullough *et al.* (1983) found the same, as did Prince and Bentler (1972).

From our data, interviews, and correspondence with TVs, such early cross dressing is almost always interpreted as enjoyable and non-

Table 5. Before the Age of 18, How Much
Information Did You Receive Concerning
Human Sexual Topics (Birth Control,
Intercourse, Masturbation, etc.)?

Extremely little information	37%
Less than my friends	15
About as much as my friends	38
More than my friends	5
Considerably more than most	5

Table 6. Before the Age of 12 Did You
Participate in Cross Dressing Activities?

Never	22%
Once or a few times	29
A few times each year	25
About once a month	11
About once a week or more	13

threatening in retrospective self-reports, although considerable guilt, at least in the early years, is often also a consequence. However, Stoller (1968a, 1985c) reasons that such early cross dressing may be a humiliating experience for a young boy or a threat to masculine gender self-perceptions if it is precipitated by another person, especially a woman or a girl. He sees such an event as having causal significance. Prince (1976) believes that through cross dressing, however this occurs in the young transvestite-to-be, there is an "awakening" of the feminine self—that is, the feminine gender component that Prince assumes to be biologically laid down. Learning explanations of the significance of this early cross dressing would point up the opportunity for positive reinforcement of cross dressing very early in the sexual history. Whatever approach or combination of explanations ultimately emerges as most correct, the significance of these early experiences with gender deviant and taboo behavior seem self-evident. Early cross dressing behavior and the affective experiences associated with this are virtually certain to be critical antecedent learning experiences fundamental to the later unfolding of complete cross dressing, and the later emergence of a cross-gender identity (see Chapter 8). This seems all the more important in view of the fact that a substantial percentage of our transvestites experienced their first orgasm in association with a cross dressing activity.

First Orgasm and Cross Dressing

We asked: *Was any kind of cross dressing, partial or complete, associated with your first orgasm?* The responses were: Yes 37%; No 63%.

For those who favor a learning-based explanation of transvestism, this link between cross dressing and initial orgasm would seem especially important. In fact, it may be highly significant both in the origin and perseverance of transvestism regardless of the explanatory theory favored. There is much evidence that the practice of transvestism is, at least in the early years of cross dressing, a highly erotic and orgasmic activity that is, for many but not all TVs, an important source of sexual

Table 7. At Approximately What Age Did You
First Experience an Orgasm?

Age	Percentage
5–10	4
10–15	79
15–20	18

expression (e.g., see Croughan *et al.*, 1981). We shall present additional data concerning the sexual side of cross dressing when we review the results of the Cross Dressing Inventory completed by our subjects. There can be no debate about the central importance of sexual excitement and masturbatory reinforcement so far as the early years of transvestism are concerned. Table 7 describes age of first orgasm, and Table 8 gives the circumstances surrounding this event.

Again, neither of these questions suggests anything unique about the first orgasmic experiences of these subjects. We shall continue along this track by considering the initial orgasmic experience in more detail. Table 9 contains data bearing on first orgasm associated with masturbation, heterosexual activity, and homosexual activity. The three questions were phrased as follows:

- At what age did you first masturbate resulting in orgasm?
- At what age did you first have heterosexual activity resulting in orgasm?
- At what age did you first have homosexual activity resulting in orgasm?

As shown in Table 9, all except 39 subjects said they had never experienced homosexual orgasm. The ages of these sexual experiences do not seem remarkable; it is risky to assume that the averages given are

Table 8. What Were the Circumstances Surrounding Your
First Orgasm?

Circumstance	Percentage
During sleep	18
After masturbation, alone	67
After masturbation, not alone	4
Activity with female	7
Activity with male	0
Other	4

Table 9. Ages for First Masturbation, First Heterosexual Orgasm,
First Homosexual Orgasm

Activity	Mean age	S.D.	N
First masturbation orgasm	13.3	3.0	108
First heterosexual orgasm	18.9	4.4	108
First homosexual orgasm	25.4	9.5	39

early or late since the emergence of sexual behavior is known to be
linked to religious training, socioeconomic and ethnic factors, and many
other determinants that make comparisons difficult. As we see it, these
data do not suggest any unusual pattern of sexual development in transvestites (other than their cross dressing). Far more qualitative information will be needed to establish how developmental sexual experiences
may contribute to transvestism.

Concerning the fact that about one-third of our subjects had had a
homosexual experience with orgasm, we can only surmise that such a
finding is in harmony with the widely assumed breadth of such experience within the male population (Kinsey *et al.*, 1948).

Presented with various age ranges on our survey form, our subjects
were asked to report average number of orgasms per week for each age
range. The results are given in Table 10. These data are very similar to
the classical findings that, for men, frequency of sexual orgasms peaks
in the mid-twenties with a gradual decline thereafter, and that for most
men, the frequency does not reach zero even in the seventies and
eighties (Kinsey *et al.*, 1948). None of our transvestites reported zero
sexual orgasms regardless of age. Our oldest subject was 83.

These results touch the surface of an important issue, for cross
dressing may significantly enhance the sex life of the transvestite. For

Table 10. Try to Recall As Accurately As Possible Your Average Number of
Orgasms per Week Regardless of How This Occurred

Age	Mean	S.D.	Median	Range	N
15–20	5.0	5.0	4	0–35	105
21–30	6.0	5.5	4	0–34	106
31–40	4.8	4.2	4	0–25	95
41–50	3.5	2.6	3	1–17	54
51–60	2.3	1.5	2	1–6	30
61–70	1.7	1.0	1	1–3	7

example, a few of our subjects have kept diaries and other records of sexual outlets during extended (several months) periods of cross dressing and non-cross-dressing periods. While these data have not been acquired from a large number of subjects or as part of a formal project, the tentative indication is that sexual outlets are approximately double in rate during cross dressing periods, compared to non-cross dressing periods. Again, this must be considered nothing more than an interesting hypothesis pending a properly conducted data-based project. When we speak of enhancement of the sex life of the transvestite through cross dressing, we do not imply such activity has a positive impact on the marital sex life. As we shall discuss later, cross dressing appears to become a competitive substitute for participation in marital sex. Lest this be overgeneralized, we can also add that some of our subjects' wives noted that cross dressing contributed positively to both the intimacy level of the marital relationship and to marital sex.

Adolescent Sexual Shyness

These statistics for initial sexual experiences are what would be expected in a predominantly heterosexual male sample in our culture. They seem to point toward a sexual history not unlike that of most male youth. A somewhat different view is obtained, however, upon examining the more qualitative aspects of their sexual histories. In our survey we asked each subject to describe his youthful feelings about his own sexuality and about dating using this short-answer question: "As a teenager and young adult, what kinds of feelings did you have about your own sexuality and your ability to compete for dates? How sexually bold or sexually inhibited were you as a young person?" Table 11 provides a summary of the responses classified into four levels.

It is very common for teenagers and young adults to report feelings of shyness especially relative to sexual or intimate relationships. We must not, therefore, rush to conclude that sexual inhibition or lack of heterosexual practice in dating are definitive contributing factors in the

Table 11. Ratings of Adolescent Sexual Shyness

	Percentage
Very inhibited, very shy	35
Somewhat inhibited or shy	31
Not inhibited or shy . . . average	25
Bold and confident . . . very active	10

formation of transvestism. What we can assert on the basis of the data is that heterosexual cross dressers appear to have histories representing all degrees of sexual inhibition—from exceptionally shy through very bold—but that about two-thirds tend toward the shy end of this continuum, and about one-third are very inhibited in their adolescent and young adult years.

Cross Dressing Behavior

We asked: *At what age did you have your first experience with cross dressing, either partial or complete?* Mean age was 11.5 (*S.D.* 9.7). Median age was 9. The range was from 2 to 60 years. For 92% of our subjects, this initial cross dressing was limited to partial, not complete cross dressing. The remaining 8% reported cross dressing completely even on this first occasion. Because this age range is so extensive, it is useful to examine the distribution for responses to the above question which are given in Table 12.

Over half of our transvestites did some kind of partial or complete cross dressing before the age of 10; Prince and Bentler (1972) reported 54%. Eighty-five percent did so before the age of 15. Again, this is not an unusual finding. Such evidence of early involvement in cross dressing has partially blinded us to the fact that such behavior may emerge very late in life, although this is atypical. Transvestites who start this behavior late in life have not been studied as a unique group. Judging from our own case histories, such late developing transvestism is most likely following a divorce, death of the spouse, or some other major life stressor, but we cannot report such facts in a sufficiently large subsample to present this as more than an interesting observation. We think the

Table 12. Age of First Cross Dressing

Age	Percentage
Before 5	10
5–10	43
11–15	32
16–20	5
21–25	3
26–30	1
31–35	2
Over 35	4

emergence of cross dressing for the first time in the age range from 40 to 60 supports the thesis that cognitive scripts underlie transvestism. In these older men we would speculate that a very long "incubation period" preceded their first actual experience with cross dressing and that this period included fantasy-based script construction in which fetishistic stimuli associated with cross dressing became a central theme. Another important but tentative point is that these older men did not start cross dressing in response to any kind of cross-gender identity. As we see it, they began exactly as do the more numerous teenage cross dressers—in a very fetishistic manner. The learning of a cross-gender identity comes much later. Put more directly, it appears that men may proceed through a predictable series of stages of transvestism regardless of the age of commencement. For the case of a man who became a cross dresser in his early sixties and a secondary transsexual at 74, see Docter (1985).

If one essential difference between fetishism and transvestism is complete cross dressing by the transvestite, then we shall be especially interested in facts pertaining to such complete cross dressing. We shall now report when complete cross dressing first occurred in our sample, what the circumstances were, how much practice preceded the first venture out in public, and when a femme (woman's) name was adopted. Public presentation of the pseudowoman, the adoption of a name, and the ownership of all that is required for complete cross dressing are all closely connected with the formation and development of the cross-gender identity. It is important, therefore, to note the extensive years of practice as a transvestite which typically precede these events. Our subjects were asked: *At what age did you have your first experience with complete cross dressing? Definition: "Complete" means everything needed to appear in public.*

Mean age was 26.5 (*S.D.* 11.8). Median age was 25. The range was from 4 to 59 years. It seems clear that if the concept of transvestism is defined to include the necessity of complete cross dressing (as opposed to fetishism) the emergence of this pattern of behavior is far removed from the origins of cross dressing in early childhood. One way of conceptualizing the formation of the group we now label transvestites is to think of them as having developed out of a more heterogeneous group of fetishists who, for unknown reasons, do not progress into transvestites. Some would speculate (Freund *et al.*, 1982) that the underlying reason is the transvestite's propensity for experiencing cross-gender identity only when cross dressed. The fetishist, it would be argued, has no such gender identity development; he is satisfied with the use of women's clothing for sexual arousal and they serve no other purpose. We shall therefore be especially interested in looking for clues concerning causal factors in the shaping of the cross-gender identity. As taken up in Chapter 8, we believe it is the social role-playing, and all that goes with this, which is causative in the evolution of the cross-gender identity. Notice the great variation in age for this first experience with complete cross dressing as shown in Table 13.

We asked: *At what age did you first go out in public while cross dressed for at least one hour?* Mean age was 32.4 (*S.D.* 12.2). Median age was 42. Range was 12 to 63 years. (Twelve individuals reported never having gone out in public cross dressed.) As with the age of first complete cross dressing, we see evidence of substantial passage of time prior to the first public presentation of self while cross dressed. Prince (1976) has regarded this public exposure as a highly significant and perhaps psychotherapeutic experience. We believe this social experience serves as one of the major opportunities for the formation and strengthening of the feminine self, a term we use synonymously with cross-gender identity. What is certain is that this stepping out of the "closet" of privacy and often secrecy is an event which culminates very extensive rehearsal and practice. In many cases from our sample, which is heavily weighted with members of cross dressing clubs, it is the opportunity for club membership and for the safety and encouragement this offers which makes possible the initial venture into a social setting. Such club meetings are certainly not public events, but the coming and going to the meeting is semipublic. Transvestites usually have intense fantasies of how rewarding it would be to go out in public, cross dressed, and to be accepted as a woman. But the enactment of such fantasies usually occurs considerably after the origins of cross dressing. Table 14 gives the distribution for ages of first cross dressing in public.

Another way of addressing the same question is to ask: *How many years of experience with cross dressing did you have before you owned your first complete outfit of women's clothing?* Mean number of years was 15.2 (*S.D.*

Table 13. Age of First Complete Cross Dressing

Age	Percentage
Before 10	8
11–20	23
21–30	40
31–40	14
41–50	8
51–60	7

Table 14. Distribution of Ages for First
Cross Dressing in Public

Age	Percentage
Before 10	11
11–20	10
21–30	37
31–40	16
41–50	14
51–60	11
61–70	1

11.3). Median years, 12. Range was from 1 to 44 years. (Three said they never owned a complete outfit of women's clothing.)

We asked: *How many years of experience with cross dressing did you have before adopting a femme name?* The mean was 21.2 years (*S.D.* 12.0). Median was 20 years. Range was from 1 to 53 years. (Five said they never adopted a femme name.) What we see is that for the average transvestite it requires at least a decade, often 20 years or more of cross dressing experience, before owning a full set of suitable feminine attire, adopting a femme name, or going out in public cross dressed takes place.

Each session of transvestism requires considerable time. We asked our subjects to list what activities they engage in while cross dressed and the time a typical session required from start to finish. The average time per session was 5.4 hours (*S.D.* 2.3). Median, 6 hours. Range from 1 to 11 hours. The practice of transvestism is not a hasty sexual ritual; it is typically an excursion of several hours, often encompassing an evening, an afternoon, an entire day, or in unusual cases, a weekend. The activities described usually begin with from 1 to 2 hours of preparation with makeup and cross dressing, with the remainder devoted to either shopping, correspondence, reading, cinema or television watching, dining out, or visiting with friends. The predominant activity is nonsexual although many sessions conclude with masturbation. Data indicative of this will be described when we take up the Cross Dressing Inventory. The diversity of activity reported and the duration of a typical cross dressing session calls into question the familiar characterization of transvestism (found in many textbooks) as primarily a sexual excitant. Steiner (1985b) has expressed her opinion that this explanation is too simplistic. Little has been previously reported concerning what TVs say they do during a typical session or how long they spend doing it. Such knowledge is important to a more complete understanding of this be-

Table 15. Ratings of Benefits or Importance of Cross Dressing

Percentage	Amount of benefit or importance
0	Cross dressing is of little or no importance to me. Very little or no pleasure is derived from these activities.
4	Cross dressing is somewhat joyful and pleasurable, but not of great importance.
23	Cross dressing is an important source of joy and pleasure for me.
34	Cross dressing is highly pleasurable and brings exceptional joy.
22	Cross dressing is extremely pleasurable; it brings greater pleasure and joy than other pleasurable activites in my life.
17	Cross dressing is a super-pleasure for me. No other activity gives me as much delight. Peaks of exceptional pleasure and joy are obtained.

havior because, as many have argued, it seems to almost certainly involve multiple sources of reinforcement.

Our subjects were asked to rate the benefits or importance of cross dressing; the results are shown in Table 15. Almost 40% say their cross dressing is "extremely pleasurable" or a "super-pleasure." That leaves 60% of the sample who appear to be implying that they have multiple sources of pleasure and joy in life, and cross dressing is simply one of them.

We also asked our subjects to rate the possible harmful effects of cross dressing experienced; the results are given in Table 16. Roughly half of our subjects say their cross dressing has "never had harmful consequences" or that these have been "slightly harmful"; the remainder

Table 16. Ratings of Harmful Effects of Cross Dressing as Experienced

Percentage	Amount of harm
23	Cross dressing has seldom or never had harmful effects for me or upon others in my life.
31	Cross dressing has occasionally had slightly harmful consequences for me or upon others in my life.
23	Cross dressing has led to somewhat harmful consequences for me or upon others in my life.
14	Cross dressing has led to clearly harmful consequences for me or upon others in my life.
6	Cross dressing has had very seriously harmful consequences for me or upon others in my life.
3	Cross dressing has had extremely harmful consequences for me or upon others in my life.

report more serious harmful effects. It may surprise those who see transvestism as a psychiatric disorder that 23% of these transvestites consider it to be little or no problem. The issue of what should be clinically diagnosed as a psychiatric disorder goes beyond our immediate concern. But given these data, we may ask if it makes sense to consider all transvestites alike from a psychiatric viewpoint. Should transvestism preclude induction into the military services? Should transvestism preclude issuance of a security clearance? As with all judgments about people, especially where psychiatric labels are involved, the most reasonable approach is to base decisions on the facts of individual cases rather than diagnostic labels alone.

We also asked: *"Did you experience a 'stage' or period of years when having women's clothing directly associated with masturbation was important to you?"* Sixty-six percent indicated that this was the case ($N = 119$). This supports Brierley's (1979) view that transvestism typically has an early stage in which fetishism is predominant and a later stage in which a shift in gender identity is seen.

Initial experience with complete cross dressing typically occurred during the young adult years. While 10% reported complete cross dressing prior to age 10 and 24% prior to age 20, 38% first engaged in complete cross dressing during their twenties. Thirteen percent first cross dressed in their thirties, 8% in their forties, and 7% after age 50. While the origins of complete cross dressing may be in youth or in early childhood, it appears to have required many years for this behavior to take its final form for at least 30% of our sample. Examination of the development of individual histories reveals marked differences in age of onset and time required to move from no cross dressing or partial cross dressing into full cross dressing behavior.

Perceived Attitudes of Wives

Our 90 married subjects were asked to rate how they believed their wives felt about cross dressing using the 7-point descriptive scale shown below. The results are given in Table 17. The assessment of wives' attitudes is confirmed by independent ratings given by wives who said much the same thing as did their husbands. The survey results will be discussed in our chapter concerning wives. While 28% of the wives are described by these husbands as near the bottom of this attitude scale ("Clearly negative . . . or Highly negative . . . ") approximately the same percentage fall into the top two categories ("Highly supportive . . . or Somewhat supportive . . . ").

Table 17. Which Best Describes Your Wife's Feelings about Cross Dressing?

Percentage	Husband's rating of wife's attitude
12	Highly supportive and eager to participate and assist. Likes it.
15	Somewhat supportive. Few negative feelings or none.
9	Slightly supportive. Few negative feelings.
16	Evenly balanced between supportive and negative.
20	Slightly negative. Some supportive help but not extensive.
18	Clearly negative feelings but tries to be somewhat supportive.
10	Highly negative. Mostly nonsupportive. Strongly dislikes it.

Part II: Explanations for Cross Dressing

In previous studies, transvestites have not been asked in a systematic way to evaluate their own explanations concerning their cross dressing. However, we assumed that such subjective impressions might, at the least, clarify the question of how these individuals explain their behavior to themselves. It is well know that such subjective reports may be self-serving, biased for many reasons, and perhaps totally erroneous. We can question, for example, whether anyone of us can correctly list or rate the motives or explanations behind his or her behavior no matter how conscientious the effort. Such pitfalls call for extreme caution in the examination of results from a rating scale designed to assess how transvestites explain their cross dressing.

Sixteen explanations for cross dressing were extracted from major articles concerned with transvestism. These represented motivational, reinforcing, and theoretical explanations. They were selected to offer a spectrum of explanations although it was not feasible to list all possible explanations. We believe our list is reasonably representative of the most frequently cited contributing factors associated with transvestism. Each explanation was rated independently of the others. Subjects were asked to use a rating scale which contrasted "less important" from "more important" explanations.

Subjects were asked to consider these 16 explanations for cross dressing, to rate each using a 6-point scale to describe " . . . how important this explanation is as applied to you . . . ." Further, they were asked to make these ratings for two time periods, during the "early cross dressing years," and "at present."

The 6-point scale is shown below and ranges from "very unimportant" through "most important of all." This terminology was used to encourage the evaluation of the relative importance of each of the 16 statements, although if the rater wished to do so he was free to rate each with any of the 6 scale values. All but a few subjects distributed their ratings across the various explanations. The rating scale used was: 1. Very unimportant to you. 2. Slight importance. 3. Some importance. 4. Highly important. 5. More important than most others. 6. Most important of all.

Explanations for the Early Time Period

Here are the results, in Table 18, listed in rank-order of importance from the most important to the least important for the time period, "early in your cross dressing years." Ranks are based on the mean rating so that high means indicate "most important" and low numbers comparatively unimportant. The full content of item definitions shown in the Explanations measures are given in the Appendix.

For the early period in cross dressing careers the highest rated explanations pertain to (in descending order):

- Sexual arousal (item 2) (*highest rating*)
- Erotic fantasy (item 8)
- Compulsive motive to cross dress (item 14)
- Pleasure getting (item 1)
- Anti-boredom (item 7)
- Role playing/role relief (item 4)

Table 18. Ranked Mean Ratings for Explanations of Cross Dressing for the Early Period

Rank	Mean	S.D.	Mean ratings of explanations for cross dressing: early years
1	4.6	1.6	As sexually arousing (See Appendix for item definition)
2	3.8	1.7	As erotic fantasy
3	3.5	1.9	As a compulsion
4	3.3	1.5	As pleasurable behavior
5	2.9	1.6	As anti-boredom behavior
6	2.6	1.5	As role-playing and role relief
7	2.6	1.6	As expression of the "girl within"
8	2.3	1.7	As anti-loneliness behavior
9	2.2	1.4	As multiple rewards
10	2.2	1.3	As achievement of feminine identity
11	2.1	1.6	As due to damaged sense of masculinity
12	2.1	1.3	As an outlet for emotional expression
13	2.0	1.4	As multiple personality
14	1.9	1.5	As a substitute for intimacy and closeness
15	1.7	1.2	As dependency behavior
16	1.5	1.1	As part of a femme lifestyle

The five explanations rated lowest for the early time period are (in ascending order):

- Feminine life style (item 5) *(lowest rating)*
- Dependency (item 11)
- Intimacy and closeness (item 10)
- Multiple personality (item 12)
- Emotional expression (item 9)

Explanations for the Present Time Period

In order to see how explanatory attributions changed over time, we shall now examine the means of ratings, listed in rank order, from the most important to the least important, for the present time period in the cross dressing career. These results are given in Table 19.

The explanations considered most important for this time period are far different from those most highly rated for the early cross dressing time period. Here are the top rated explanations for the present time period (in descending order):

- Pleasure (item 1) *(highest rating)*
- "Girl within" (item 16)
- Multiple rewards (item 13)
- Role-playing/role relief (item 4)
- Feminine identity (item 3)

Table 19. Ranked Mean Ratings of Explanations for the Present Period

Rank	Mean	S.D.	Mean ratings of explanations for cross dressing: present time
1	4.9	1.3	As pleasurable behavior
2	4.3	1.7	As expression of the "girl within"
3	4.3	1.5	As multiple rewards
4	4.1	1.6	As role-playing and role relief
5	4.1	1.6	As achievement of feminine identity
6	3.9	1.4	As part of a femme life style
7	3.9	1.5	As an outlet for emotional expression
8	3.8	1.7	As a compulsion
9	3.5	1.5	As anti-boredom behavior
10	3.3	1.6	As multiple personality
11	3.3	1.8	As erotic fantasy
12	3.3	1.4	As sexually arousing
13	2.8	1.7	As anti-loneliness behavior
14	2.7	1.6	As a substitute for intimacy and closeness
15	2.5	1.6	As dependency behavior
16	2.0	1.6	As due to damaged sense of masculinity

The explanations rated of least importance are these (in ascending order):

- Damaged masculinity (item 15) (*lowest rating*)
- Dependency (item 11)
- Intimacy and closeness (item 10)
- Loneliness (item 6)
- Sexual arousal (item 2)

Our transvestites are saying that the most important explanations for their cross dressing early in the cross dressing career have to do with sexual and erotic factors and with experiencing a compulsion to cross dress. This is associated with sexual excitement and helps to overcome boredom. However, late in the cross dressing career most of the highest rated explanations have changed. Nonerotic pleasure has moved to the top of the list, followed by several items dealing with feminine gender expression and with the sense of receiving multiple rewards from cross dressing. Hence, the "present time" ratings show diminshed sexual factors and much stronger rating of cross-gender identity explanations.

Table 20 shows changes in ranked importance for 16 explanations at two time periods. A minus indicates a drop in importance from the early cross dressing period to the "present time" ratings. (These are listed in the order of importance shown for the early period in Table 18.)

Table 20. Changes in Ranked Importance of 16 Explanations of Cross Dressing from Early Cross Dressing to the Present Time[a]

Change in rank	Explanation
−11	As sexually arousing
− 8	As erotic fantasy
− 5	As a compulsion
+ 3	As nonerotic pleasure
− 4	As anti-boredom
+ 3	As role-playing/role relief
+ 5	As the "girl within"
− 5	As anti-loneliness
+ 4	As multiple rewards
+ 6	As feminine identity
− 5	As damaged masculinity
+ 5	As emotional expression
+ 2	As multiple personality
0	As intimacy and closeness
0	As dependency
+10	As femme lifestyle

[a]Each step in the ranking was counted as one point.

Analysis of Variance for Early *vs.* Present Time Period Means

The data for the early and late periods were subjected to a two-way analysis of variance for repeated measures and the F values are given in Table 21. We may conclude that the 16 means for explanations, taken as a set, differ significantly from each other. Also, the early *vs.* late ratings are markedly different, with the late ratings much higher than the early ratings. Finally, the interaction term indicates that the time period for which explanation ratings are made significantly influences the size of these ratings.

This change in motivation or perhaps in the kinds of reinforcement derived from cross dressing has been described previously by several researchers. For example, Brierley (1979) strongly emphasized what he believed to be a shift from an early "fetishistic stage" to a later "gender identity stage" although he did not acquire data to document this process. An intriguing suggestion by Brierley is that the process of transvestism may entail a self-fulfilling trip down the path of gender deviance. The idea is that the more the transvestite cross dresses, the more he is inclined to do so. Further, the resulting cross-gender behavior progressively comes to be self-perceived as a necessary and desirable aspect of himself. While Brierley does not go so far as to speculate that the end result of this could be the syndrome of secondary transsexualism, this possibility is an obvious potential end result of years of practicing to be a woman. For the heterosexual transvestite club members we are studying, however, such an outcome seems not to occur in more than about 5% of those who begin as fetishistic cross dressers. Such club members, we must remember, tend to be high-functioning persons who are more or less satisfied with their pattern of transvestism. As Buhrich and Mc-Conaghy (1970) have pointed out, there may be another subgroup of fetishistic cross dressers who, for gender and sexual orientation reasons, are more directly inclined toward a transsexual destination. These marginal transvestites may belong to cross dressing clubs, but in our experi-

Table 21. Two-Way Anova for Explanations Means during Early and Late Periods

Source	F-test	DF	p
Explanations means	25.4	15	<.0001
Early *vs.* late period	215.4	1	<.0001
Interaction	12.9	15	<.0001

ence they are not likely to value this group membership as much as do the less gender deviant cross dressers.

Concerning the evolution of the transvestite career, Virginia Prince (1976) has strongly underscored the erosion of sexual motivation in favor of the later expression of the "girl within"—that is, the expression of a cross-gender identity. This thesis has been very widely communicated to the heterosexual transvestite clubs through their magazines and newsletters, and the girl within idea seems to appeal to many of these cross dressers. As we have shown above, the girl within explanation finished seventh for the early period rankings of explanations, and second for the present time period. But now we must ask, Are the subjects we studied simply "playing back" the explanations they have most often heard from others? Have these become attributions which make sense to them in the quest for some kind of understandable theory to explain their cross dressing? Of course, it is possible that such attributions may fit closely with the belief-system of the transvestite and that this is why the girl within idea seems so well established. As yet, the final word is still out. We are justified in assuming from several lines of evidence, some of which we will present below, that there is indeed a developmental process associated with transvestism, and what these individuals have told us about this process through their rating of causal attributions at two different time periods may offer some useful clues for further investigation.

Principal Components Analysis of Explanations for the "Early Time Period"

Ratings for the early period were subjected to a principal components analysis using the varimax rotation procedure. Three factors emerged which accounted for 32%, 14%, and 10% of the variance of this data set. The factor loadings are shown in Table 22. The three factors identified are discussed next.

Factor 1: Cross Gender Identity/Pleasurable Affect

Factor 1 accounts for 32% of the variance of this measure. The Explanations items which load most heavily on this factor are those pertaining to:

- Item 3: expression of a feminine identity or cross-gender identity (loading, .83)

Table 22. Principal Components Analysis from Explanations Ratings for the Early Time Period

Explanation	Factor 1	Factor 2	Factor 3
1. Pleasure	.66	.05	.09
2. Sexual arousal	−.08	−.13	.81
3. Cross-gender identity	.83	.14	−.09
4. Role relief	.82	.16	.14
5. Femme lifestyle	.79	.00	.01
6. Anti-loneliness	.23	.41	.46
7. Anti-boredom	.37	.25	.65
8. Erotic fantasy	.04	.18	.83
9. Emotional expression	.25	.74	.02
10. Intimacy	.08	.66	.17
11. Dependency	.08	.75	.17
12. Multiple personality	.57	.45	.12
13. Multiple rewards	.50	.20	.33
14. Compulsion	.07	.24	.70
15. Damaged masculinity	−.07	.61	.10
16. "Girl within"	.29	.68	.06

- Item 4: cross dressing affords relief from the masculine role (loading, .82)
- Item 5: enjoyment of a feminine life style (loading, .79)
- Item 1: gaining nonerotic pleasure from cross dressing (loading, .66)

Factor 1 appears to be measuring the subjective experience of pleasure, fun, relaxation, retreat from the demands of the masculine role, and of gaining this through the taking on of a temporary cross-gender identity. This factor is nonerotic. It is important to note that the variable most highly loaded on Factor 1 and on any factor in the entire matrix is item 3, which pertains to "achievement of feminine identity."

Factor 2: Emotional Expression

Factor 2 accounts for 14% of the variance of this measure. The Explanations items which load most heavily on this factor are those pertaining to:

- Item 11: able to become more dependent when cross dressed (loading, .75)
- Item 9: ability to express emotions (loading, .74)

- Item 16: expression of the "girl within" (loading, .68)
- Item 10: as substitute for intimacy and closeness (loading, .66)

The items appear to have in common various expressive feelings said to be beneficially achieved through cross dressing.

Factor 3: Sexual Excitement

Factor 3 accounts for 10% of the variance of this measure. The Explanations items which load most heavily on this factor are those pertaining to:

- Item 8: enactment of erotic fantasies (loading, .83)
- Item 2: sexual arousal (loading, .81)
- Item 14: feeling a compulsion to cross dress (loading, .70)
- Item 7: cross dressing as an anti-boredom tactic (loading, .46)

Factor 3 appears to tap sexual excitement produced by cross dressing, the feelings of a compulsion to cross dress, and the overcoming of boredom through this behavior.

Principal Components Analysis for Explanations during the "Present Time Period"

This analysis yielded three components having virtually identical variables as listed for the early time period, although some of the loadings were quite different. The only major change from one factor to another was a shift in item 16 (expression of girl within) from its earlier loading on Factor 2 to Factor 1. This appears to strengthen the interpretation of Factor 1 as measuring cross-gender identity and other closely related attributions.

Part III: Frequency of Cross Dressing during Early, Middle, and Late Stages

Previous studies have reported changes in the frequency of cross dressing throughout a subject's life (e.g., see Croughan et al., 1981) but the matter has not been explored well. So far as we know, there has never been an analysis of such changes for stages of development in the cross dressing career. It is certain such careers vary greatly, so forcing comparisons into decades of age or any other format may yield means which are impossible to interpret. For this reason, we asked our subjects to define their own eras or stages of cross dressing based on their own experience.

Ideally, the study of this topic would include such variables as activities while cross dressed, the reinforcers which may be identified, the stimuli most likely to control cross dressing, and the frequency of the activity. We do not have all such data, but as a start in what may be considered the behavioral analysis of transvestism we shall provide an analysis of frequency of cross dressing at three stages or periods of life.

Identification of Stages or Periods

Subjects were asked to *"Divide your life into stages or periods having different patterns of cross dressing. Use any basis you wish for establishing these stages or periods. The important thing is to show how your actual cross dressing changed over the years."* Subjects were then instructed to list, for each stage, their "average cross dressing per month." The unit of measure used in this analysis will be, therefore, the frequency of cross dressing sessions per month.

There is great diversity in the duration of these stages. For example, some younger subjects said they could identify an extensive early period, followed by a brief middle period (as while married for a few years), followed by a much longer period. Older subjects might view their stages or eras of development quite differently. Often, however, they involved these major considerations:

- *The early stage.* This typically begins prior to age 15 and ends, for example, with leaving home for an apartment, college, marriage, full-time employment, or entry into the military. Privacy and independence are low. This is believed to be a more fetishistic stage (Brierley, 1979) compared to the successive periods.
- *The middle stage.* During this period there is often much greater privacy and independence permitting increased cross dressing. For those married, the clothing of the wife becomes an optional source of garments. For those not married, far greater privacy may facilitate cross dressing. For all, this is a time for learning, meeting other transvestites, reading about cross dressing, and for the growth of their desire to make improvements in the techniques of feminine appearance.
- *The late stage.* There is movement out of the closet and into clubs or other public settings. Cross dressing becomes a more social process rather than a secretive one. A feminine name is selected and apparently there is development of the "second self" (Ovesey &

Person, 1976; Prince, 1976). Brierley (1979) has also discussed this identity stage.

We reviewed the stages identified in the self-constructed histories of each subject. It was simple to recognize the early and late stages, and we used our best judgment in selecting the middle stage which seemed most representative of such an era in the transvestic career. Since our subjects used many different bases of judgment in making their selection of stages, we did not attempt to set up standard criteria for the definition of the middle stage. Typically, this was chronologically in the middle of the cross dressing career of each subject.

One complication is that our transvestites ranged in age from 20 to 83 and there are, therefore, great differences in their number of years of experience with cross dressing. Obviously, our youngest subject did not have the opportunity to experience the possible developmental changes reported by some older transvestites. For this reason, we shall first present the data for all subjects and then a second analysis in which subjects above the median age of 42 are compared with younger subjects.

While this approach to examination of the cross dressing history is far from exact, it is one way to group information across subjects whose lives have unfolded in various ways and where changes have occurred at quite different ages. It is important to note that these hypothetical stages do not reflect a forced division of the life span into predefined segments such as decades; each subject constructed his own divisions and identified the ages at which changes in cross dressing occurred.

When all the subjects are grouped together we find statistically significant differences between the means for frequency of cross dressing across the three stages. Using the t-test for paired subjects, significant differences between means for frequency of cross dressing are observed when the stages are compared to each other. The results are shown in Table 23.

We may say with confidence that these means differ significantly. An important consideration is whether there was an age effect in which

Table 23. t-Tests for Frequency of Cross Dressing Events per Month at Three Stages

Stages compared	Mean X	Mean Y	t	p
Early *vs.* middle	5.5	8.0	4.15	<.0005
Early *vs.* late	5.5	11.1	14.0	<.0005
Middle *vs.* late	8.0	11.1	3.36	<.005

the younger men differed from the older subjects. A two-way analysis of variance was calculated for a repeated measures design involving the same subjects viewed in three time periods of the cross dressing career (early, middle, and late stages). We shall identify this as Factor A. The division of age groups simply involved splitting the distribution at the median age of 42. Hence, we have six cells representing three stages of cross dressing and two age conditions.

There are two issues: (1) Are the means for stages of the two age groups statistically different? (2) Is there a significant interaction between the means for stages and the age variable? The results are given in Table 24. These data indicate that there are significant differences in the frequency of cross dressing across the three stages, and that these means are not age-dependent. Let us now examine the mean frequencies for cross dressing at different stages as shown in Table 25.

These data show that for all subjects, whether grouped as younger or older or taken as a whole, regardless of age, there are statistically significant differences in the reported means for frequency of cross dressing per month at three stages. The differences between means for younger *vs.* older subjects are not statistically significant. There is no interaction effect between age and stages. For all subjects combined, there is about twice as much cross dressing reported for the later stage than in the early stage.

The frequency of cross dressing at one stage is not highly predictive of this rate at another stage. The Pearson correlations for these comparisions were (early–middle) .42, (early–late) .02, and (middle–late) .35. The first and third of these are significant beyond the .001 level but since only about 18% of the variance is explained for the highest of these we may conclude that the frequency rates at one stage are not very predictive of rates at a subsequent stage.

Most of these subjects say they can recognize an early stage of cross dressing which closely related to masturbation. Here is the question we asked and the responses: *"Did you experience a 'stage' or period of years when having women's clothing directly associated with masturbation was important to you?"* The responses were: Yes 66%; No 34%.

Table 24. Two-Way Anova for Means of Frequency of Cross
Dressing per Month

Source	F-test	p
Factor A (stages)	16.77	<.0001
Factor B (age)	1.0	>.25 (not significant)
A × B	2.43	>.10 (not significant)

Table 25. Group Means for Frequency of Cross Dressing per Month during
Three Stages for Younger and Older Subjects

	Early	Middle	Late	N
Young subjects	5.9	9.3	10.4	52
Older subjects	4.4	6.6	12.1	49
All subjects	5.5	8.0	11.1	101

There is some evidence from the reports of others that fetishism is diminished as the years pass (Brierley, 1979; Stoller, 1985c), but not for all transvestites. Buhrich and Beaumont (1981), for example, reported a survey of cross dressers in the United States and Australia in which they found only about 20% to 25% saying they experienced "no fetishism" compared to earlier years. About 40% said their fetishism was diminished, while 24% said it remained the same. In the United States, 11% of these men indicated increased fetishism in later years, and in Australia the percentage was 14. Their subjects were members of transvestite clubs. Pooling all of their 212 subjects, the average age was in the low forties which is quite similar to the sample our data is based upon.

Conclusions Concerning Stages of Cross Dressing

Our research support the following conclusions about frequency of cross dressing during early, middle, and late stages:

1. With the passage of time and the gaining of experience, there are marked increases in the frequency of cross dressing of most transvestites who participated in this study. Beginning with an average cross dressing frequency of about six times monthly at the early stage, the average rate is almost double this for the later stage. Heterosexual transvestism may be characterized as behavior very likely to increase in frequency with years of experience. Data from individual case histories show marked variability in the frequency and developmental pattern of cross dressing; there is no single pattern. But for the group as a whole, the general trend over time is toward substantially increased frequency.
2. Frequency of cross dressing at different stages is not significantly different as a function of age.
3. Frequencies during the early and middle stages are not predictive of frequencies for the late stage.

4. Late stage frequencies are about twice the amount seen in the early stage regardless of the age group sampled.
5. The matter of "stages" may be as complex as the situational and personal adjustment factors influencing the lives of each subject. While Brierley's (1979) thesis of an early "fetishistic stage" and a later "identity stage" may be correct as indicative of general trends, the two-stage view would seem too restricted to account for the life span changes described by our subjects. We believe that reported increases in frequency of cross dressing at the middle and late stages may involve such factors as: discovery of multiple reinforcers, availability of time, greater privacy, revelations made to the wife and her acceptance, greater self-acceptance of transvestism, and joining a TV club.

Part IV: Bem Sex-Role Inventory

The Bem Sex-Role Inventory (Bem, 1974, 1981a,b) is designed to measure the extent to which an individual describes himself (or herself) as having personality features considered desirable and traditional in our culture for either a man or a woman. The unique feature of this test, unlike many earlier efforts to assess masculinity or femininity, is that a person can identify either or both the masculine or feminine qualities which he or she thinks apply. Hence, by comparing a subject's self-description with suitable norms, it is possible to classify each individual in one of four ways:

1. As traditionally sex-typed in the feminine direction.
2. As traditionally sex-typed in the masculine direction.
3. As androgynous—having strong masculine and feminine characteristics.
4. As undifferentiated—having weak masculine and feminine characteristics.

Bem describes her test as follows: " . . . the BSRI is based on a conception of the traditionally sex-typed person as someone who is highly attuned to cultural definitions of sex-appropriate behavior and who uses such definitions as the ideal standard against which her or his own behavior is to be evaluated" (1981a, p. 4).

Although the BSRI has been extensively utilized during the 1970s and 1980s, there is some doubt that it measures what it purports to measure. For example, Spence and Helmreich (1981) argue that it measures " . . . expressive and instrumental personality traits . . . " but that such trait clusters are not much related to " . . . global self-images of masculinity or femininity . . ." Bem has responded to this critique (1981c). We pursue our Bem data with due recognition of the difficulty of creating sex-role measures, such as the BSRI, and of demonstrating their construct validity.

The test contains 20 personality characteristics which are "stereotypically feminine," such as affectionate, gentle, understanding, sensitive to the needs of others, and 20 which are "stereotypically masculine," such as ambitious, self-reliant, independent, and assertive. There are 20 additional characteristics which serve as filler items. For each of these 60 descriptive terms the subject rates how closely it applies to her or to him using a 7-point scale which ranges from Never through Always and which is labelled at each of the 7 points.

Two things are most important to note about this test: First, each subject earns a score on both the feminine and masculine dimensions (see the four possible classifications listed above); and second, the norms reflect the social desirability of these personality characteristics as judged appropriate for women and men by our culture, not merely the actual test scores earned by women and men. To interpret the results, therefore, you must ask: To what extent is this person responding in a "traditional," sex-stereotypic manner in relation to femininity or masculinity?

Our subjects were classified as Feminine, Masculine, Androgynous, or Undifferentiated using the median split-procedure advocated by Bem (1981a). Talamini (1982) reported that transvestites, apparently similar to our subjects, described themselves on the BSRI as highly androgynous. As will be described, our results are markedly different from his.

Procedure

Subjects were mailed the Bem record sheet with its instructions and examples as part of the research packet. They were first asked to take the test and to respond simply "as yourself." Then they were asked to take the test again, either cross dressed or not cross dressed depending upon their preference, but to respond as their "femme self." We therefore have the opportunity to divide our transvestite sample into two subgroups for this test: cross dressed *vs.* non-cross dressed. And we also have each subject describe himself in two ways: "as yourself," and "as your femme self."

All 110 subjects took the Bem and described an "as yourself" condition; 109 of these also described a "femme self" condition. Of the latter, 49 responded while dressed in their feminine attire and 44 elected not to dress. For the remainder, we were not told if they were cross dressed or not, so we shall exclude them from this part of our analysis. Nor do we know which subjects, if any, elected to take the "as yourself" condition while dressed, as we did not ask them. We have no proof, of course, that subjects actually did cross dress or did not in connection with this test taking, so we report their statements without independent confirmation.

Bem Results

When asked to describe themselves simply "as yourself" our subjects described themselves as slightly less masculine and as slightly more androgynous than the Bem standardization group which consisted mainly of college students. These ratings are given in Table 26. The first column of data (TVs) shows how our 110 transvestites rated themselves. The second column of data (Bem male norms) shows the number of individuals within a hypothetical group of 110 who would be expected to fall into each of the four sex-role categories, according to Bem's normative data.

As noted above, Talamini (1982) reported a very high rate of androgynous self-reports from his 50 heterosexual transvestites. We compared his data with our transvestites' self-ratings. The results are shown in Table 27.

A chi-square was also computed to compare Talamini's BSRI data with the Bem male norms and the result was a chi-square of 158.0, $df =$ 3, and $p < .001$. It is clear that either his subjects are describing their sex roles in radically different ways than have our subjects or Bem's normative group, or else something unknown is accounting for these enormous and unlikely differences. Perhaps there was something unique about the way we (or Talamini) instructed subjects or used the Bem norms for classification, or in the manner in which the tests were scored.

Table 26. BSRI Ratings "as yourself" Compared to Male Norms

Taken "as yourself"	TVs ($N = 110$)	Bem male norms ($N = 110$, expected)
Feminine	16	13
Masculine	36	46
Androgynous	33	22
Undifferentiated	25	29

Chi-square: 8.84 (goodness of fit) df: 3 $p < .05$

Table 27. Chi-Squares for BSRI Ratings of the Talamini Sample *vs.* Present Sample

Groups compared and condition	Chi-square	p
Talamini's TVs *vs.* present group "as yourself"	91	<.001
Talamini's TVs *vs.* present group "as femme self" (for both comparisons, *df*: 3)	25	<.001

When our TVs describe their femme selves they greatly downplay both masculine and androgynous characteristics. They describe themselves as very traditionally feminine in sex role attributes. These data are given in Table 28, together with Bem's norms for college women. Obviously, the college women are describing themselves as far less stereotypically feminine and as far more androgynous than our transvestite sample.

Now let us compare the same information for subjects who told us that during the femme self rating (at least) they chose to take the test while cross dressed. We shall call this the "dressed group" and compare it to the "not dressed" counterpart. Keep in mind that for the dressed group, knowledge that they were dressed while taking the femme self part of the BEM procedure is based on unverified subjects' reports. We also do not know whether some may have been dressed during the first part of the test ("as yourself"). We shall first examine the dressed group (Table 29), and see how they chose to describe themselves, both *as themselves*, and as their femme self. Then we will examine the same comparison for the not cross dressed group.

It is clear that this cross dressed group is stating a major change in self-descriptions based upon their views of themselves when as themselves compared to when as their femme selves. Now let us consider the

Table 28. BSRI Ratings "as your femme self" Compared to Bem Norms for Women

Taken "as your femme self"	TVs ($N = 109$)	Bem norms for women ($N = 109$, expected)
Feminine	43	64
Masculine	13	7
Androgynous	33	18
Undifferentiated	20	20

Chi-square: 19.84 *df*: 3 *p* <.001

Table 29. Dressed Group BSRI Ratings "as yourself" and "as your femme self"

BSRIs	As yourself ($N = 49$)	As femme self $(N = 49)$
Feminine	11	32
Masculine	11	2
Androgynous	14	8
Undifferentiated	13	7

Chi-square: 63.92 *df*: 3 *p* <.001

data for the group that took the BSRI while not cross dressed as shown in Table 30. Again, we see statistically significant differences between the descriptions when as themselves *vs.* when as their femme selves, but in this example we have subjects who were not cross dressed while taking the BSRI.

Let us now compare the dressed and not dressed groups. As is shown in Table 31, the groups differ significantly when describing themselves as themselves, but the groups do not differ beyond chance variation when they describe their femme selves.

For unknown reasons, the dressed and not dressed groups' descriptions when as themselves are quite different from one another. In contrast, they are very similar in how they perceive their femme selves as is shown in the data. There is the clear indication here that the men who elected to cross dress while taking this test describe themselves as less masculine and more feminine compared to transvestites who did not cross dress while taking this test. One interpretation is that the group which cross dressed during the test may have experienced greater cross-gender identity than the other group, as suggested by the data in Table

Table 30. Not Cross Dressed Group BSRI Ratings "as yourself" and "as your femme self"

BSRIs	As yourself ($N = 44$)	As femme self ($N = 44$)
Feminine	5	26
Masculine	19	1
Androgynous	11	6
Undifferentiated	9	11

Chi-square: 345.4 *df*: 3 *p* <.001

Table 31. BSRI Ratings from Two Groups: Cross Dressed and Not Cross
Dressed Taken "as yourself"

Taken "as yourself"	Dressed group (N = 44)	Not dressed group (N = 44)
Feminine	10	5
Masculine	10	19
Androgynous	12	11
Undifferentiated	12	9
Chi-square: 10.35 *df*: 3 *p* <.02		

31. This line of reasoning emphasizes the hypothesis that a higher percentage of "marginal transvestites" (Buhrich and McConaghy, 1970,
1977b) elected to cross dress while taking the test. According to Buhrich
and McConaghy, these marginal TVs may be expected to experience
stronger cross-gender identity feelings than do fetishistic transvestites.
We cannot demonstrate this given the present data alone, but assuming
the decision to cross dress or not cross dress during the test was not a
random variable, an explanation based on Buhrich and McConaghy's
"fetishistic" and "marginal" subgroups would seem plausible.

In Table 32 the BSRI ratings are given for the dressed and not
dressed groups when the subjects were asked to complete the inventory
"as your femme self." Very strongly sex-typed, stereotypically feminine
attributes are favored by both groups. These ratings which project the
femme self may reflect the cross-gender identity said by Freund *et al.*
(1982) to be seen in heterosexual transvestites only when they cross
dress. If such intense gender-identity changes do, in fact, characterize
these subjects it is certainly possible that they might provide stereotypically feminine ratings of themselves because of such intense feelings. A

Table 32. BSRI Ratings from Two Groups: Cross Dressed and Not Cross
Dressed Taken "as your femme self"

Taken "as your femme self"	Dressed group (N = 44)	Not dressed group (N = 44)
Feminine	29	26
Masculine	2	1
Androgynous	7	6
Undifferentiated	6	11
Chi-square: 5.12 *df*: 3 *p* >.20 (not significant)		

less complex explanation would rely upon attribution theory. According to this theory, these cross dressers will "explain" their cross dressing through reliance upon ideas such as the "girl within." A simple extension of this line of thinking might lead cross dressers to make highly feminine ratings of themselves when replying as their femme selves to sustain the consistency of their own theory of cross dressing. Summarizing the BSRI results:

1. Our TVs rate themselves as less masculine and more androgynous than the Bem normative group.
2. Our findings differ markedly from those of Talamini (1982) who reported a much stronger androgynous component in his transvestite group.
3. Our TVs rate their femme self in a more stereotypically feminine manner compared to the Bem norms for women.
4. The dressed and not dressed groups are quite similar when describing their femme self; these ratings tend very strongly toward stereotypically feminine attributes, far exceeding what women say about themselves.
5. There is a significant difference between the dressed and not dressed groups when they describe themselves "as yourself." We have noted several hypotheses which may explain this. One of the more obvious possibilities is that men who elect to take the Bem test while cross dressed generally perceive themselves as having more feminine personality characteristics than the not dressed group. Another possibility is that the dressed group differs in the direction of having greater gender discordance than the not dressed group.
6. Research with sex role ratings may prove useful in the differential assessment of fetishistic transvestites *vs.* marginal transvestites (Buhrich and McConaghy, 1970, 1977b).

Part V: The Cross Dressing Inventory

The paramount motivation in the early stage of transvestism invariably has been said to center on sexual arousal often leading to orgasm, and a history of sexual excitement to cross dressing is the key diagnostic point differentiating transvestism and transsexualism. Hence, there is no issue concerning the central importance of fetishistic cross dressing, at least in the early stages of transvestism. But on the other hand, there is also evidence that what begins as a highly sexual behavior can cool to virtually a nonsexual behavior for at least some inveterate transvestites (e.g., Brierley, 1979; Buhrich & Beaumont, 1981; Prince, 1976; Stoller, 1985c). We are left with the question: If sexual excitement is not the primary motive for transvestism in those subjects who report virtually no fetishistic significance to cross dressing, then what motives are important?

Desexualization, for some, takes place across a cross dressing career in which the frequency of transvestic episodes greatly increases. We have presented data bearing on this in both the "Explanations" section, and in the "stages of cross dressing" material earlier in this chapter. Now we shall turn to data from the Cross Dressing Inventory.

This inventory was constructed to assess fetishistic behavior, fantasies, cross-gender identity, heterosexual–homosexual orientation, sexual behavior, and various behaviors associated with cross dressing. The contents of this inventory are listed in the Appendix.

Subjects were asked to rate each statement on a 7-point scale, ranging from "Never or almost never true" through "Always or almost always true." A pilot version of the inventory was completed by twelve heterosexual cross dressers who helped to edit and refine the original items and who suggested many additional items.

We shall discuss the principal components structure of this inventory later. For now, let us simply examine the items upon which there was the strongest agreement from our sample of heterosexual transvestites. The means and standard deviations for the 10 top-ranked items are given in Table 33.

Taken at face value, these items appear to reflect the following content:

- Heterosexual orientation
- Persistence of the reinforcement value of cross dressing
- Feeling more "alive" or excited when cross dressed
- Sometimes becoming sexually excited when reading about cross dressing
- Cross dressing as positive and helpful
- Daydreaming of the pleasure of cross dressing/daily fantasies on this theme
- Wanting to cross dress whenever possible
- Gaining a pleasant feeling of exhilaration

Except for the fifth item in Table 33—"(I) become sexually excited when I read about cross dressing"—none of these most highly rated items expressly deals with sexual excitement. Several items within the inventory offered such an option, but the most highly rated descriptions pertain to heterosexuality, feeling pleasurable excitement, and a desire to engage in fantasy about cross dressing and to cross dress as often as

Table 33. Top Rated Items from the Cross Dressing Inventory in Rank Order

Mean	S.D.	Rank	Item
6.2	1.4	1	(#52) My behavior has been exclusively or almost exclusively heterosexual.
6.1	1.5	2	(#42) I don't think I could completely give up cross dressing even if I really wanted to.
5.7	1.8	3	(#40) I'd like very much to attend a 10-day cross dressing meeting where I could remain cross dressed the entire time.
5.4	1.4	4	(#3) I usually feel more "alive" or more excited when cross dressed.
5.4	2.1	5	(#36) I sometimes become sexually excited when I read about cross dressing.
5.4	1.7	6	(#49) All things considered, cross dressing has been a positive and helpful part of my life despite occasional difficulties.
5.3	1.8	7	(#7) I daydream at least once every day about the pleasure of cross dressing.
5.2	1.7	8	(#9) I usually want to cross dress almost every time there is an opportunity.
5.2	1.8	9	(#35) I have pleasant fantasies about cross dressing almost every day.
5.1	1.9	10	(#32) Very few activities give me as pleasant a sense of exhilaration as does cross dressing.

possible. Surprisingly, 15% of our transvestites said cross dressing was "usually not" or "never" a sexual experience; Buhrich and Beaumont (1981) reported 10% using a similar question. Here is the distribution of responses to the item: "Cross dressing is almost always a somewhat sexual or erotic experience for me" (Table 34).

Similar results are seen for all other fetishistic items in the Cross Dressing Inventory. From about 15% to 25% of the transvestites say

Table 34. Responses to: Cross Dressing Is Almost Always a Somewhat Sexual or Erotic Experience for Me

Never or almost never true	5%
Usually not true	11
Sometimes but infrequently true	11
Occasionally true	17
Often true	15
Usually true	17
Always or almost always true	24

Table 35. Responses to: Over the Years, Cross Dressing Resulted in an Orgasm (Percentage of Cross Dressing Episodes)

Less than 10% of the time	13%
Between 10% and 25% of the time	24
Between 25% and 50% of the time	14
About 50% of the time	16
Between 50% and 75% of the time	10
Over 75% of the time	11
Over 90% of the time	12

erotic and sexual feelings are not associated with cross dressing activities. An even stronger indication of the diminished sexual component is seen when subjects are asked about cross dressing and orgasm (Table 35). For this sample, just about half of our subjects said they experienced an orgasm 50% or more of the times they cross dressed. Sexual excitement can be highly reinforcing without orgasm, and it seems certain that many transvestic cross dressing episodes are nonorgasmic. Clearly, we need a more thorough assessment of the reinforcers which do operate to sustain transvestic behavior and to make it so highly valued. As an experimental effort to move in that direction, a principal components analysis of the Cross Dressing Inventory was done, and we will now turn to this analysis.

Principal Components Analysis of the Cross Dressing Inventory (CDI)

Although our sample of 110 transvestites is larger than much reported research on this topic, this number of subjects is considerably smaller than required for a principal components analysis in which each of the 75 items in the CDI would be treated as variables. We therefore combined items believed to be tapping the same variance into eight content areas. Please refer to the Appendix which gives the item statement for each of the numbers of questions listed below. We thereby obtained average scores for each of the eight sets of items shown; these eight scores were then treated as variables in our principal components analysis. In Table 36 are shown the eight variables and the CDI question numbers from which each was developed. (Refer to the Appendix to find the specific statement of the questions referred to by number in the table.)

The goal in the construction of the CDI was to have an inventory

Table 36. CDI Items Comprising Each of Eight Variables

Variable	CDI items included in each of eight variables (see Appendix)
1. Sexual excitement	#1,3,15,19,21,24,27,28,33,34,36,61,75
2. Relaxation-pleasure	#2,7,32,40,49,68,69
3. Heterosexuality–homosexuality	#52
4. Cross-gender identity	#5,8,18,31,37,38,39
5. Cross dressing intensity	#9,35,42,73
6. Sado-masochism	#16,17,26,41,43
7. Hormones, electrolysis	#10,11
8. TS reassignment	#8 (also in Variable 4), 13,14,51

which would measure several dimensions of behavior, fantasy, and feeling states as reported by transvestites. We were especially interested in the eight variables listed above because they seem central to the present conceptualization of transvestism. This inventory is still in the pilot stage of development and so proper caution is required in making generalizations from the results. A principal components analysis (varimax rotation) yielded three variables with eigen values in excess of one, and the respective loadings are listed in Table 37.

Factor 1: Cross-Gender Identity

This factor accounts for 34.4% of the variance of the CDI. We believe the item content, as answered by this transvestite sample can reasonably be interpreted as tapping variance which measures self-attributed cross-gender identity. This interpretation, like all naming of factors extracted

Table 37. Principal Components Extracted from Cross Dressing Inventory

CDI variable	Factor 1	Factor 2	Factor 3
7 Hormones	.92	.08	.06
8 Transsexualism	.92	.06	.14
4 Cross-gender identity	.85	.14	.28
1 Sexual excitement	−.07	.77	.32
6 Sado-masochism	.04	.71	−.02
2 Relax/pleasure	.43	.05	.76
5 CD intensity/persistence	.26	.32	.74
3 Heterosexuality– homosexuality	−.31	−.50	.54

through procedures of this kind, is dependent upon the exercise of judgment and logic. Ultimately, its construct validity will have to be demonstrated by methods showing correlations with other better established indices, such as behavioral measures or other testing procedures. We have listed the item statements representing CDI Variables 7, 8, and 4 which are very strongly loaded on Factor 1:

Variable 7 (Hormones, electrolysis)

- If given the opportunity I would like to take female hormones (or I have already done so).
- If given the opportunity I would like to have my beard removed through electrolysis (or I have already done so).

Variable 8 (Transsexual surgery)

- I frequently wish I could live permanently as a woman.
- If given the opportunity I would like to have breast implants (or I have already done so).
- If given the opportunity I would definitely choose to have complete gender reassignment surgery at some time in the future (or I have already done so).
- I consider myself to be primarily a pre (or post) operative transsexual.

Variable 4 (Cross-gender identity)

- When cross dressed I seem able to throw off my male identity and take on a feminine identity which is quite different.
- One of my favorite fantasies involves having sex with a man while I am in the role of a woman.
- I feel as if I have a different personality when I'm cross dressed.
- I'd choose to be cross dressed at least 90% of my life if I could do it without hurting anyone else.
- I often think of how pleasant it would be to live full time as a woman.
- I have the goal of living full time as a woman for at least one year or longer sometime in the future (or I have already done so).

Factor 2: Cross Dressing with Sexual Excitement

This factor accounted for 18% of the variance of the CDI with high loadings on Variables 1 and 6 (.77 and .71). A loading of -0.50 was shown for homosexual erotic orientation. We believe this factor is measuring intensity of fetishistic interest in cross dressing and in closely related sadomasochism and homosexual behavior. The person who is most sexually responsive to many questions about cross dressing fetishism is also answering in the same direction concerning other sexually excitatory fantasy and behavior (sadomasochism and some degree of homosexual interest). Here are the questions which comprise Variables 1, 6, and 3:

Variable 1 (Sexual excitement)

- Cross dressing is almost always a somewhat sexual or erotic experience for me.
- I usually feel more "alive" or more excited when cross dressed.
- Lovemaking is more pleasurable if I am wearing one or more articles of feminine apparel.
- Touching elegant lingerie usually gives me some sexual excitement.
- Some specific articles of clothing or makeup have an especially powerful effect on my sexual arousal.
- Cross dressing brings me as much or more sexual pleasure as any other kind of sexual behavior.
- I often become sexually excited when I think about cross dressing.
- I sometimes become sexually excited by reading or seeing ads or pictures of beautiful feminine clothing, shoes, or makeup.
- I sometimes become sexually excited when I shop for women's clothing, shoes, or makeup.
- I sometimes become sexually excited when I read about cross dressing.
- I sometimes have a fantasy in which I am cross dressed and I become sexually excited while with a woman.
- Over the years, cross dressing has resulted in an orgasm _____ percent of the time.

Variable 6 (Sadomasochism)

- When having fantasies about cross dressing I often have strong ideas about being punished or disciplined.
- When having fantasies about cross dressing I often have strong ideas about being humiliated.
- I prefer to mix cross dressing with being tied up or tying someone else up.
- When having fantasies about cross dressing I often have strong ideas about sadism or masochism mixed with cross dressing.
- Creating a small amount of pain in yourself can add to the enjoyment of cross dressing.
- My behavior has been exclusively or almost exclusively heterosexual (negatively correlated with Factor 2).

Factor 3: Cross Dressing and Relaxation/Pleasure

This factor accounted for 20% of the variance of the CDI and the highest loadings were on Variables 2 (relaxation/pleasure/exhilaration as reinforcers for cross dressing), Variable 5 (intensity and persistence of cross dressing motivation and behavior), and Variable 3 (heterosexual preference).

None of the other identified factors was sufficiently strong to be considered significant. (These variables involve a total of 12 items on the CDI.) The correlations among the three factors were: 1 *vs.* 2 = .06; 2 *vs.* 3 = .20; and 1 *vs.* 3 = .23, which supports the conclusion that they are independent of each other.

The CDI self-report measure is in the process of development, and it is presented here as a potential research tool along the lines of the more extensively developed measures of Blanchard (1985a,b), Freund, Langevin, Satterberg, and Steiner (1977), Freund *et al.* (1982), and measures described in the extensive report edited by Langevin (1985b). A high research priority should go into the development of better procedures for the assessment of such constructs as fetishism, gender identity, sexual orientation, and cross-gender identity.

Chapter 7

Wives of Transvestites

Several reports describe the wives of transvestites (Beigel, 1963; Fein-bloom, 1976; Prince, 1973; Stoller, 1967; Talamini, 1982; Wise, Dupkin, & Meyer, 1981) but most of these are based on very few cases. The wives were seen by Stoller (1967) as inadequate women, inclined to either succor their husbands through overindulgence or to humiliate them by dressing them as women, thereby threatening their masculinity. We did not see these personality features in the 21 wives we have interviewed and followed for 4 years, nor does this group seem to lack self-esteem as suggested by Feinbloom (1976). Both Prince and Talamini expressed a more positive view of the wives of TVs.

Virginia Prince's book, *The Transvestite and His Wife* (1973), was written largely from the perspective of the cross dressing husband. It describes cross dressing as a benign interest while emphasizing that the transvestite cannot stop this behavior. Prince concludes that transvestism can enrich a marriage if the wife will accept it. The book includes several letters from wives describing their experiences with cross dressing, their attitude changes, and examples of how cross dressing improved their marital relationships. Absent, however, is any evidence indicative of how a larger sample of wives may feel about cross dressing within the family. This book has been widely circulated within the TV club movement and it has been a major source of information for many wives. For example, it was the most frequently reported source of information about transvestism according to the wives in our sample, and it was also often noted as a resource by the transvestites in our survey. Many of the wives, however, commented that the book is not an entirely satisfactory source of information about cross dressing. Some describe it as a "hard sell" for transvestism. Others object to the rating scheme Prince employed which evaluates the level of acceptance shown by wives along a graded scale (A, B, C, etc.).

Talamini (1982) interviewed 50 wives of cross dressers and reported that 60% were able to accept their husband's transvestism, while 40% were not. We are not told the meaning of accept as applied here, other than Talamini's reference to such wives as showing "active participation, empathy, or tolerance of cross dressing when the husbands did not engage in it in their presence" (p. 33). Perhaps these "acceptant" wives show great diversity in their tolerance for cross dressing. It would seem likely that most of them either knew other wives of cross dressers or had some kind of transvestite club affiliation. This is an important point, for as Talamini notes, the network of TVs, their wives, and the organizations which support them constitute a social subculture, however small, which has its own values, roles, and status assignments. Wives who are strongly unsympathetic to the goals of these support groups may find such groups unrewarding. One of the strongest values and goals of these clubs and organizations is the acceptance or tolerance of cross dressing. Wives who express strong support, even encouragement of cross dressing, earn high status from the TV members and other wives.

Concerning the 40% of Talamini's wives who do not accept cross dressing, we are told that their adjustment is "difficult" and that "strains are evident." Some are said to show "envy or self-doubt" because the husband is perceived as more attractive as a woman than is the wife, or because he is more proficient in housekeeping while cross dressed. In contrast, we have never met or corresponded with a wife who cited either of these reasons as basic to her distaste for transvestism. Other sources of strain included excessive self-admiration by the TV husband when cross dressed, and fear that a sex change operation might be sought.

Seventy percent of Talamini's sample of wives reported having children, and of this group, 37% or 13 couples had informed their children of the husband's transvestism. However, in only one case had the father been seen cross dressed by the children. Talamini gives no details concerning the ages of the children or when, why, or how they were informed, although this would seem to be very important. He reports that the couples noted no adverse effects upon informing their children. None of these children cross dressed or revealed any other indications of cross-gender identity or deviant sex role behavior. Despite the absence of details, this is an important report since it is the only data we are aware of dealing with the impact of transvestism upon children. We shall not attempt to propose a future research project here, but it is obvious that providing information to children is one thing, while the frequent modeling of a cross-gender role (e.g., very frequent cross dressing) within the family would be another. The age of the children when informed about or shown cross dressing would also seem to be very important. Related issues pertaining to children raised by homosexual or transsexual parents have been discussed by Green (1978).

Survey Procedure and Results

A survey form designed to elicit various information from the wives of our transvestite subjects was included in the research packet sent to all participants. Sixty-four of our 110 male subjects were currently married. Eight of these preferred not to ask the wife's participation. Judging from brief notes of explanation, this was usually due to either a conviction that the wife would not participate or to the husband's feeling that inviting the wife's participation would create problems. In any case, we believe approximately 56 couples represented the maximum possible sample. A total of 35 wives' survey forms were returned, yielding a return rate of 63%. Among the 35 were 4 from long-term partners who indicated they were not married. Since the information they contributed appeared useful, we have included these 4 cases along with the other 31 wives.

Duration of Marriage

Fifty-eight percent of these wives were married more than 10 years. Twenty-one percent were in the 5- to 10-year range, and 21% were married less than 5 years.

Number of Times Married (Wife)

Eighty-seven percent of these wives had been married once, 10% twice, and 3% had married three times. This sample is overwhelmingly comprised of women who are currently in their first and only marriage.

Number of Children, This Marriage

Forty-one percent reported no children within the present marriage. Eighteen percent had a single child, 32% had two children, 6% three, and 3% reported five children. Regretfully, we did not acquire religious affiliation data which would be essential to compare these birth rates with normative rates.

Knowledge Concerning Transvestism

Our survey included this question: *Before discussing cross dressing with your husband, how much information on this topic did you have?* Eighty-five percent reported "practically no information" or "misleading information." Eleven percent reported having "some information but not much," and one wife reported "a great deal of information."

Initial Interpretation of Transvestism

Wives were asked: *What were your main ideas about cross dressing when you first tried to understand this behavior? What did this behavior mean to you?* There was much diversity across the 35 responses although some trends are clear. Seven wives initially perceived cross dressing as "gay." Four saw this as "a fetish" or a form of "sexual release." Five theorized some sort of mental abnormality might be involved. Three saw this as simply "peculiar" while others noted "a personality quirk," "a harmless compulsion," or "a biological problem." Three noted their main worry concerned threats to their marriage or sexual life. The remainder viewed cross dressing as "confusing," "ridiculous," or as "a perversion," and one feared a sex change operation might lie ahead.

Sources of Information

Our survey asked: *What have been the most important sources of information you have relied upon concerning cross dressing?* Many wives noted more than one source and we have therefore combined the responses according to source. The frequency of citations is shown in Table 38.

While written materials are the major source of information, many wives commented that finding useful materials in libraries was frustrating. Although few titles were cited, it appears likely that materials published by transvestite organizations provide the major source of information. Except for those who consult psychologists, counselors, and friends, there would appear to be a closed information *loop* within the transvestite group. Husbands obtain information from their organizations and from wherever else they can obtain knowledge, and pass it along to their wives who share it. From time to time, issues and theories are taken up at club meetings with outside "experts," but such exchanges do not seem frequent. We may conclude that the typical wife is left with few options in her search for information.

Table 38. Citation Frequency for Sources of Information Concerning Cross Dressing (*N* = 33)

Frequency	Source of information
21	Books, magazine articles, literature from organizations
10	My huband
5	Other cross dressers
4	Wives of cross dressers
4	Psychologist/counselor
3	Television programs
2	Friends

Husband's First Revelation of Cross Dressing

Sixty-two percent of our 31 wives reported being told about their husband's transvestism after marriage, 29% prior to marriage, and 9% gave unclear descriptions of the timing.

Cross Dressing and Sexual Behavior

Wives responses to this question: *How does cross dressing seem to influence your husband's sexual behavior? That is, how does a dressing session affect him?* The results are shown in Table 39. The view of wives confirms a point made in Chapter 6 from TVs' reports of their sexual behavior while cross dressed: This behavior represents a highly erotic experience for many, but not for all. Thirty-three percent of these wives tell us their husbands show no change or a reduction of sexual behavior when cross dressed. We are not attempting to take sexuality out of transvestism, especially since two-thirds of these wives point toward heightened sexual arousal in their husbands. However, if we want to account for the one-third not sexually aroused, it seems simplistic to characterize cross dressing as *nothing more* than a procedure for enhancing sexual excitement—a description often seen in psychiatric and psychological texts.

Frequency of Complete Cross Dressing

In previous surveys, wives have not been asked to describe the frequency of their husband's cross dressing. We asked: *How many times per month does your husband completely cross dress . . . that is, sufficient to go out in public?* Thirty wives provided data. Fifty-seven percent said 1 to 4 times monthly; 30% said from 5 to 9 times. Three percent reported from 10 to 15 times monthly, and 10% said 30 times per month. These reported rates are close to what would be predicted from the average frequencies we reported in Chapter 6 using data given by TVs. We did not ask this

Table 39. Wives' Rating of Impact of Cross Dressing on Sexual Behavior ($N = 33$)

Percent	Impact on sexual behavior
33	Greatly increases his sexual behavior
22	Somewhat increases
12	Slightly increases
27	Neither increases or decreases his sexual behavior (no effect)
3	Slightly decreases
0	Somewhat decreases
3	Greatly decreases

Table 40. Wives' Attitudes toward Cross Dressing by
Husbands

N	Attitude toward cross dressing
4	I love it. It's a great pleasure for me.
5	I like it very much. It brings much added joy to me.
3	I like it somewhat. It brings me a little joy.
3	I like it but just a little on rare occasions.
7	I neither like it nor dislike it. I am neutral.
1	I dislike it just a little.
9	I dislike it somewhat. It causes me unhappiness.
1	I strongly dislike it. It causes me much unhappiness.
2	I hate it. It's a major problem for me.

frequency question in exactly the same way for husbands and wives, but in 25 cases we were able to assemble similar reports for each. The coefficient of correlation for these scores was .80.

Attitudes Toward Cross Dressing by Husbands

Wives were asked to rate their present attitude toward cross dressing by their husband using a 9-point rating scale. The descriptive statements and the number of wives indicating each are shown in Table 40. The wives were in nearly equal number on the like–dislike ends of this scale, with seven squarely in the middle. Keep in mind that we did not hear from about 37% of the wives eligible to respond in this survey, and therefore we do not know what their attitudes may be. However, in some cases the husband made it clear that his wife's feelings about cross dressing were strongly negative. We can only speculate, therefore, that most of the wives who did not respond to the survey would probably place themselves toward the dislike end of this rating.

Problems as Seen by Wives

We know of no previous quantitative report indicating what wives say are the problems associated with cross dressing by their husbands. Our survey included a set of 26 problem statements and the wives were asked to rate each using a 7-point scale. Two summary statistics are reported. First, a count of the number of wives who indicated an item was a problem regardless of seriousness. Second, the average seriousness was rated for each item (based on the sum of the problem scale ratings divided by the number of wives who said a given item was, to some degree, a problem). As will be seen, each of the items was a problem for some of the wives, and some of the items presented difficulties for most of the wives. Here is the question posed on the survey: *Please rate the following "problems" as to whether they apply to you. Consider each in terms of what cross dressing means to you. Rate each one using this scale: N/A, does not apply to me; 0, no problem; 1, a very slight problem; 2, a slight problem; 3, a moderate problem—not especially difficult; 4 , a difficult problem; 5, a great problem; 6, a very great problem.* The results are listed in order of frequency of citation in Table 41. We believe four main areas of concern can be identified and these concerns are the topics for discussion next.

Security Issues

The greatest concern of most of these wives is that the cross dressing not be revealed to others. Twenty-five wives expressed some degree of concern for the item: "I'm troubled by the possibility of visitors find-

Table 41. Problems Identified by Wives of Transvestites

N	Average rating	Problem
25	3.7	I'm troubled about the possibility of visitors finding out.
20	3.1	Cross dressing creates tensions within the marriage.
19	2.8	My husband fails to realize people may notice telltale signs.
18	3.7	Cross dressing might in some way be harmful to our children.
17	3.0	Cross dressing might in some way be harmful to our relationship with relatives or close friends.
17	2.9	Too much time is devoted to cross dressing.
16	2.6	He suffers guilt or other emotional reactions from cross dressing.
16	2.5	Purchases of clothing may lead to discovery.
16	2.3	It is difficult to keep clothing and makeup hidden at home.
15	3.7	Cross dressing has had a harmful effect on our sex life.
15	3.1	Too much money is spent on cross dressing activities.
15	2.9	It has become too much of a total interest.
15	2.5	He fails to use proper caution or security measures.
14	3.8	When blocked from cross dressing he is hard to live with.
14	3.6	Cross dressing has become a source of disagreement.
13	2.1	Our social life has become too restricted.
11	3.7	Increasingly, he wants to live in the role of a total woman.
10	2.5	He is upset if I refuse to participate in some (TV) activity.
9	2.5	Someday he might decide to become a transsexual.
8	2.6	He has difficulty keeping his agreements about cross dressing.
8	2.0	Cross dressing takes priority over other work or obligations.
7	3.9	He wants me to assist him in cross dressing or makeup.
6	3.5	He insists that I go out with him when he's dressed.
6	1.8	His dressing sessions take too long.
5	1.8	He is upset if I refuse to go out with him when he's dressed.
2	1.5	Cross dressing leads to increased alcohol usage.

ing out." Nineteen indicated concern that "My husband fails to realize that people may notice tell-tale signs of cross dressing."

The TVs we have interviewed vary greatly in their concern for security, but very few are insensitive to the possible consequences of public disapproval of cross dressing. Some of the most experienced and publicly visible TVs (and TSs) have gone to great lengths to keep their male identity separate from their cross dressing activities. Virginia Prince, for example, has appeared on radio and television discussing transvestism but never publicly uses her real family name. At a lesser recognition level, we know of men who take leadership in organizing and sponsoring TV outings and who use their real name on the return address of printed mailings—certainly not a secure procedure.

Some TVs report that they have risked possible detection while cross dressed only to wonder in quieter moments how they could possibly have shown such poor judgment and such a lack of restraint. For some, there seems to be a weakening of reality testing associated with being cross dressed. Perhaps the experience of heightened arousal and excitement which seems to accompany the transvestic experiences of some also involves a "suspension of judgment" as one TV put it. However, it appears very apparent that the ability to test reality is not lost, as it would be in a psychotic episode or in drug intoxication. Rather, there seems to be a temporary pushing aside of caution, restraints, and clear thinking about the consequences of actions.

The hindsight, reflective evaluation of some cross dressers is often expressed as something like, "I don't know how I could possibly have taken such a risk . . . ." Unusual risk taking seems to be most common in the early years of venturing out in public while dressed. For example, one TV said: "When I first started going out as Irma I felt I had to do things I would never do today, such as going to the same coffee shop 'dressed' where I have lunch every day." Another noted: "For years I felt that I had to establish challenges and things to conquer as a woman; now that I have accomplished them, I am content to do my favorite things without the special challenges."

But for the wife there is no special excitement, no suspension of judgment. She may therefore be especially uncomfortable with risk taking and with virtually any possibility of detection. All are perceived as threats to her security and to the social status of the family.

Tensions within the Marriage Owing to Cross Dressing

Twenty of the wives said "Cross dressing creates tension within the marriage." We have seen that our sample of wives is both highly experienced with cross dressing and at least half have positive feelings about this. And so, if this sample of wives reports tension as a problem, we can safely anticipate that most other wives would report as least as much discomfort if not more. The spectrum of concerns in the present inventory of problems offers some hints as to what the particular sources of tension and disagreement might be. For example, the wives tend to be uncomfortable with many of the investments of resources necessary to support cross dressing. These include devoting too much time, spending too much money, restricting social activities, interfering with family relationships, and risking harm to the children. At least some of these might be reduced through negotiation and compromise if the particular concerns about cross dressing can be identified.

Possible Harm to Children

The question of whether cross dressing should be revealed to children has usually been resolved by TVs in a very conservative way; that is, by keeping the topic or the practice of cross dressing entirely secret. In our experience, it is the rare couple which informs young children about transvestism. For the most part, those who have written about transvestism have urged that children not be given this information. However, no study of the impact of cross dressing upon children has ever been reported other than Talamini (1982). The TV parents we have interviewed have been very sensitive to the potential hazards of discussing cross dressing with young children. It seems obvious that children form complex parental relationships and that gender role deviations are highly meaningful to children. While the fetishistic cross dresser may not experience any significant cross-gender leanings, his apparent transformation into a woman could easily be interpreted by a child as having profound gender (not simply appearance) significance. Children want and need parents who are predictable, available, caring, and dedicated to their families. The risk of giving young children information about the cross dressing of the father seems to us to be far greater than any good which could be served by being "open and honest," or by teaching children to be accepting of diversity. These goals, however meritorious, can be achieved without using cross dressing as a family experiment in education.

Effect on Sex Life

Fifteen wives indicated that cross dressing " . . . has had a harmful effect upon our sex life." In contrast, only a few noted that cross dressing had had a strongly positive impact upon their sex life (Table 41). This topic has not been adequately considered in the research literature.

When sexual problems do arise, it is likely that the husband has come to prefer his erotic cross dressing to the marital sexual relationship. Masturbation while cross dressed becomes the favored sexual technique, and often, the almost exclusive sexual outlet. But we must be cautious here, as our sample is small and one might be tempted to generalize. We know from the reports of the husbands, for example, that the decline in sexual activity is closely related to age—a fact that has been well-established at least since the reports of Kinsey and his associates (Kinsey *et al.*, 1948). There is much that remains unclear about the quality and quantity of marital sex in TV marriages. The survey statements of even a few wives point up the need to explore this avenue much more thoroughly. It is important to know if there is often a history in these marriages of failure or inadequacy within the sexual relationship, and if so, to what extent this may be attributed to the husband's cross dressing sexual outlets.

Transvestism and Marital Sex

The marital sex life of the fetishistic heterosexual cross dresser contains a paradox. On the one hand, he feels most sexually alive while cross dressed. As Stoller (1968a) noted, this cross dressing is merely a "detour" through which masculine sexual strivings are being expressed—despite all the feminine trappings. On the other hand, the wife is typically turned off in the presence of a crossed dressed husband. Even wives who are most understanding and cooperative in assisting their husbands with cross dressing frequently demand no cross dressing in bed. The result is often a strengthening of masturbation while cross dressed.

In marriages having less traditional fidelity and commitment there may be an active search for women or men who are turned on by transvestism. The following "personal ad" of such an individual was published by a TV magazine:

> EILEEN: Mid-50s. Married but wife isn't "into it." Love frilly things. Can entertain from 8 *a.m.* to 5 *p.m.* Monday through Fridays. Lonely. Age no barrier but like small, sexy people.

This undisguised, sexually oriented advertisement can hardly be expected to strengthen sexual ties within a marriage. But given the paradox we have posed, what alternatives are there for the wife and the husband who want to sustain or enhance their sexual relationship? How can the intense sexual energies of the heterosexual TV be channeled toward the wife rather than away from her? The following four suggestions come from wives who believe they have developed compromises which work successfully for them.

Close Your Eyes and Let Him Do It. This is not a popular solution but it has worked for some wives. The idea is to put their own sexual feelings and needs aside, shut out the reality of a cross dressing husband, and simply submit to his sexual overtures when he is cross dressed. Our survey does not tell us directly how TV husbands may respond when confronted with such an attitude, but the tactic would seem to have very strong disadvantages.

The typical TV (as with many men) wants a wife to show initiative as a sexual partner. We find evidence for this, for example, from item 63 on our Cross Dressing Inventory (see Appendix). He prefers that she will take sexual leadership at least some of the time and function as a highly motivated partner. In short, he wants a wife's sexual pattern to be just the opposite of those who passively say, "do whatever you want . . . ." Our assumption is that this approach is most likely to be attempted in older couples with a history of cool sexual relationships, and with little variety in sexual practices.

Take It Off—Wash It Off. This approach may be considerably more useful for some couples. The idea is to end the cross dressing session immediately prior to having sex. The partners mutually recognize that the husband becomes optimally aroused while cross dressed, so to take advantage of this without destroying the wife's sexual motivation, he takes off his feminine attire just prior to having sex. For those couples who say this does work, it seems to have the advantage of giving each partner most of what he or she wants. The ability of the partners to negotiate and compromise may be the key to making this tactic work.

Using a Fetish. Some wives can tolerate or even enjoy the husband's use of a single fetish although the entire cross dressed appearance is unacceptable in association with sex. This tactic calls for finding out what is and what is not acceptable to each of the partners as an enjoyable fetishistic sexual excitant. Fetishes, especially women's undergarments and lingerie, have long been recognized as having strong erotic significance. Learning to use this potential asset may assist some couples in the construction of a more satisfying sexual relationship.

Verbalization of Sexual Scenarios. The verbalization or enactment of sexual scenarios may be sexually enhancing for some couples. The objective is to join together in creating a sexual fantasy which taps the sexual themes exciting to each partner. Of course, there are no best or ideal scenes since this is a highly individualistic matter. Perhaps the greatest payoff from this creative effort may be the sharing of sexual fantasies. For some, this can lead toward greater intimacy and a deepening of the marital relationship. But unless the woman feels comfortable with unusual sexual themes it may be best for her to proceed with caution. It is common for TVs to enjoy fantasy themes of gender reversal, homosexuality, bondage, humiliation and the like. While this is nothing to be alarmed about, such themes may be very strong turn offs for some individuals.

Positive Factors in Marriage Attributed to Cross Dressing

We recognize that our sample of wives of TVs is probably biased so as to include an unusually large percentage of women who feel positively about their husband's cross dressing. But this sampling bias need not detract from the information we were given concerning positive impacts of transvestism as viewed by some wives. Many of the following observations came from wives whose attitudes about cross dressing are clearly negative. Our survey form asked this question: *Does cross dressing add anything positive to your marriage?* Twenty-two wives did give a positive response (see below); seven responses were negative; and six were ambiguous responses, as they noted something positive but not directly connected with the marriage. Here are the verbatim responses:

"Since TV matters have become more open we've seen our best years . . . . He has become more understanding toward me and others. He has become more calm and he's stopped trying to prove his manhood."

"It's made for an excellent sex life at times. If he dressed more often it would be even better because it makes him more affectionate, sensitive, understanding, and like a good friend."

"It has changed my sexual freedom as a woman by letting me experience what makes me happy and what feels good. It's helped out our communications."

"It led us to counseling and that helped our marriage tremendously . . . despite the cross dressing issue."

"When I see how much he enjoys it and how well he passes, it gives me pleasure."

"My husband is more considerate and caring when he is dressed."

"The dressing adds closeness and he is then relaxed and happy; that makes me happy. His dressing has had an effect on my day-to-day appearance."

"It enabled me to feel closer to my husband."

"It makes us closer. We share clothes, makeup, etc. He is more comfortable now that everything is in the open, and that makes for a healthier relationship."

"There is a greater feeling of togetherness and closeness."

"It makes us more open with our feelings. Our sex life is always good."

"It has forced me to accept something that I don't like but can't change . . . so it has made us closer."

"It has made for more happiness and variety."

"After dressing, he becomes more relaxed and more responsive sexually and emotionally."

"Even when partially dressed it is much easier for him to be relaxed and sensitive. He is able to communicate easier and to be more loving."

"It makes him interested in my clothes, my feelings as a woman, my needs, and it is just plain fun to shop together."

"I feel he is a little more understanding of my feelings. He enjoys going shopping with me. He has made me more aware of my appearance."

"He is much more complimentary toward me and he seems to have a different personality. Maybe he is more relaxed."

"My husband is a more sensitive and caring person when he's dressed. He is more solicitous of my needs . . . he is a softer person."

Most of the positive responses concern interpersonal or affectional changes in the husband said to be facilitated by cross dressing. The most common are enhancement of closeness, greater consideration of the needs of the wife, ability to express feelings, mood improvement, and greater capacity for intimacy and sexual participation.

Negative Factors in Marriage Attributed to Cross Dressing

The survey form also asked this question of the wives: *Does cross dressing detract from your marriage or your own life?* Twenty-three expressed some kind of negative impact, eight denied any negative impact, and four cannot be classified into either category. The main concern expressed was that the husband would somehow be *discovered*, and that this would threaten his job, his friendships, the status of the family, or harm the relationships with his own children. The second most frequently cited difficulty was diminished quality of the sexual relationship. Note that security and sexual concerns were cited earlier when the wives were asked to specify problems related to cross dressing; this replication is some confirmation of internal reliability. Here are some of the representative negative responses:

"Cross dressing creates a barrier in our marriage because of the stress, tension, and conflict of feelings it brings out. The cross dressing habit is a very expensive and time-consuming hobby."

"The main fear is security. Sometimes he puts more thought and planning into his dressing than he does for what we do as a family. He's more excited about the club meeting than taking me out."

"The security of our personal life, family life, work, and our 4-year-old daughter—to keep that part of our life a secret is a strain."

"Having to tell lies and keep secrets is not healthy. His shaved legs and hands make him less sexy to me and our sex life suffers. I don't like protecting his 'image' from the kids."

"I'm in constant fear of family or friends learning about this situation. I'm always listening for footsteps on the porch, fearing a neighbor will drop in."

"I do not feel married. I feel like I'm living with a female and it's very depressing."

"Just a fear of someone exposing him to hurt him."

"It limits our choice of friends and the friends we can be around."

"I fear that he might get caught and embarrass us, or that our son might find out."

"It interferes sexually to a certain extent. Also, the fear that others will find out."

"Drop-in company can pose a problem. Shaved legs around the pool are a problem."

"I feel he risks exposure."

"Financial expenses—because he has to buy tall sizes. And sometimes I want to be romanced by the good-looking man I married."

"It has affected our sex life."

"He's not content unless we live in a city that has a support group."

"He refuses to talk with me about it. I'm not sure how far he wants to go with it."

"I don't enjoy sex because—when he is dressed up—it makes me feel like I am having sex with a woman and that makes me sick."

"I worry that he'll be caught dressed as a woman and that would embarrass our family. Also, he could lose his job. He spends money extravagantly for a person who is otherwise miserly in his spending habits."

"It affects our sex life and our social life."

Choice of Marital Partner: An Hypothesis

The marital issues raised by transvestites are unique compared to other more commonly seen problems within marriages, but they are by no means entirely different. A key question concerning any kind of marital difficulty is what the motives, needs, and personality characteristics of the partners may be. We must ask, What led them to find and select one another as partners in the first place? While all TVs are no more alike than all their wives are alike, we believe that some cross dressers do have similar sexual histories. A pattern of preadolescent and adolescent sexual shyness and poor self-confidence in the male sex role during those years, is frequently reported. Assuming that is the case, we believe there is an hypothesis that explains the characteristics that some TVs look for in their prospective wives and vice versa.

The husbands.   We believe there is good evidence that these men show diversity in many personality attributes and that there is no unique TV personality. But there are some very common personality characteristics. Some of these men men tend to be somewhat compulsive, organized, and precise in style. They are more likely to be mechanical, quantitative, and cool in interpersonal relationships, although many establish and maintain warm friendships. The single most important attribute in terms of frequency seems to be a history of adolescent shyness in the male sex role, that is, reticence, and lack of experience and success in approaching girls during these years. But we are all aware that such characteristics can commonly be found in men who never cross dress. Despite this, we believe there is great significance in the cross dresser's frequently expressed history of adolescent fear of intimacy with women. Here is what some of them told us in response to a question concerning adolescent sex role development:

"I've generally been afraid of beautiful women . . . [and] it's a fear of being masculine around women."

"I was cautious or slightly shy. A loner. Not a bold hero."

"I dated steady girlfriends but I didn't have sex with them. I was a loner."

"I was an introverted, inhibited person. I was not a great lover."

"I was sexually inhibited because of the Catholic Church, and I agreed with them totally."

"After an accident I took on an 'ugly duck' theory of myself . . . I had dates but no close relationships."

"I was extremely inhibited sexually but this did not lead to trouble in getting dates."

"I was somewhat shy and uncomfortable around girls. Although I dated frequently, I had a good self-image and interests, but I was sexually inhibited."

If we accept that shyness and lack of sexual experience in dating during adolescence are common among TVs, we may then ask to what extent such a history might be a factor in the selection of a particular kind of wife.

For example, might such TVs be more likely to date and marry one of the local glamour queens, or a less flamboyant, more sexually reserved young lady? We suggest that the TV is strongly inclined to choose a wife whom he perceives as capable of helping him to express his sexual feelings, but also one who is basically quite conventional, stable, and sensitive to social mores. If this is correct, the TV selects a wife who is apt to be sexually reserved; certainly not the "swinging single" type or one likely to prefer unusual avenues of sexual expression. The profile of the woman we have in mind would come closer to being an attentive mothering type rather than a provocative sex symbol.

As might be expected, such wives often respond to the first discussion of transvestism, before or during a marriage, with shock, alarm, confusion, disappointment, shame, anger, or with a sense of loss. These are the initial reactions most often reported by wives with whom we have communicated.

The Wives. Looking at the marriage from the perspective of the wife, she selects a man who she thinks will be a good provider, not too demanding a sex partner, conventional, controlled and cautious in human relationships—again, certainly not a swinging single. The partners think of each other as reliable and stable, not sexually demanding, and as sharing conventional attitudes especially where intimate relationships are concerned. But as we have noted, when the husband's transvestism becomes evident to the wife, either through accidental discovery or disclosure by the husband, most wives report feeling stunned and amazed. The following are a representative sample of their survey responses:

"I thought of it as a perversion . . . ridiculous . . . abnormal . . . but I loved my husband and realized it was something I would have to get accustomed to . . . "

"It was a total shock! I was disgusted! I felt it had to be homosexual . . . "

"I wasn't sure of anything. I was very naive about a lot of sexual behavior. I thought he was going to have a sex change."

"At first, I thought it must be a temporary condition, limited to fetish garments. I didn't feel threatened. I was understanding, sympathetic, and relatively unconcerned."

"He told me before our marriage. I thought he just had a high sex drive that wasn't satisfied and that after we were married a while the desire would lessen."

"I felt abandoned. I wondered why I hadn't suspected anything before being told."

"I felt my husband must be emotionally and mentally unstable. I felt very negative. I was confused and afraid of the unknown . . . threatened, angry, hurt, embarrassed, humiliated, and had feelings of jealousy."

"I was very confused. I left and went home not knowing if I would ever come back."

"I felt sorry that others were unkind to him and punished him . . . but more and more he wants less and less to be my husband, and I can't accept living with my husband as a woman on a long-term basis."

"I thought it was a harmless compulsion . . . I was relieved because I had suspected that there was another woman. I could accept anything but another woman. I view cross dressing as a handicap that my husband cannot overcome."

"I thought cross dressing was primarily a sexual release. I was rather excited about it and was eager to be a part of it."

These selected statements from wives point up the diversity of their reactions. The most frequent themes reported in our survey were feelings of surprise, distaste, uncertainty, confusion, and a fear that cross dressing must somehow relate to homosexuality. The point of this discussion, therefore, is that the sexually conventional or reserved wife is ill-suited to be transformed into a wife who can participate in the TV's games of erotic cross dressing. The idea of having sex with a man dressed (to any extent) as a women probably will be very distant from her own ideal sexual script. But after the TV husband has emerged from his closet, shared his secret, expressed his feelings, and has pled for understanding, his next aim is to invite his wife to participate in some kind of cross dressing-related sexual activity. If we are correct about her attitudes, her conventionality, her needs, and her sexual script—the husband's plan is doomed to failure. The end result of this mismatch may be his withdrawal of sexual energies from within the marriage; his other pseudowoman self will come to be preferred as a sexually exciting "partner," always available, with everchanging variety and erotic enticements in harmony with his sexual script.

Patterns of Marital Adjustment

Let us consider some of the tactics we have observed TV couples attempting to use in their efforts to live with actively practiced transvestism by the husband. We shall do this by describing several patterns of adaptation or interactive "games" enduring over an extended period. Two important preliminary points are these: First, most couples employ a combination of games. Second, marital success is obviously not dependent merely upon how the cross dressing is managed. More important is the basic character of the marital relationship and the quality of personal adjustment seen in the partners as well as their commitment to each other.

The Isolation Game

The tactics of the isolation game call for each partner to withdraw and seek satisfaction elsewhere. It involves much denial of real problems and feelings. There is much cover-up, lying, and deception on the part of the husband. Intimacy is lost. Mutual commitments are diminished. The partners attempt to isolate transvestism by pretending that it does not exist. Here are the main elements of this game.

1. Each partner attempts to deny the reality of cross dressing and this behavior is separated and isolated from the wife through secret sessions of transvestism. The husband fabricates reasons for absences from home and for money spent on cross dressing.
2. There is little meaningful communication about feelings, frustrations, sexuality, or cross dressing.
3. The husband searches for others like himself. He joins a club, corresponds with other TVs and builds a circle of new friends with whom he feels comfortable.
4. Marital sex takes second place to the sexuality associated with cross dressing. This is typically solitary masturbation while cross dressed.
5. The wife becomes increasingly angry but cannot fully express these feelings. She holds her husband responsible for damaging her life and their marriage.
6. The husband is less angry and frustrated as he finds ways to express his transvestism. His new interests, new friends, and new ways to spend time and money take priority over investments in his wife. He cannot understand why she has become so resentful and angry.
7. Often the couple remain married, especially when children are involved, but the relationship is not very rewarding to either partner.
8. Each may look toward a long-term goal of divorce, for example, when the children are out of the family, following retirement, or at some other time of major life reorganization.
9. When there is a divorce and remarriage by the husband, it is usually to a woman far more informed and able to tolerate transvestism than was the earlier wife. Not infrequently, a new wife is selected who is to some extent sexually aroused by cross dressing. Little is known about the success of second marriages by TVs.
10. In rare cases, when the partners are strongly committed to each other and share many common interests, the isolation game can help mask the problem of cross dressing. The irritation of transvestism is avoided by pretending that it does not exist.

The Personal Growth Game

The personal growth game is characterized by struggles on the part of each partner to understand and respond to the needs of the other. A

high measure of mutual respect and concern for the partner is imperative. Each partner must be motivated for personal growth, change, and
adaptation to the changing environment of the marriage. Transvestism
may be regarded as an unwanted interference, but it is also accepted as a
part of reality and not as something about to disappear. Here are the
main elements of this game.

1. In this scenario the partners put aside the fear and discomforts
   associated with cross dressing and engage in intensive discussion of what this means to them, both individually and as a
   couple.
2. There is a quality of genuine concern and respect for the well-
   being of the other person. Despite inevitable changes in their
   respective comfort levels, each partner is committed to the belief
   that their marriage will not only survive, but it will grow stronger
   and more satisfying.
3. There are great differences among couples in how the marital sex
   life is affected. For some, transvestism facilitates stronger and
   more mutually satisfying sexual experiences, although most
   wives ban cross dressing from their actual sexual relations. For
   others, there is a gradual decline in their sex lives together.
   Despite their mutual respect and concern for each other, for the
   TV cross dressing becomes more sexually rewarding than marital
   sex.
4. As one TV stated: "When marriages work the wife usually takes
   some part or some interest in transvestism." Whatever this may
   be, it is a powerful way to show respect and caring. Even the
   slightest demonstration of acceptance or encouragement by the
   wife is highly valued by the cross dresser.
5. The wife meets other TVs and their wives and comes to the
   conclusion that new friendships can be rewarding for her as well
   as her husband.
6. The most frequently noted effect of cross dressing according to
   wives is that it brings great pleasure to the husband which then
   accrues to her benefit. It may be this insight by the wife, together
   with the desire to help her husband, which are the most critical
   starting points for constructive management of cross dressing
   within a marriage.
7. The husband perceives both the anguish of his wife and her
   desire to be helpful. He modifies his behavior by following nego-
   tiated rules and guidelines which are most valued by her. There
   is considerable variation among TVs in their ability or willingness to abide by their agreements.
8. With the passage of time, cross dressing takes a place among the

various activities and sources of pleasure which make each marriage unique. Transvestism generates less unpleasant emotion and less conflict than initially seen.

The Double Message Game

In this game, transvestism is out in the open but the partners are not honest in their efforts to handle this. They deny their feelings, pretend that all is well, communicate falsely in hope that this will help, and generally fail to establish bridges essential to long-term marital satisfaction. Here is some of what we have observed in these relationships:

1. The husband professes that his marriage is the most important thing in the world to him. He says he will do anything to save his marriage and to strengthen it. But he persistently behaves otherwise. He breaks the rules they have agreed upon. He is a law unto himself. He believes that he must have what he wants when he wants it.
2. Like most wives of TVs, this wife would prefer that cross dressing did not exist. However, she has difficulty expressing this directly because it seems very rejecting. Instead, she buries and conceals her feelings and, at first, pretends to be accepting and supportive. She occasionally buys a gift for "the other woman" and assists her husband in cross dressing. Together with verbal approval, these outward signs of acceptance are really a mask for her feelings of contempt, anger, and frustration.
3. The husband incorrectly assumes his wife really enjoys his cross dressing and asks her to become more involved in purchases, club activities, and other TV events. The more she does, the more he asks for.
4. The wife continues to mask her feelings but becomes increasingly uncomfortable. She is becoming fed-up. As time passes, there are occasional episodes of anger, tears, and accusations.
5. Neither partner is eager to seek marriage counseling. If they do so there is sufficient ambivalence that little progress is made. For both, it is more comfortable to conceal feelings than to discuss sources of conflict.
6. There is progressive withdrawal from each other and, at a time of unusual stress, the marriage may end.

The Mother Game

The themes of this game are dependency and subordination by the TV; he seeks to transfer the responsibility for his need-fulfillments in all

areas to his wife—the idealized, all-giving mother. Perhaps he has selected a wife who was comfortable with certain managerial and leadership tasks. But it is highly unrealistic for him to assume that she ever
expected to take on such responsibilities with regard to his cross dressing. Here is the scenario for this game:

1. The husband seeks a wife who will function in a mother-like
   relationship with him, giving direction, control, and parental au-
   thority to his life. He wants to be dependent, to be passive, to be
   controlled—but at the same time he resents this. As with teenagers there is both a need for compliance and a contradictory
   desire to break away from parental jurisdiction.
2. In general, the wife is pleased to be cast in the role of mother.
   She is more comfortable calling the shots, managing, giving directions, and issuing orders. However, she is not interested in
   giving direction to her husband's cross dressing, and has no
   desire to encourage this behavior.
3. The husband values his cross dressing and wants his wife to give
   the same love, direction, approval, and control to this activity as
   she may be giving to other activities he enjoys. He wants his wife
   to help improve his feminine image and teach him how to be a
   girl. These responsibilities do not appeal to the wife.
4. Instead of showing unconditional acceptance and approval of
   cross dressing, the wife begins to take charge by telling her husband what he can and cannot do, when to do it, where to do it,
   and how much to spend on cross dressing. Since she has been
   effective in the past by being a no-nonsense leader in the family
   she continues to use this managerial style. She is surprised to
   discover that her husband resists her efforts to regulate or control his transvestism.
5. The husband attempts to break away from the dominance of his
   wife and cross dress as he wishes. As he does so, she tries harder
   to take control. More orders are issued. There are threats, rules,
   and demands by her.
6. When the wife becomes aware that she is losing this battle,
   despite her husband's promises to mend his ways, she becomes
   angry and resentful. She may consider his cross dressing to be
   out of control, although he may see this very differently.
7. The outcome of this power and growth struggle will depend
   largely upon the wife's ability to share control over cross dressing and to partially give up the mother role. On the husband's
   side, the challenge will be whether or not he can take steps to
   carry out his cross dressing in ways which are either satisfactory

to his wife, or at least offer minimal annoyance to her. Possibly, he will learn that as he takes responsibility for his expression of transvestism he can also do so in other areas of his life. The experience of discovering and working on his own dependency needs may help him to become a more assertive person.

Cessation or Frustration of Cross Dressing

The experience of intense frustration upon cessation of cross dressing, or in response to the blockage of cross dressing, has been long recognized. Thirty-three wives responded to this question: *From the standpoint of personal adjustment, what effect does stopping cross dressing have upon your husband, if any?* Overwhelmingly, wives report irritability and other unpleasant emotional responses to cessation of cross dressing. Twenty wives indicated their husband became tense, frustrated, moody, unhappy, or angry. Twelve said the husband had never stopped cross dressing, and one said cessation had "no effect."

The wives' views of the effects of cessation can be illustrated by reviewing their written comments. Here are some examples:

"My husband becomes very tense and frustrated. Resentment toward me builds up and he doesn't care if he pleases me or not. He becomes less tolerant of other people. He becomes moody, depressed, short-tempered, and generally loses interest in the family, job, friends, and other aspects of life. He becomes less interested in his hobbies or in improving things around the house. He likes to hit the road and get away for total freedom."

"He doesn't stop. I tell myself that cross dressing brings my husband happiness or some sort of release or that it provides an outlet for his particular sort of personality, and so long as he is safe and provokes no embarrassment I can accept it."

"He became very unfriendly, angry and uncomfortable. He would not work at anything. In fact, it was 2½ years of 'his/her' not being dressed that almost led to our breaking up."

The wife of a professional who takes a day off each week to stay at home cross dressed said this: "During the year he didn't dress he felt like a caged lion with no escape. It was a lonely existence when he couldn't share his feelings with anyone and he thought he was the only person on earth with those feelings. I also think stopping or trying to stop leads to depression which could be more serious and damaging than cross dressing." We did not ask husbands for their self-descriptions of how it feels to stop, but one TV with over 50 years of cross dressing experience and a happy marriage of almost this length said, "When I stop, and I often have tried to give it up, it's as if my entire world turns grey. The joy and happiness that I usually get from many activities is reduced. The peaks of satisfaction and pleasure are gone."

These and other similar kinds of reports are important sources of corroboration for the view that cross dressing is a mood-altering experience. It is a self-regulated behavior offering the powerful rewards of tranquilization, joyful excitement, high exhilaration, a focusing of attention with ensuing stress reduction, and intense pleasure and erotic gratification. As we see it, the reports of feminine feelings or feminine identity are not so much the essence of this experience as they are convenient labels or explanations passed from one TV to the next. Such labels have been given great prominence in transvestite club publications, but most likely they are incomplete attributions. However, speaking in terms of the familiar explanation of cross dressing as "expression of feminine feelings," the TV can present his behavior to himself and to others in nonsexual terms. As we previously noted, these men are usually somewhat ashamed of the erotic and sexual aspects of their cross dressing. It is somewhat understandable, therefore, that they would offer a more neutral description of TV motivation. For them, the explanation of cross dressing on the basis of "feminine feelings" provides a comfortable and plausible theory for cross dressing. To firm up this explanation, he often speculates about vague, but possible, physiological or hereditary causes of transvestism, as a way in which to reduce personal responsibility for his behavior.

Survey Wives' Comments to Prospective Wives of Transvestites

We invited the wives to comment concerning any advice they might offer women who planned to marry cross dressers. Here are some representative responses:

"Be certain you can cope because you will not change your husband's behavior."

"Read as much as you can about it . . . verbalize your opinion, your fears and concerns . . . find out what his feelings are . . . and it is very important to meet other cross dressers."

"Realize that this is just the way he is and to make him give up cross dressing is wrong."

"Talk openly about your feelings and fears . . . and talk to other wives of cross dressers."

"Strongly recommend counseling for the couple prior to marriage. Be with him and experience the cross dressing behavior so you can test your acceptance of this. Project the effects of cross dressing on your children and on your parenting."

"Before marriage read a lot of books about cross dressing and be sure you know what you are doing."

"Very difficult to advise . . . but a woman would have to be accepting and comfortable with the habit before marriage and still be prepared to make adjustments. I think I would find it very difficult to recommend marriage."

"Either you totally accept it or forget it. There is no in-between. It will not go away. If you really love him and understand this need of his you'll have a beautiful marriage."

"It is more difficult to live with transvestism than you would think. Most cross dressers have the hope to be TSs one day."

"Go for it. You would be surprised at how wonderful the entire experience can be if you go into the situation with an open mind and a loving heart. It can enrich your mind too!"

"My advice is don't marry a cross dresser!"

"Learn to understand it, accept it, and enjoy it. If you can't handle it don't get married."

"See him dressed before you marry. The full effect can be emotional and scary. And know that it won't go away with lots of tender love and care."

"You shouldn't feel pity . . . as if this were a plight. You should not use this as a form of blackmail. Praying once in a while doesn't hurt either."

"Realize it is a compulsion that will not go away. You can set some limits but it is a strong need. Don't do what you aren't comfortable with."

"Relax. Don't make a big deal out of it."

"Know what he wants from dressing. Be sure you can accept him for what he is. Don't expect him to change. If you know before marriage, be with him when he's dressed a few times."

"Don't marry a cross dresser."

"Accept the fact that his cross dressing won't go away and will probably increase with his introduction to other cross dressers. Share your feelings with a close confidant. This was extremely important for me."

Summary

The wives of transvestites have not been the target of much systematic research. The sample of wives we are working with is believed to overrepresent partners who accept and even encourage cross dressing. Over 80% of this group has been married over 5 years, and an even higher percentage has never been divorced. About two-thirds of them have children. They seem to be an unremarkable group of women from a personal adjustment standpoint, unusual only in the sense that they unexpectedly found themselves in a marriage with a transvestite husband. Their main concerns regarding this problem—and most of them would consider it at least a problem if not a serious matter—is security. They fear the consequences of discovery of their husband's semisecret cross dressing, for him and the family. Many of these men go out in public or into semipublic situations, cross dressed—some very often and most at the rate of once or twice a week. Another concern producing tensions within the marriage is the use of resources—time, money, energy, and emotional involvement—extensively devoted to the transvestic behavior. Hence, some wives complain of the restriction of their social life, interference with family relationships, and difficulties keeping the cross dressing secret from their children. Most wives with children report they attempt to shield their youngsters from any knowledge of the father's cross dressing. Another problem identified is the reported negative impact cross dressing has upon the sex life of the couple. Often, it is alleged that transvestism promotes an alternative sexual outlet which is usually adverse to the happiness of the wife. Several approaches to coping with this are described, but for some wives, sexual factors related to cross dressing remain a major area of difficulty. In attempting to deal with these concerns, most wives receive a good deal of information and help from several sources—literature is the most common resource, with other TVs and wives of TVs, friends, psychologists, and other counselors also available to assist. The husband's efforts with regard to candor and information giving are also crucial.

Sometimes this struggle to adapt asks more of the couple than they have to give and the pattern of growing apart is seen. For others, the stress of transvestism has been converted into an opportunity for personal growth, and both partners gain individually along with the strengthening of the marriage. Wives use many strategies in an effort to fit the sexual excitement of cross dressing into the marriage, and some are surprisingly successful. Many others prefer not to have cross dressing in any way associated with their sexual relationship, but considerable evidence from the wives was noted that supports the long-held view that blocking or stopping cross dressing has marked emotional consequences for the TV. Finally, these wives offer a considerable range of comment to prospective wives of cross dressers.

Chapter 8

A Theory of Heterosexual Transvestism and Secondary Transsexualism

A theory of heterosexual transvestism should attempt to explain the origins of this syndrome, the developmental process which seems basic to its many expressions, and the ultimate behaviors which emerge. It should encompass the entire range of transvestic behavior, from fetishism through secondary transsexualism. Of greatest importance is the necessity to conceptualize heterosexual transvestism as a multistage developmental process, heavily dependent upon cognitive structures, and as a means of generating intense positive reinforcement and changes in mood.

Transvestism is no more understandable using a brief time-slice approach than any other behavior. People change greatly over the life span, and so do the manifestations of heterosexual cross dressing. We will emphasize cognitive processes as having a causal role in the origins and expressions of transvestism, and we shall emphasize change and development as critical to understanding this behavior. Finally, while we are interested in all types of related cross dressing phenomena— from fetishism to transsexualism—our conceptual focus will be narrowly directed to the heterosexual transvestite. Therefore, when we refer to secondary transsexualism in this chapter, we shall restrict this to the transvestic type of secondary transsexualism (see Chapter 2).

As we have attempted to show with our own data and through the analysis of the work of others, the heterosexual transvestite behavior pattern typically requires many years to shape, and major changes occur during the transvestic career. We will give attention to these changes or stages of transvestism as our theory is presented. Our ideas incorporate themes from several earlier theories, but more than anyone else, Buckner (1970) has influenced our thinking; what follows owes much to his creative insights concerning the "career" of transvestism. His view of the experienced transvestite emphasizes the pseudorelationship between the cross dresser and his imaginal "partner." It is the social character of this pseudopairing which most interested Buckner. We agree that this is important for many transvestites, but our theoretical scheme has a different emphasis. We are especially interested in two things: first, how the cross-gender identity develops, and second, what the outcome is of efforts to integrate this within the self system. Some organizing ideas and assumptions are presented in the next several sections as a foundation to the five-stage theory to be proposed.

Foundations of a Theoretical Model

We shall rely upon three major streams of influence or foundational themes to guide our theory development. These are: (1) biological determinants of behavior, (2) learning processes and behavior, and (3) the self system and gender identity.

Biological factors are basic to the development of sexual behavior and it is through biological mechanisms that physical and psychological development is made possible. The unfolding of the sex drive, the innately reinforcing attributes of sexual arousal and sexual behavior, and the maturational and physical growth processes which underlie adult sexual conduct are inextricably influenced by our biology. All behavior is channeled through biological processing. There is no disputing that many biological factors contribute heavily to transvestism and perhaps some are critically important. But we also believe that biology alone cannot explain the diversity within human behaviors, sexual or otherwise. We must, therefore, give necessary weight to learning factors.

Operant-learning theory, with its emphasis upon the control of behavior through schedules of reinforcement, has a central place in the proposed theory. It is very probable that transvestites have learned much of their fetishistic and cross-gender behavior as part of a multitude of learning experiences punctuated by reinforcers which strengthen specific behaviors. Innate as well as learned reinforcers are no doubt involved.

Social-learning theory emphasizes modeling and imitation as key components in the learning process. Identity, gender identity, identification, cross-gender envy and numerous other aspects of cross-gender behavior may be interpreted within the framework of social-learning theory. It is widely thought that all gender presentation is influenced by social learning to some extent, and that specific gender-linked behavior, such as clothing preferences, are highly dependent upon such learning. Role-modeling, imitation, and sex role typing all depend upon social learning from our most formative years.

Self theory and gender theory are vague and troublesome conceptual schemes, but what they deal with is central to transvestism. We shall assume that ego development processes can, for our purposes, be best understood in terms of the operations of the self system and its subordinate systems. While the formation of this hypothetical management system—the self—remains more of a research target than a well-documented body of knowledge, we are impressed by the many contributions which are being made by developmental and object relations theorists (see, e.g., Kernberg, 1976). Similarly, we place high value on Hilgard's (1977) model of the mechanisms that may enable the dissociation of parts of the self from other parts, of the interlocking systems of shared consciousness, of the interactive communications among subsystems, and of the multiple control capabilities within the self system.

Ideas Basic to Theory Development

A Spectrum of Cross Dressing.   Cross dressing is manifested for many reasons in males and females, ranging from fetishism through several variations of heterosexual transvestism (in men), and in both primary and secondary transsexuals. We have reviewed these types and their classification in Chapter 2. While a good theory should attempt to account for all of these variations, great differences do exist along several dimensions across this spectrum. This is especially obvious, for example, when contrasting the behavior of homosexually oriented cross dressers with their heterosexual counterparts. Similarly, there is no erotic association with cross dressing observed in the primary transsexual, while such feelings are present in the heterosexual transvestite and the secondary transsexual (TV type). While theorists, ultimately, must attend to such differences, our immediate focus will be upon one group only—the male heterosexual transvestite.

Developmental Changes.   We believe that the motives, reinforcers, and controlling stimuli associated with heterosexual transvestism change radically across the extensive course and development of this behavior pattern. The secretive, guilt-producing, highly sexual cross dressing of the 14-year-old gives way to bolder cross dressing experiments as the years pass. But far more than appearances and clothing change. The masturbatory sessions of youth are supplanted by efforts to present a pseudowoman in social situations, and to receive acceptance and praise as this person. The guilt of adolescence is replaced by believing there is a right to have the feminine self expressed from time to time, and that this is harmless. This *social practice* of being a woman is believed by us essential to the formation of a cross-gender identity. Our conceptualization, therefore, gives emphasis to the changing patterns of cross dressing across the life span of the transvestite. A key set of issues is concerned with why such developmental changes are manifested.

Learning Processes.   In the absence of evidence favoring a predominantly biological model of transvestism, learning processes offer the strongest explanations for this behavior. Very likely, transvestism involves a combination of classical conditioning, operant conditioning, and social-learning events. By emphasizing learning factors in transvestism, we do not intend to disregard the biological mechanisms which support general arousal changes, sexual excitement changes, and emotional states. But present indications are that transvestites, as a group, are not different in their biology, and therefore, we cannot invoke biological processes to specifically explain their cross dressing behavior.

Heterosexual Preference.   As defined, our group of transvestites are, at the least, predominantly heterosexual in their preferred object choice. There is some bisexuality within this category, as noted by virtually all investigators concerned with the topic. We shall confine our effort here to the predominantly or exclusively heterosexual transvestite. The predominantly homosexual cross dressers we have known do not, for the most part, have histories similar to the heterosexual transvestite.

Absence of Gender Dysphoria.   In individuals with a history of substantial and sustained gender dysphoria, one invokes the concept of transsexualism. Transvestism does not incorporate such intense negative gender feelings. As Stoller observed 20 years ago (1968a), transvestites are, for the most part, "unremarkably masculine," except when cross dressed, and most are satisfied to remain that way. But a theory of transvestism needs to account for heterosexual cross dressers who seem indistinguishable from their transvestite friends, but who ultimately elect to become secondary transsexuals. It is these rare cases which most clearly reveal the extreme changes occasionally seen in transvestism across the life span.

Individual Differences.   We believe that transvestites do not have anything even roughly akin to identical personal histories. Substantial individual differences appear to be present among transvestites in virtually all aspects of personality and interpersonal behavior. It would appear that their common behavior, transvestism, resembles a *final common path* with many points of origin rather than a unitary road of development. But this is not to say that no similar developmental experiences are possible. Just as some persons occupying a particular vocational role may have some common learning experiences leading to such work, transvestites may also represent a wide variety of human differences, each quite unique, but with a few threads of common history.

Self System Theory.   We believe that self theory can greatly contribute to the understanding of both the cognitive and affective components associated with transvestism. We have discussed the importance of both identity theory and self theory in Chapter 4. Although this is not the only hypothetical construct advocated to account for the complexities of ongoing behavior, it is one of the oldest ideas and, we think, one of the best. Transvestites may help us to understand the operations of the self system. Some, for example, seem able to turn off their masculine gender identity and turn on a feminine gender identity. We believe that self (or ego) mechanisms proposed by Hilgard (1977) and discussed in Chapter 4, support these changes. In our theory we shall employ his postulates of shared consciousness and of a duality of the self.

Explanatory Constructs.   In Chapter 1 we identified four explanatory constructs which constitute the unifying themes of this book: sexual arousal, pleasure, the sexual script, and cross-gender identity. To us, these constructs seem critical to the explanation of transvestism in its many and changing expressions. Of these four explanatory ideas, only sexual arousal has been reduced to an objective operational definition— as exemplified by the studies of Masters and Johnson (1966) and in phallometric research (e.g., Bryne, 1977). The remaining three are undoubtedly very complex, multidimensional variables which await both refined analysis into their component parts and subsequent operational definition.

Definitions of Four Major Explanatory Constructs

Sexual Arousal or Sexual Excitement

We shall use these terms interchangeably and treat them as synonymous. We regard cognitive, autonomic, central nervous system, and muscular response phenomena as innate or conditioned accompaniments of sexual arousal. For our purposes, sexual arousal will be used in a very general sense to refer to *all preparatory cognitive, autonomic, and muscular responses associated with the sexual response pattern* (Masters & Johnson, 1966). Although sexual arousal consists of responses, these are cue-producing responses which generate external feedback and sustain a build-up of sexual excitement. This excitement is assumed to be innately reinforcing. We believe that learned erotic preferences (discriminative stimuli) provide the cues that channel and direct sexual arousal.

Feelings of Pleasure

We conceptualize pleasure as *a cognitive process interpretable at the subjective report level as "feeling good, feeling happy, feeling joyful" and as a state which is associated with intrinsic positive reinforcement.* That is, people learn how to produce this state, to find stimuli which lead to this state, and to emit behaviors which produce this state because it is positively reinforcing to do so. It seems likely that such neurologically based feeling states are, at least, to some extent, supported by limbic system processes. The roles of several neurotransmitters, collectively called endorphins, have become fairly well-established (Bolles & Fanselow, 1982). A key point in our theory is that transvestism is not usually driven by unpleasant motives, such as anxiety. More likely, we believe, this behavior is the product of "pull motivation" in the form of highly positive, valued, delightful expectations of pleasure. As we use the term, pleasure will exclude any erotic components in order to clarify the difference between nonerotic pleasure and sexual arousal.

The Sexual Script

When erotic preferences are honed and perfected into a set of cognitive schema and repeatedly reinforced, these preferences are said to form a sexual script. We mean nothing more than an organized, selective, coherent, recognizable and enduring set of erotic mental stimuli. This script has powerful cue significance and provides the focus of controlling stimuli for transvestic sexual arousal and/or pleasure-seeking behavior. The sexual script, in our usage, is entirely internal and cognitive, but the attentional priority given this script as a format for action may be controlled by either internal or external stimuli. The transvestite may "decide" that he wishes to have a cross dressing session, thereby responding to internal stimuli. Conversely, as a stimulus to cross dressing, he may respond to such external cues as time of day, day of week, being left alone at home, being in a hotel room with time available, or looking at a sexually exciting photo, person, or literary product.

Gender Identity and Cross-Gender Identity

Gender identity is defined as *the unity of our subjective sense of being masculine, feminine, or ambivalent, to a greater or lesser degree, especially as experienced in self-awareness and behavior* (derived from Money & Ehrhardt, 1972, p. 4). Cross-gender identity is defined by, *the subjective sense of belonging to the gender opposite one's anatomic sex in the absence of long-standing gender dysphoria.*

Some heterosexual transvestites report strong feelings of cross-gender identity when cross dressed and only in that condition (for example, Freund *et al.,* 1982), but the phenomenon has not been studied well beyond this descriptive level. While some transvestites do report strong feelings of gender dysphoria, this is atypical. Such feelings may be predictive of a desire to experiment with living in a transgender or transsexual mode.

Gender identity, cross-gender identity, and gender dysphoria are best conceptualized as variables having differential significance for an individual depending upon either situational or long-term events. We find it useful to think of gender identity, cross-gender identity, and gender dysphoria as evaluative components of the self-system, or more specifically, of those subsystems of the self which deal with gender-related self-perceptions and self-evaluations.

A Five-Stage Theory of Transvestism

Stage 1: Antecedent Developmental Factors

Transvestism does not grow in just any kind of soil. We think it is more than a matter of simply releasing an existing inborn feminine self which has been suppressed by gender role socialization (Prince, 1976). In the theory which follows, we shall propose that a cross-gender identity comes about as a product of extensive social reinforcement of cross dressing. But how does this begin? What predisposes some young boys to first engage in nonerotic cross dressing, and then to link this to the powerful motivational and reinforcing systems of sexual responding? Understanding these questions and coming up with some possible answers may offer a key which unlocks the learning processes basic to transvestism. We need to know what prepares these youth to become fetishists and what channels their learning into the particular behaviors which propel them along the road of heterosexual transvestism. We next examine some critical antecedents of fetishistic cross dressing.

Individuation-Separation Phase of Development.   During the individuation-separation phase of very early human development transitional objects provide reinforcement by contributing to feelings of security, safety, and love (Kernberg, 1976). The theory is that a transitional object, such as a favorite blanket, serves as a symbolic substitute for the security afforded by the mother. The object is transitional because it provides a kind of bridge between needing closeness to the mother and feeling secure in the mother's absence. For most children there is progressive growing apart from the mother and a developing awareness of the individuality of oneself. But many impediments to smooth development may cause some infants to experience failure in this process of separating from the mother and in the building of a self-identity. Another requirement of this very early stage is the gradual comprehension that neither outside "objects" nor the self are entirely good or bad. Reality-testing abilities, the formation of ego boundaries, and the security necessary to become independent, and to grow stronger, are all critically important developmental issues during these earliest years. When serious problems impede separation and individuation development, according to object relations theorists, they result in syndromes of the borderline or narcissistic personality (Beitel, 1985; Bowlby, 1969, 1973; Masterson, 1981). As postulated by Person and Ovesey (1974a), these earliest developmental difficulties are most likely to be seen as antecedent components of the most intense cross-gender identity difficulties as in primary transsexualism. We believe they are not likely to be antecedent factors in the higher-functioning transvestites who are strongly represented in our research sample. These transvestites have had a better start in the earliest years of development, and their early fetishism is best explained by some developmental factors associated with the onset of adolescence rather than very early experience.

Women's Clothing as Discriminative Stimuli.   In our culture, youth are provided extensive training, both about gender differences in clothing, and also concerning ways in which certain clothing may have erotic or sexually arousing significance. Specific kinds of women's apparel, such as underwear or high-heeled shoes, are culturally defined as having more than utilitarian significance. The preadolescent boy has received extensive training about the unique stimulus value accorded certain women's clothing, and about the exclusivity of these properties as garments available only to women. The important point is that all of this social learning strongly establishes a unique set of stimuli as discriminative stimuli associated with erotic arousal. Under certain conditions, these stimuli generate sexual excitatory responses. These learning experiences are the foundation for fetishism. While some unique personal experiences no doubt play a part in the further development of a sexual script, it is not the deflection of personality into psychopathology which is important, but rather a particular learning process which will ultimately lead to adult transvestism. Very importantly, we will argue that there is typically no cross-gender identity "problem" basic to transvestic script formation. The cross-gender identity will emerge much later, after much fetishistic practice with cross dressing, and even then it will become a "problem" for only a few cross dressers.

Sexual Maturation.   There is no way to rule out the possibility that biological factors, such as a possible gender system within the brain, may contribute to deviant gender behavior. But we shall not rely upon this line of theory. Rather, we will stay as close as possible to the observable. One thing of which we are certain is that the processes of social development interact with increases in sex drive to encourage behavior associated with sexual arousal and sexual responding in the preadolescent years. This interactive process has been discussed in a theoretical statement concerned with erotic orientation by Storms (1981). These social and biological developments during early adolescence promote many variations of sexual responding as documented by Kinsey *et al.* (1948). Cross dressing in its most elementary forms often can be seen in children long before the adolescent years, but it is during these teenage years that the first strongly sexual link between fetishistic cross dressing and sexual reinforcement through orgasm, is evidenced (see Chapter 6). This pairing of fetishistic cross dressing and sexual satisfaction is invariably a part of the adolescent cross dressing pattern, and is basic to the development of transvestism.

Learning Gender Envy.   Some boys develop intense feelings of gender envy due, at least in part, to their strict sex role socialization. Theirs is the view that girls have it better in many ways. These feelings of envy may center around competition for love and security—both very basic human requirements. We believe the stresses and strains of early adolescence, with its intense new sex role demands, may exacerbate feelings of gender envy and gender inadequacy in some young boys. Women are valued not only as potential sex objects, but because of their perceived advantage as passive-receptive participants in sexual relationships. In identifying with the sex role of a woman, the youthful cross dresser defends himself against the threat of actual rejection by women and consequent loss of self-esteem by inventing his own sexual partner and experiencing sexual excitement and reinforcement in this pseudosocial "partnership" (Buckner, 1970).

Heterosexual Preferences.   Another antecedent factor is the formation of a well-established heterosexual orientation. It seems logical to assume that an attraction to women, as erotic or sexual objects, or to their clothing as sexually charged symbols is most likely to be an essential ingredient of transvestism. These men come to treasure their fantasies not only about clothing and appearances, but later, fantasies of functioning in many roles as a woman. Some homosexual boys with effeminate interests cross dress, as described by Green (1974, 1979, 1987), Zuger (1966, 1978), and others, but their motives for cross dressing are believed to have different roots than in the heterosexual adolescent.

Sexual Inhibitions.   Inhibitions about intimacies with girls will restrict sexual experience in the young adolescent. It is well known that a considerable range of adolescent sexual behavior is seen in the general population, as discussed by Kinsey *et al.* (1948) and by Gagnon and Simon (1973). Fear of failure, early rejection experiences, sexual guilt, lack of assertion, and many other personality features may be presumed to inhibit some youth from heterosexual experimentation. Stoller (1968a, 1974, 1985c) has noted that the psychodynamics basic to all fetishism, and presumably the paraphilias as well, is the perception of women and their bodies as dangerous. For some of these adolescents (presumably the future transvestites) the alternative of experimenting with erotically arousing women's clothing comes to be highly valued and promotes satisfying reinforcements.

The above examples point up how different interactive processes shape cross dressing behavior, regardless of whether it initially begins in the very early years or just prior to adolescence. The necessary steps are highly specific stimulus-discrimination learning (women's clothing as erotic symbols), intense identification with the roles of women (gender envy), heterosexuality, and ultimately, the evocation of sexual arousal with fetishistic cross dressing. The glue which holds these interactive processes together is the emerging sexual script. At the heart of the matter are cognitive changes which facilitate affective changes—not the other way around. As these cognitive schemas take shape around cross dressing and cross-gender themes, the beginnings of fetishistic cross dressing are seen.

Stage 2: Fetishistic Cross Dressing

Fifty-three percent of our transvestite sample reported some cross dressing experience before the age of 10. These early cross dressers have often been viewed in the literature as little more than a subgroup of the fetishistic preadolescent cross dressers who experiment with transvestism as sex drive increases rapidly in the years immediately preceding adolescence. We believe partial cross dressing before the age of 10 is usually not primarily an erotic activity, although a few subjects describe it as highly erotic, even at a very early age. In the case of nonsexual cross dressing, an attractive explanation is the transitional object hypothesis, which holds that this behavior is a response to the clothing of the mother for the purpose of experiencing security, reassurance, or love (Ovesey & Person, 1976). These security blanket responses are perhaps the most familiar examples of substitutive or compensatory behavior predicted by object relations theory. Presumably, conditioning processes can account for the acquired emotional significance of nonhuman objects. That transitional objects can take on extremely significant meanings to the young child appears self-evident. The clothing of the mother, being highly available, are a natural choice as conditioned stimuli and as secondary reinforcers. This line of reasoning is powerfully supported by the affectional research of Harlow (1958), which showed how infant monkeys, separated from maternal contact from birth, clung to their "cloth mothers" and valued these substitutes as emotional supports when faced with fearful stimulus objects.

When persistent cross dressing begins very early, perhaps before ages 7 or 8, we propose that it may be predictive of a transvestic career in which fetishism is less important, in the long run, than cross-gender identity. Our reasoning is that such cross dressing appears not to be motivated by intensification of the sex drive, which is probably a major motivating and reinforcing factor for transvestites who begin cross dressing at the outset of adolescence. Rather, these early cross dressers may begin this behavior because of unfulfilled dependency or security needs. Such developmental deficits, then, may be more common in the marginal transvestite group. For the marginal transvestite, the erotic aspects of cross dressing will emerge a few years later.

Thirty-two percent of our sample had their first experience with cross dressing in the range of ages 10 to 15. (Combined with those under 10, the cumulative total comes to 85 percent.) From the descriptions of how this early cross dressing begins and what behaviors actually occur, it is clear that for many of our TVs this early cross dressing is not primarily sexual. But for others, cross dressing is strongly associated with sexual excitement during early adolescence. For example, one-third of our subjects reported their first orgasm took place during some kind of cross dressing activity.

As the sex drive strengthens in the period just prior to adolescence, around ages 11 or 12, the fetishistic aspect of cross dressing becomes important, as reported by almost all heterosexual transvestites. It is for this reason that a history of sexual arousal to cross dressing is part of the definition of transvestism in DSM-III-R (American Psychiatric Association, 1987). We believe that the antecedent learning steps which result in these garments becoming perceived as sexual objects are complex. They appear to involve the conditioning of sexual responses prior to adolescence. An example would be the "forbidden fruit" message (see Chapter 5) given to boys about women's intimate attire—lingerie, panties, stockings, nightgowns, and high heels, especially. But for our immediate purpose it is enough to note that, in fact, they have acquired sexual arousal significance. Put more formally in learning terms, these garments have become discriminative stimuli for sexual arousal and sexual responding.

The fetishistic cross dressing of these early years of the transvestic career typically do not involve cross-gender identity, certainly not in the form that will develop later. Specific stimuli evoke sexual arousal, and soon masturbation promotes orgasmic reinforcement in a very high percentage of the transvestite population. This is a major step in the strengthening of cross dressing and sexual behavior, but there is no attempt, for most, to even contemplate the full impersonation of a woman or to attempt to role play a woman in a public setting. All of that is yet to come.

The early cross dressing behavior of the transvestite is not the product of any single motivation, personality characteristic, or learning experience. It is the product of several interacting developmental processes which are, together, transforming the youth into a man. A key point is to view these processes as interdependent, interactive, and as highly driven by cognitive factors. The sexual script is becoming increasingly explicit. Taken together, they represent the shaping forces which are basic to becoming a transvestite. We move on now to the adolescent years, and to the immensely powerful physical and social changes which they entail. To summarize, the four factors which we believe contribute most to adolescent transvestism are:

1. *Adolescent sex drive development.* Biology is basic to the major motivational and maturational changes which define adolescent development. A growing capacity to become sexually aroused and sexually motivated is fundamental to the development of fetishistic cross dressing. Intense orgasmic responses are paired with cross dressing.

2. *Social learning and social development.* Fetishistic cross dressing is shaped, in part, because of the social learning experiences of transvestites. For example, they may learn of the radically different sex role expectations assigned men and women as sexual partners. For many reasons, the young male may turn from such challenges if other alternatives, such as the fetishistic use of female-substitutes have been learned,

and if these alternative stimuli are subsequently reinforced. The highly conflicting messages concerning sexual behavior given to the young as part of the socialization process contribute to the probability that heterosexual responding may be inhibited, conflictual, or otherwise troubled. But only a few become transvestites, because (a) specific antecedent discrimination learning, and (b) actual reinforcement of cross dressing must occur for the process of transvestism to begin and to unfold into its later stages.

3. *Development of heterosexual identity.* Transvestism is a heterosexual phenomenon, but the important point is that it is so because men who do not have erotic preferences for feminine stimuli (clothing) will not become fetishistic cross dressers. There is no generally agreed upon set of principles that accounts for heterosexual *vs.* homosexual development, and our present concern has nothing directly to do with this issue. What we can say is that, however the heterosexual erotic preferences are formed, such development and preference is imperative to the learning which underlies transvestism. Storms (1981) has provided a theory of erotic orientation development which stresses the interaction of sex drive, social development, and social learning processes and we have found his discussion very pertinent.

4. *Transvestic stimuli become secondary reinforcers.* With each cross dressing episode there is assumed to be an inherent reinforcement experienced which strengthens and sustains these responses. Many transvestites think of the intense strength of cross dressing expectancies as a "compulsion" to cross dress. But rather than refer to compulsions, we shall emphasize the progressive strengthening of the sexual script. The reported feeling of an individual that he "must" cross dress is organized around very specific sexual expectancies, and subsequent orgasmic reinforcement is highly predictable. At the same time, all of the stimuli associated with this transvestic responding tend to become secondary reinforcers. Clothing, makeup, places, times, the textures and sensations of the entire cross dressing episode—all become secondary reinforcers. On the cognitive side, various expectancies are being formed which will become the building blocks for future complete cross dressing, and for presentation of the feminine self in social situations.

Throughout this early period partial cross dressing is much more likely than complete cross dressing. This is largely a practical matter, as the youth has neither the resources nor the privacy to arrange for a complete cross-gender self-presentation, however much he might enjoy the prospect of this in fantasy. And so it is through fantasy that the elaboration of the transvestic experience must first be sought. With increasing experience in fetishistic cross dressing, the young transvesitite comes to daydream of himself as a beautiful woman having a unique appearance harmonious with his developing sexual script. But in order for this script to take on the full significance that it will have during the coming periods of transvestic development, there will have to be time, practice, cognitive reorganization, experiments with alternatives to transvestism as a sexual excitant (such as dating or marriage), and more than anything else—privacy and resources to expand the experience of cross dressing. Lest we err and think of this early period as mainly fantasy, we need only be reminded that the average frequency of cross dressing during the early period for our subjects was about 6 times per month; very likely, this represents a significant part of the total sex life of many of these subjects.

The importance of the mirror as a desired, even necessary, device deserves comment. As Buckner (1970) has noted, it is through the reflected image of the pseudowoman that the young transvestite develops his "partner." Nothing more clearly provides a clue into the experience of the transvestite than does the mirror. The cross dresser never wants to perceive himself as his male self in the mirror; he wants to see images, stimuli, and many variations of his dream girl. The mirror offers him endless reflections of his ideal pin-up; the one "girl" who will never reject or disappoint; a predictable, reliable partner in the adventures of sex.

Stage 3: Complete Cross Dressing, Cross-Gender Identity, and Cognitive Dissonance

This stage begins at about age 18, when many adolescent males start to function quite independently from parental supervision and control. Whatever the age, this stage begins with the critical step of having greater separation from parental involvement, and of becoming able to allocate one's own time. Going to college, joining the military service, having one's own apartment, and getting a job—each of these is an example of the increased freedom which sets this stage apart.

Marriage used to be far more common in the years immediately after high school, and for many of our TVs, this event marked the first important break with parental control. Increased freedom has the following behavioral implications for the young adult cross dresser:

1. There is an increase in the average frequency of cross dressing from about 6 times monthly to about 8 times per month.

2. Partial cross dressing is gradually replaced by complete cross dressing and the use of a wig and makeup appropriate for appearance in public. This is a critical developmental process, because the formation of the cross-gender identity and the subsequent cognitive dissonances as-

sociated with this depend upon the emergence of a sexual script in which the transvestite transforms himself into a "woman" and takes the gender role of a woman in public settings. All of this builds and reinforces both the sexual script and the progressively stronger sense of cross-gender identity.

3. A cross-gender identity is learned both through fantasy, and increasingly, through cross dressing experiences which involve public self-presentation. Social reinforcers play a major role in this identity learning. The sexual script is further developed and consolidated both through solitary fantasy practice and through social interactions while cross dressed. With several years of practice there will be growing confidence in the appearance of this pseudowoman. This will be followed by progressively more bold public exposure and risk taking, greater social reinforcements, including new friendships, and the taking of a feminine name. *The taking of a feminine name should be viewed as a major "rite of passage" for the transvestite; it is the transvestite's most explicit statement that a cross-gender identity has emerged.* Passing in public may reinforce validation of the feminine self, a feeling that one's secret life is indeed kept secret through successful passing, and very importantly, it may reinforce a reduction of negative self-evaluation given the evidence of social acceptance (or even of being ignored). The feelings of guilt and shame associated with social deviance are thereby replaced by feelings of triumph, much in line with Stoller's view of sexual excitement (1976).

4. Formation of the cross-gender identity is a long-term process. In Chapter 6 we presented data which strongly support this conclusion. Here is a summary of that information: Among our subjects, 79% did not appear in public cross dressed prior to age 20; at that time, most of the subjects had already had several years of experience with cross dressing. The average number of years of practice with cross dressing prior to owning a full feminine outfit was 15. The average number of years of practice with cross dressing prior to adoption of a feminine name was 21. Again, we have factual evidence indicative of the considerable time required for development of the cross-gender identity.

5. There is substantial cognitive dissonance (anxiety, depression, tension, periodic guilt, and threats to self-esteem) associated with developing a cross-gender identity and in perceiving oneself as a transvestite. All aspects of this gender deviance are socially disapproved, if not taboo, for males in our culture. This discomfort and emotional tension is characteristic of the ambivalence and conflicting motivation seen in this stage of transvestism.

6. As social reinforcers become increasingly valued by the transvestite, cross dressing in isolation loses its appeal; the thrill of interacting with the beautiful "woman" in the mirror wanes. For some, there is a

gradual reduction in fetishistic cross dressing. But for others, cross dressing continues to be a major stimulus for masturbation and orgasm. A few are able to incorporate some aspect of their cross dressing into their heterosexual encounters, but this is uncommon. The most sought after transvestic opportunities require social interactions in semipublic settings. All types of desired social activities are reported, for instance, eating out, shopping, visiting libraries, museums, bars, travel, and vacations in feminine garb.

7. Revelations about transvestism to prospective wives are not typical for TVs prior to the first marriage, but after several years of marriage, transvestite club members usually reveal their fantasies and cross dressing practices to the spouse. Many wives are initially very uncertain about the meanings of transvestism to their marriage and their future, but most gradually become somewhat more accepting with experience and knowledge. Whatever acceptance a wife may show helps to strengthen both the sexual script and habitual routines of cross dressing.

8. Often there is a reduction in the frequency and intensity of the marital sexual relationship; transvestism may "take the edge off" sexual responding with the wife. In its place, the erotic component of transvestism becomes the major sexual outlet.

9. A cross-gender identity is being constructed in harmony with the sexual script. This subsystem maintains an unstable relationship with the primary self system. Despite far greater self-acceptance as a transvestite than was seen in the first stage, there is guilt, uncertain self-esteem, and persistent efforts to terminate this deviant habit. These "purges" often include destruction of cross dressing paraphernalia.

Psychodynamically, the transvestite is now experiencing conflict within the self system between his primary identity (I am a socially conforming heterosexual, a good person deserving of approval) and his cross-gender identity and transvestic fantasies (I enjoy dressing like a woman and imitating a woman; when dressed I have fantasies of being a woman including, perhaps, having sexual encounters with men). These self-perceptions are not compatible. The resulting cognitive dissonance motivates intense efforts to meet other transvestites, to obtain information about cross dressing, and to affiliate with transvestite clubs and support groups.

This third stage often proceeds through the thirties and forties although there are large variations as to duration. The most significant changes which will occur as this stage gives way to the fourth stage are the manner in which the cognitive dissonances of Stage 3 are resolved. The transvestite has had to live with three major cognitive dissonances:

First, he values his cross dressing as much as virtually any source of satisfaction in his life—not simply his sexual life, but compared to any satisfactions; however, he also recognizes the significant social deviance this entails. With his desire to appear cross dressed in public, he takes risks which are not harmonious with his view of himself as a conventional, rule-keeping good citizen and good husband. While he cannot give up transvestism and does not wish to do so, he feels locked into a conflict between behavior which brings him some of his most joyful experiences, and self-evaluations which are highly negative. He does not perceive a way to resolve this dissonance, especially since he has experimented with purges on the one hand, and with increases in his cross dressing on the other.

Second, he is confronted by a subjective reality which is dissonant. He says to himself something like this: "I recognize that I am a man and that I can never become a woman, yet my most intensive daydreams and my sexual script include strong fantasies in which I identify with taking the role of a woman." These competing aspects of identity threaten self-esteem.

Third, the heterosexual transvestite is ambivalent and threatened by his own cross-gender fantasies of having sex with men while cross dressed and of striving to be attractive to men. While the range of reported fantasy concerning this is very great in subjects we have interviewed, for the many who do experience such daydreams, the fantasy encounter has unmistakable sexual overtones which are threatening to self-perceived heterosexuality. It is therefore a highly conflictual fantasy (or motive).

Figure 3 provides a schematic model of the five stages being discussed. As we have noted, some individuals progress from one stage to the next while others do not. While the arrows in Figure 3 indicate movement in one direction only, some individuals may change in a reverse direction.

In the fourth stage of transvestism, we shall see that for most transvestites, the cross-gender identity becomes satisfactorily integrated into the self system; it becomes a compatible subsystem. But for the marginal transvestites (Buhrich & McConaghy, 1977b) the cross-gender identity will be split off in a dissociative-like process which promotes tension and instability.

Stage 4: Resolution of Cognitive Dissonance—Path A and Path B

Two pathways may be identified in Stage 4, each indicative of how the cognitive dissonances and struggles experienced between the cross-gender identity and the primary self are managed.

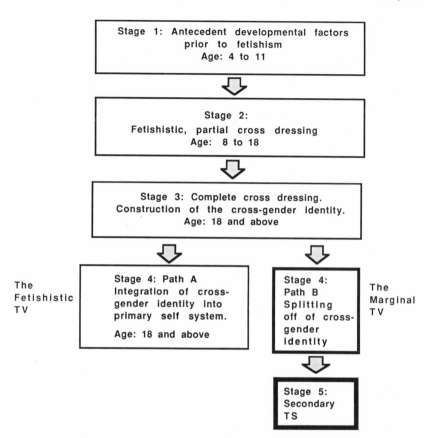

Figure 3. Sequential diagram of a five-stage theory of transvestism and secondary transsexualism (TV type). It is believed that a large pool of individuals experience the necessary antecedent conditions (Stage 1) to become fetishists. Most of these men, however, do not become fetishistic cross dressers (Stage 2). Those having certain unique developmental learning experiences and the formation of a sexual script favoring cross dressing become partial cross dressers. After several years, they develop skills to support complete cross dressing (Stage 3). A cross-gender identity is then developed, along with considerable cognitive dissonance. Gender and identity conflict can be resolved in either of two ways (Stage 4). If the cross-gender identity is split off from the self system, there is an increased probability of transgenderism or, less frequently, secondary transsexualism (TV type) is the result (Stage 5).

Path A: Integration of the cross-gender identity into the self. In Path A, we hypothesize harmonious integration of the cross-gender identity into the self system. It becomes a compatible, ego-syntonic, highly valued subsystem in close communication with the primary self and with other subsystems. It is integrated into the whole self and takes its place among other subsystems, clearly subservient to the primary self.

Path B: Disintegration of the self / dissociation of the cross-gender identity. In path B, we hypothesize a splitting off of the cross-gender identity. This subsystem becomes a renegade within the self, competing for expression, threatening the primary self, and generating intensely egodystonic feelings because the cognitive dissonances of Stage 3 have not been satisfactorily resolved. These individuals are akin to the marginal transvestites of Buhrich and McConaghy (1977b). They are the never satisfied transvestites described by Benjamin (1966) who manifest some transsexual features. Many of these transvestites will explore cross-gender living, seek feminization through surgery or hormones, and some will ultimately apply for transsexual reassignment. A very few will become secondary transsexuals. It is this marginal group, we believe, which resembles the "phallic woman" variation of transvestism noted by Stoller (1968a). This transvestic type begins with fetishistic cross dressing and then shows a " . . . gradual emergence over the years of nonerotic desire to sense himself intermittantly as a woman and to pass as one" (p. 177). Stoller saw in this group a more marked disturbance in gender identity compared with a more fetishistic group, and emphasized the time element in this process (requiring many years to develop).

As to the causes underlying the development of Path A or Path B, we can only assume, as others have (Ovesey & Person, 1976), that this must be a reflection of differences in the level (or age) of developmental difficulty, the intensity of traumatic events, or such other experiences as may have contributed to difficulties in the maintainance of an integrated self system.

As noted earlier, we believe the psychodynamics involved in the temporary cross-gender identity change during cross dressing may parallel the neodissociative mechanisms of hypnosis presented by Hilgard (1977); we discussed this in Chapter 4. In brief, the theory is that a primary or master self system has many affiliated subsystems which maintain interactive communication and control links with other subsystems and with the primary self. Under special conditions, such as hypnosis or intense stress, a subordinate subsystem can usurp the controls of the primary system and take over the management of the self—a process that results in a "shared consciousness." The present hypothesis is that such a mental mechanism may be fundamental to the behavioral and affective changes frequently seen in transvestites when cross dressed; in the most extreme cases, the cross-gender identity defeats the primary self. These men become transgenderists or secondary transsexuals.

The idea that transvestic experience may entail a dual representation of the self has been extensively described at a subjective-experiential level by Prince (1976), who sees the existence of a second self (a feminine self) as part of our biological heritage. Prince reasons that men are born with a feminine gender component but that our socialization suppresses the expression of this. We are not concerned here with the issue of whether gender is biologically set—as self-experienced male or female person—or whether we may have a combination of both gender predispositions built in. What is important is Prince's insight into the significance of having a feminine self regardless of the source of such self-perceptions. Along the same line, both Money (1974) and Ovesey and Person (1976) have discussed the possibility that transvestism can be conceptualized, in part, as due to a dual representation of the self, or to use Hilgard's (1977) term, a shared consciousness.

Experiential Aspects of Stage 4.   In Stage 4, there is a feeling of becoming another person, of putting the primary identity aside, and of temporarily (when cross dressed) taking on the appearance, the personality, and the gender orientation appropriate to women. In Path A transvestites this occurs only in association with cross dressing. This temporary identity exchange and bending of reality is perceived as pleasurable, joyful, and as an exhilarating experience. For these men, Stage 4 is likely to endure throughout life, without major behavioral changes. This is especially probable where circumstances make possible the regular practice of transvestism, including frequent public appearances of the pseudowoman.

Similar feelings of great pleasure are sometimes reported by the Path B group, but their unresolved cognitive dissonances motivate them to seek more frequent and more extended cross dressing episodes. They are more likely to apply for various body feminization procedures (e.g., cosmetic surgery), and to take greater risks, as in the use of female hormones.

In Stage 4, frequency of cross dressing increases to an average rate of about 11 sessions per month, which is twice the average rate of Stage 2 (early fetishistic cross dressing). This may be an artifact of greater privacy and increased opportunity for cross dressing sessions, or it may, at least in part, be a product of the stronger cross-gender identity.

There is a need for variety and change in all aspects of transvestism; it does not remain static. New experiences are sought, such as attending cross dressing conventions, establishing new social ties while cross dressed, and finding new risks and adventures in the role of a woman (e.g., air travel, attempting to get a job as a woman, going to a physician cross dressed, enrolling in an adult education class, and the like). There is decreased reliance upon marital sex.

Various stimuli may facilitate or interfere with the temporary behavioral expression of the cross-gender identity. Some examples: The combination of having privacy and time to cross dress, for some, appears to be discriminative stimuli for cross dressing. Having plenty of time to "get in the mood" is essential to experiencing the cross-gender identity shift. Conversely, some transvestites report difficulty establishing this shift when the wife or someone else is present who communicates masculine role expectancies to the transvestite. Such persons tend to become unwanted reminders of reality.

As the cross-gender identity strengthens, fantasies of being a woman and having sex with a man while cross dressed are acknowledged. The more intense the cross-gender identity, as in Path B, the stronger the yearnings to experiment with sexual relations with men while the transvestite is cross dressed. This is less commonly seen in transvestites who have weaker cross-gender identity, stronger fetishistic interests, and in persons who are inhibited about sexual experimentation.

Stage 5: Secondary Transsexualism

Movement to Stage 5 is uncommon, and when it does occur we think it represents an attempt to resolve the incompatible gender dissonance experienced by individuals in Path B who cannot satisfactorily integrate the cross-gender self into their self system. The cross-gender self forces a reorganization of the self system. A new (feminine) self takes charge. These men, formerly periodic, heterosexual cross dressers, have now joined the ranks of those living full time in the cross-gender role. They are gradually moving toward hormonal and surgical reassignment.

For the most part, these men have been described as homosexually inclined (although many have predominantly heterosexual histories), unhappy, conflicted, frustrated individuals, often with significant psychopathology (Buhrich & McConaghy, 1977b; Person & Ovesey, 1974b; Wise & Meyer, 1980).

We have followed six secondary transsexuals over a period of approximately 4 years, and some of these men contradict the profile described above, at least in part. None regrets the transsexual decision. A dramatic example of a high-functioning transvestite-turned-secondary transsexual is the case of a World War II navy commander who became a transsexual at the age of 74 (Docter, 1985).

Chapter 9

Summary and Conclusions

We have presented descriptive information, a review of the literature, some new research data, and a theory concerned with the heterosexual variations of cross dressing. We define these behavior patterns as encompassing fetishism, fetishistic and marginal transvestism, transgenderism, and secondary transsexualism (transvestic type).

When a *heterosexual* male presents himself to others with the appearance of a woman, and strives to imitate a woman, there is a confusing paradox. On the one hand, we have a more or less socially conventional male, often married, who seems to function satisfactorily in his various male roles. But on the other hand, he lives a secret second life dominated by fantasies of being a temporary, periodic woman, and he derives extraordinary exhilaration and delight in this. Despite the social disapproval which would almost surely accompany the public disclosure of his transvestism, he devotes much of his fantasy life and some of his time to periodic cross dressing. As the cross dressing behavior continues over several years, his interest in this activity grows progressively stronger. For some, it takes on a compulsive quality roughly akin to an addiction—at least, that is how some TVs describe the intensity of their feelings. When cross dressing is blocked the result is frustration, tension, and irritation. When the behavior is resumed, there is an immediate sense of relief, joy, and happiness. Some analgesia may be reported, general arousal level and autonomic variables are markedly increased, and attention is sharply focused upon the cross dressing experience. All of this seems triggered by cognitive stimuli organized around a long-established sexual script. We have attempted to describe the interplay of heterosexual interests, gender envy, and the culturally defined significance of women's intimate apparel as erotically tinged body symbols—all of which may play a part in the formation of transvestic sexual scripts.

For reasons that may be very different from one heterosexual transvestite to another, cross dressing, and all that goes with this, typically promotes an alteration of mood which is highly satisfying. But there is more involved than simply touching or putting on women's clothing. If tactile or visual stimuli were sufficient to produce the desired mood changes, then transvestites would probably be touching and visualizing their favorite items of women's apparel, rather than wearing them and venturing into public places. For most transvestites, there is a long-term learning experience which moves from a largely fetishistic interest in women's clothing toward efforts to present oneself in public as a woman. TVs report that there is a special delight in passing as a woman in public. The men who do this report that they feel like a different person when they are cross dressed—that they have acquired a second self or an alternate identity. Were such cross-gender identity feelings to be sustained, we would begin to think of transsexual motives to explain the cross dressing of the transvestite. But when the cross dressing episode ends, our TV reverts entirely to his masculine role behavior—a change which is not seen in transsexuals. Only a few TVs progress in the direction of transgenderism, and fewer still apply for sex reassignment surgery in their later years (secondary transsexualism, TV type). The history, the psychodynamics, and the sexual orientation of the secondary transsexual are radically different from the primary transsexual pattern.

Procedures and Thematic Constructs

Our procedures have involved four main sources of information. First, we have reviewed the technical literature bearing on transvestism and transsexualism. Second, we have collected survey and test information from 110 heterosexual transvestites during the period 1980–1985. Third, we have obtained extensive histories and maintained regular in-person communications over a period of about 8 years with 40 transvestites (most of whom also participated in our survey). Finally, we have had a counseling relationship with 15 transvestites and some of their wives extending from a few weeks to several years.

In Chapter 1 we note the different theoretical approaches which have previously been used to describe and explain cross dressing behaviors. It seems to us that all approaches deserve our consideration and none can be excluded. Hence our model is multidisciplinary and draws from biological, psychodynamic, and social-learning principles.

Four thematic constructs are proposed as unifying ideas. These are: sexual arousal (and sexual excitement), pleasure getting, sexual scripts (as cognitive guides to action), and cross-gender identity. These organizing ideas are critical to the five-stage theory of transvestism and secondary transsexualism which we offer.

Terminology and Classifications

We need to specify the meanings of terminology in order to communicate about cross dressing behavior. Chapter 2 presents a rationale for adopting terms to denote different patterns of cross dressing behavior. Considerable overlap among these categories is seen. While we reject the medical or illness model as a way to conceptualize this behavior, we see much benefit in using terms having international meaning, such as transvestism and transsexualism, rather than in inventing new terms. Therefore, without implying any psychiatric or diagnostic labelling of cross dressing behaviors, we have used the following terms: fetishism, fetishistic transvestism, marginal transvestism, transgenderism, and secondary transsexualism (TV type). These five behavior patterns comprise the spectrum of heterosexual cross dressing. Our main interest is in these variations, but in order to clarify similarities and differences among these variations and the homosexual variations of cross dressing, we define the later as well. The homosexual variations include: primary transsexualism, secondary transsexualism (homosexual type), female impersonators (on stage), and so-called drag queens. The distinction between heterosexual and homosexual variations of cross dressing is supported by growing evidence.

Primary transsexualism is defined as involving long-standing gender dysphoria originating in earliest childhood, a conviction that one's anatomical sex is different from one's gender identity, and an absence of any history of fetishistic cross dressing. A well-established homosexual orientation is seen. Throughout the present report, however, we are concerned with heterosexual variations of cross dressing and cross-gender identity. Women do not appear to become heterosexual transvestites, except in the rarest of cases, and secondary transsexualism has not been clearly established in women. Our focus, therefore, is entirely upon men.

Review of the Literature

Transvestism and transsexualism have existed throughout history with various behavioral expressions across different cultures. There are believed to be between 6,000 and 10,000 postoperative transsexuals (combining men and women) in the United States. No reliable method has been developed to estimate the incidence of heterosexual transvestism, and guesses concerning incidence rates vary widely.

Over the past 75 years, there have been extensive descriptive reports pertaining to all kinds of cross dressing behavior, most of which have been derived from either clinical case material or from observations of transvestites belonging to cross dressing clubs. We present a summary of these findings and use this information as the basis of the recommended terminology. In our view, the greatest weakness in many of these reports has been the absence of sufficient developmental perspective. Too often, transvestism especially, has been discussed as if the behavior observed at a given time were the whole story; our emphasis is on the processes of change over a long time span. This developmental perspective is a central point emphasized throughout our report.

The most important contemporary research pertaining to transvestism includes efforts to clarify behavior patterns and terminology, the development of measures of gender identity and cross-gender identity, and developmental studies which highlight the erotic roots of some patterns of cross dressing. Transsexualism has been described and studied more extensively than transvestism. A major contribution has been the clarification of the very different patterns of primary and secondary transsexualism. It seems likely that most examples of transsexualism fall within the profile of secondary transsexualism, not the primary version. Theories of the etiology of transsexualism are discussed in Chapter 2. Follow-up research on the effects of sex reassignment surgery have been inadequately controlled and the definition and measurement of various outcome criteria has been unsatisfactory, to say the least. Most men and women who undergo sex reassignment seem to report that they feel happier and function better in various roles following this gender change, but the objective effects (e.g, improvements in work or personal adjustment) have not yet been adequately demonstrated. Strong assertions have been made by advocates and critics of transsexual procedures, but a definitive outcome study is still needed.

The Self System and Cross-Gender Identity

The concepts of identity and gender identity are central in both transvestism and transsexual theory. There is a growing trend to view these behaviors as dependent upon the sense of self—that is, of the cognitive schemas which underlie one's view of himself or herself. The chain of thinking is as follows: A self system exists which provides the executive apparatus essential for the coordination of behavior. A master self regulates behavior in response to changing conditions both within and from the environment. Different subsystems of the self facilitate the varied role-playing seen in ongoing behavior. The major functions of the self system include obtaining satisfaction of various needs and motives, maintaining self-esteem, and maintaining a favorable pleasure/pain balance. Ideally, during the course of development, a strong sense of self develops and different experiences are integrated into the self system. A sense of ethics, or moral values, is developed which institutes constraints upon the self. But the development of cross-gender identity feelings, for example, may be highly disharmonized with the master self or sense of identity. The gender dysphoria of the transsexual is said to be a product of this tug-of-war between incompatible gender identities. We find this model of the self system very useful in the conceptualization of transvestism. Chapter 4 discusses these ideas and offers examples of how the functioning of the self system seems to be expressed in both transvestism and transsexualism.

We believe the social behavior of the transvestite is the key to formation of his cross-gender identity. This feminine identity appears to be formed through processes known to be important in any kind of identity formation. The central concept is that in order to have a cross-gender identity it is necessary to take the pseudowoman (the cross dressed male) into public settings where social feedback is available. Over the many years required to develop a cross-gender identity, the TV seeks many opportunities to go into public situations and to present the pseudowoman in a favorable way. Sometimes he fails to obtain any particular attention from others. This is interpreted as successful passing. On other occasions, especially in connection with cross dressing club activities, he obtains praise and admiration in his cross dressed role. We propose that all of this is essential to the process of developing a cross-gender identity. The feminine self seems to function as a harmonious subsystem within the self system in many transvestites. These are the cross dressers who enjoy this behavior, feel little or no guilt about cross dressing, and who have worked through the cognitive dissonances associated with cross-gender behavior. But others do not fare so well. For unknown reasons, some TVs experience intensification of the inner struggle between masculine and feminine identities. This unpleasant tension, or gender dysphoria, may then lead to a rejection and reorganization of the self system by the feminine self subsystem, as seen in secondary transsexualism.

Sexual Scripts and Sexual Excitation

Sexual excitation unquestionably is of very great importance throughout the processes of learning which shape and control sexual responding. The preferences that underlie such responses are highly cognitive, and they are assembled into a network of ideas, expectations, knowledge, and images which constitute the sexual script. These cognitive processes have been understated in prior theory. We attempt to show the major role they play in the governance of cross dressing behaviors. The sexual script is believed to emerge from a combination of biological and social learning factors, with cultural factors playing an important part. We describe 10 attributes of sexual scripts believed to be important in the understanding of this construct.

Sexual scripts are closely tied to affective experience, such as tension reduction, the enhancement of pleasure, and innate sexual reinforcement. It is the link between these affective systems and the cognitive ideation represented by sexual scripts which gives the scripts their power and permanence. The attributes of sexual excitement are discussed, especially as they pertain to cross dressing behavior, and various theories and approaches to the understanding of sexual excitement are presented in this report.

There is a rapidly growing knowledge base pertaining to sexual excitation, although the scientific study of this topic has barely begun. Examples are given of recently developed research methods, such as phallometric measurements, which seem very promising. But it is important not to portray the heterosexual variations of cross dressing as exclusively sexual phenomena, for the motivational basis of this behavior is highly complex. Similarly, the types of rewards derived from this behavior change markedly over time in most individuals. But no matter what other variables may play a part, the sexual excitation and accompanying changes in mood almost always continue to work their influence into the motivation of cross dressing.

Because fetishistic behavior is thought to be basic to the learning which underlies all heterosexual variations of cross dressing, we consider several dimensions of research dealing with this topic. Central nervous system studies using electroencephalographic procedures with various conditions of sexual excitation in humans are described. Although important questions are being addressed, this line of research does not appear very helpful to our understanding cross dressing behavior.

We believe one of the most important and somewhat neglected aspects of cross dressing concerns the impact of this behavior upon the general arousal level. Cross dressing seems to serve as a way to promote heightened arousal and marked variations in arousal level. The focusing of attention, for example, seems to be highly controlled within a cross dressing episode. Arousal changes, as we see it, need to be considered as part of the many factors that can be positively reinforcing as part of the cross dressing behavior pattern.

We suggest three examples of learning experiences which seem basic to the development of a fetishistic interest in cross dressing. First, is learning about one's gender, including the rules and behaviors demanded within a given society and social group. Second, is learning to be envious of the opposite gender. This is the view that women have a

nssexualism. Most often, they obtained information from books,
zines, and literature supplied by TV organizations, or from their
nd and his cross dressing friends. Most described cross dressing
ing resulted in a substantial increase in the sexual excitement of
usband which may or may not have been expressed within the
sexual relationship. But 33% said there was no change or even a
e in sexual arousal. These wives split evenly along the dimension
or disliking transvestism within the family, with a few saying
neutral about this behavior. Each wife completed a problems
, rating each stated potential problem as seen by her. The
identified are summmarized by four categories (in order of
e to the wife): (1) security issues (avoidance of public discov-
nsvestism), (2) general tensions within the marriage due to
sing, (3) possible harm to children, and (4) negative effect
tal sex life. Very possibly, the adverse effects of transvestism
narital sexual relationship have been understated in the past.
wives have described tactics for incorporating some of the
ing into marital sexual behavior, although this usually re-
promise and negotiation. Nearly all wives described both
negative factors, as experienced by the wife, which had
n their husband's cross dressing. A discussion is presented
rategies or "games" employed by TV couples. There was
ete agreement that either frustration or temporary cessa-
lressing produced strongly negative affective states in the

nsvestism and Secondary Transsexualism

e theory of the heterosexual variations of cross dressing
Chapter 8. The goal is to explain all forms of this behavior
transvestism through secondary transsexualism (TV
dational aspects of these behaviors include biological
and socialization influences, and self and gender theo-
ions basic to theory development are identified and
ur major constructs seen as most important are the
throughout this book: sexual arousal (or sexual excite-
pleasure, the sexual script, and gender identity and
ity.

ith childhood antecedent developmental conditions
incline some males to develop fetishistic and trans-
ese are thought to include developmental crises dur-
n-separation phase of development, learning to be
women's clothing (and by women), sexual matura-
on of the sex drive at adolescence, learning gender

life easier and better than men. While gender envy cannot explain all
cross dressing behavior, it has been extensively cited as a factor in the
development of cross-gender behavior. Third, is learning that women's
clothing, especially intimate apparel, is "forbidden fruit" for males in
our culture. Our socialization may somehow contribute to making such
clothing especially erotic in the eyes of young boys.

Survey and Inventory Results

A survey and testing project based on 110 transvestites is described.
The sample of TVs used is thought to be biased in the direction of highly
verbal and socioeconomically successful men. It is impossible to say how
representative this group may be of the population of transvestites as
there is no feasible way to assess this population or even establish its
size, since transvestism is often a secretive behavior. Various demographic data are given. Of the 90 men who had married, 60% had never
divorced. Judging from this sample, the divorce rate of transvestites
may not differ much from nontransvestites. Most of these individuals
describe both parents as reasonably warm and affectionate; the distant
father hypothesis was not supported. There was very little report of
important family disruption, such as death or divorce of a parent, during early childhood. Overwhelmingly, these men were reared by their
natural parents. Ninety-seven percent described themselves as exclusively or predominantly heterosexual, and the remaining 3% said
they are bisexually inclined. Seventy-eight percent stated they had engaged in some sort of cross dressing activity prior to age 12. Base rates of
sexual orgasm during 10-year periods are quite similar to those reported
by Kinsey *et al.* (1948). Median age of first cross dressing was 9 years,
and for nearly all, this was partial cross dressing. We defined complete
cross dressing as wearing everything required to go out in public appearing as a woman. Median age of first complete cross dressing was 25
years.

Considerable emphasis is given to the fact that many years are
required to develop the behavior patterns of fetishistic and marginal
transvestism, and that even more time seems necessary to progress into
transgenderism or secondary transsexualism. For example, the median
age for first going out in public for at least 1 hour was 42 years. The
median number of years of experience with cross dressing prior to owning a complete outfit of women's clothing was 12 years. The median
years of experience with cross dressing prior to the adoption of a woman's name was 20 years. These findings underscore the long time period
which seems typical in the gradual emergence of transvestic behavior.

From a conditioning perspective, it seems very significant that 37%

of our subjects reported their first sexual orgasm was in association with a cross dressing episode. Our subjects confirm the reports of many other studies pointing up the close connection between cross dressing, sexual excitement, and masturbation during the adolescent and young adult years.

Transvestites' Explanations for Their Cross Dressing

We used a set of 16 explanations for cross dressing and asked our TVs to rate which reasons for cross dressing were most important to them. Ratings were made for two time periods—early in the cross dressing career, and, at present. The most important explanations for the early time period dealt with sexual excitation and erotic fantasies, pleasure-getting, feeling a compulsion to cross dress, and relief from the masculine role. For the "at present" time period sexual and erotic explanations are rated considerably lower than expression of the girl within, which is given strong importance.

The Explanations measures were subjected to a principal components analysis for both time periods, and the results were much the same for each period. Three factors were identified: Factor 1, Cross-gender identity/pleasurable affect (32% of the variance); Factor 2, Emotional expression (14% of the variance); and Factor 3, Sexual excitement (10% of the variance).

Cross-gender identity is viewed as a causal attribution, entirely subjective, and very closely associated with both sexual arousal and pleasure-getting. We reason that these latter affective and sexual arousal changes may be at the heart of what TVs refer to as their "feminine identity." Their ratings of what explanations are most important, for the early vs. at present time periods differ significantly. These changes are completely consonant with the well-known decrement in the importance of sexual factors as the transvestic career evolves over many years.

Stages of Transvestism and Frequency of Cross Dressing

Early, middle, and late stages of cross dressing were identified, and frequency of cross dressing episodes was seen to increase markedly. Regardless of whether older or younger subjects were examined, there was about twice the frequency of cross dressing sessions at the late stage than during the early stage.

The Bem Sex-Role Inventory

Our TVs described themselves as less masculine and more androgenous than the Bem normative group, but much less androge-

nously than suggested by Talamini's study (19' Our TVs described their feminine self in a ver' manner compared to Bem's norms for wom elected to take the BSRI while dressed in t' others did not. There is a significant dif' dressed group and the other group when t' yourself." We discuss several possible e> scriptions of this kind may have utility in between fetishistic and marginal transves our hypothesis that a higher percentage the inventory when cross dressed thar vestites.

Cross Dressing Inventory

An experimental Cross Dressing ated to assess various aspects of the ous self-descriptions of behavior (e cross-gender identity, heterosexua behavior). Subjects were asked t each statement. Those items with sexual orientation, (2) persistenc ing, (3) feeling more alive whe cross dressing, (5) perception and (6) frequent TV daydrea whenever possible, and ga' dressing. Concerning sexual TVs said they experienced episodes. This inventory w analysis with the followir identity (34% of the varia citement (18% of the vari tion/pleasure (20% of th

Wives Survey

Thirty-one wives Wives Survey Form, we believe this samp or favorable about t of these wives had ing children. Mos' dressing prior to fused when they

to tra maga husba as hav their h marital decreas of liking they fel inventor problems importan ery of tra cross dres upon mari upon the n Some cross dress quires com positive and emerged fro of several st nearly comp tion of cross TV husband.

A Theory of Tr

A five-stag is proposed in C from fetishistic type). The foun factors, learning ry. The assump discussed. The f themes which run ment), feelings of cross-gender iden Stage 1 deals which particularly vestic behaviors. T ing the individuatio sexually aroused by tion and intensificat envy, and formation of a heterosexual orientation. The inhibitions and shyness seen in some TVs during adolescence are discussed as important contributing causal factors.

Stage 2, often occurring during adolescence, is concerned with the formation of fetishistic behaviors involving women's clothing. At this point, cross dressing is a highly valued but secretive masturbation activity. It does not yet involve any cross-gender identity. The pairing of cross dressing with orgasmic satisfactions helps to strengthen the developing sexual script. With much practice, specific fetishistic stimuli come to be highly preferred, but this cross dressing is only partial. Most TVs require many years to develop the array of behaviors and skills necessary to carry out complete cross dressing and passing in public.

Stage 3 leads to complete cross dressing and usually requires opportunities for secrecy and extensive practice in cross dressing. Two things happen at this stage: first, there is gradually developed a cross-gender identity or "girl within", and second, this alternate identity is at odds with the primary identity or self system. The resulting conflict may be viewed as the product of cognitive dissonance. Although the TV thinks of himself as a competent male, he also values his cross dressing, and despite the frequently reported guilt and periods of abstinence, the behavior grows stronger with years of practice. The question of greatest importance is how this cognitive dissonance will be worked out. That is the subject of the next stage.

Stage 4 has two paths representing different resolutions of the cognitive dissonance described above. In Path A, there is a harmonious integration of the cross-gender identity into the primary self system. This is the TV satisfied with his cross dressing, who becomes quite comfortable with his transvestism. He has made peace with himself. In Path B, however, the cross-gender identity does not integrate itself with the primary self but initiates instead a revolt-within-the-self. This alternate identity takes over management of the self system, and the result is a desire to live in accordance with the cross-gender identity, not the former primary male identity. The immediate consequence may be transgenderism, in which there is an oscillation back and forth from one gender role to the other. We believe the Path B process to be far less likely to occur than Path A.

Stage 5 is the end product of the Path B process. The self system has been reorganized, however unrealistically, and the primary identity is now the cross-gender identity. There is a desire to live full time in the cross-gender role; there are claims (however unrealistic) of being a woman born "into the wrong body"; and the request is eventually made for sex reassignment. At this point, the behavior pattern is designated secondary transsexualism, TV type. We believe this to be a far more common route toward transsexualism than the primary transsexual pattern.

Appendix

Explanations of Cross Dressing

Instructions: Consider each explanation and then rate each for two time periods: (1) Your early years of cross dressing; (2) The present time.

Ask yourself, How important is this explanation as applied to you? Please use this scale: (1) Very unimportant to you. (2) Slightly important. (3) Some importance to you. (4) Highly important. (5) More important than most other explanations. (6) Most important of all.

1. As pleasurable behavior: You increase your joy, delight, fun, and feelings of well-being. Not mainly sexual feelings, but just feeling good.
2. As sexually arousing: At least, a mild turn on for sexual excitement or erotic feeling. May either increase or reduce feelings of sexual tension.
3. As achievement of feminine identity: An alternate sense of identity is sought and achieved. You become a different person. Your femme identity gives you greater self-esteem, confidence, good feelings about yourself.
4. As role-playing and role relief: Your identity does not really change much, but your femme role is more comfortable and rewarding for you. It is a relief to drop your less attractive male role, at least while cross dressing.
5. As part of a femme life style: You have the opportunity to meet new people, go places, do things in your femme time that are not otherwise available to you. You join TV groups which leads to pleasing social relationships.
6. As antiloneliness behavior: Through cross dressing you are able to create another "person" who exists in the mirror. You can

control this beautiful girl. She will never leave you. She offers a
form of companionship when you feel lonely.

7. As anti-boredom behavior: Cross dressing gives you a new
    sense of excitement and a higher energy level. You feel re-
    freshed and more vigorous. You are less bored. It is never dull.

8. As erotic fantasy: Cross dressing helps you sustain erotic fan-
    tasy and thought patterns. Whenever you wish you can use
    your imagination to enjoy pleasing images and thoughts
    through fantasy.

9. As an outlet for emotional expression: You create a channel for
    the expression of your emotions through cross dressing. You
    are less emotionally inhibited and more expressive. You can
    show more of your feelings when cross dressed.

10. As a substitute for intimacy and closeness: You tend to be some-
    what fearful of intimacy and closeness to loved ones, but
    through cross dressing you can achieve much greater feeling of
    intimacy and closeness. You can be more vulnerable in a loving
    way at least with some people.

11. As dependency behavior: You can allow yourself to become
    more dependent when cross dressed and it feels good.

12. As multiple personality: You seem to experience an almost en-
    tirely new personality when cross dressed. This new person is
    clearly different than your male personality. You enjoy playing
    a different role and showing an entirely different style of be-
    havior.

13. As multiple rewards: Your joy and delight from cross dressing is
    multidimensional. Some rewards are felt more strongly on one
    occasion than another. There is not a fixed order of rewards.
    Many different kinds of rewards are experienced.

14. As a compulsion: You seem partially under the control of inner
    tensions which seem to compel cross dressing activities. You are
    able to reduce unpleasant feelings through these activities. It is
    very difficult to resist these compulsion-like feelings.

15. As due to damaged sense of masculinity: Some harmful event
    has occurred in early childhood producing a powerful internal
    conflict which may be unconscious. This conflict results in ef-
    forts to master and overcome this unpleasant experience and
    cross dressing behavior is developed for that purpose.

16. As expression of the "girl within": You feel that you have both
    masculine and feminine feelings within and that our culture
    forces repression of the feminine feelings in men. You feel bet-
    ter when you are able to express the "girl within" through cross
    dressing.

Cross Dressing Inventory

Instructions: For each item, please ask yourself how true is this for you? To show how true an item is, use the scale below. Write 1, 2, 3, 4, 5, 6, or 7 beside each item. 1 = Almost never true. 2 = Usually not true. 3 = Sometimes but infrequently true. 4 = Occasionally true. 5 = Often true. 6 = Usually true. 7 = Always or almost always true.

1. Cross dressing is almost always a somewhat sexual or erotic experience for me.
2. Cross dressing is mostly a way of relaxing and unwinding.
3. I usually feel more "alive" or more excited when cross dressed.
4. I can enjoy cross dressing for several hours in practically any kind of women's clothing even without makeup or a wig.
5. When cross dressed I seem able to throw off my male identity and take on a feminine identity which is quite different.
6. When cross dressed I am mostly like my male self with just a few minor changes in my feelings.
7. I daydream at least once every day about the pleasure of cross dressing.
8. I frequently wish I could live permanently as a woman.
9. I usually want to cross dress almost every time there is an opportunity.
10. If given the opportunity I would like to take female hormones (check here _____ if you have already done so).
11. If given the opportunity I would like to have my beard removed through electrolysis (check here _____ if you have already done so).
12. If given the opportunity I would like to have facial cosmetic surgery to improve my feminine appearance (check here _____ if you have already done so).
13. If given the opportunity I would like to have breast implants (check here _____ if you have already done so).
14. If given the opportunity I would definitely choose to have complete gender reassignment surgery at some time in the future (check here _____ if you have already done so).
15. Lovemaking is more pleasurable if I am wearing one or more articles of feminine apparel.
16. When having fantasies about cross dressing I often have strong ideas about being punished or disciplined.
17. When having fantasies about cross dressing I often have strong ideas about being humiliated.

18. One of my favorite fantasies involves having sex with a man while I am in the role of a woman.
19. Touching elegant lingerie usually gives me some sexual excitement.
20. If by magic, all of my sexual and erotic feelings should disappear entirely, I think I would lose interest in cross dressing.
21. If I have the opportunity, I prefer to masturbate at least 50% of the times when I cross dress.
22. If there were a pill to eliminate cross dressing and I took it, I think it would reduce my sexual life and my sexual pleasure.
23. I can enjoy cross dressing in women's work clothes or drab clothes almost as much as a fancy outfit.
24. Some specific articles of clothing or makeup have an especially powerful effect on my sexual arousal.
25. It is essential for me to be with at least one other person to really enjoy the experience of cross dressing.
26. I prefer to mix cross dressing with being tied up or tying someone else up.
27. Cross dressing brings me as much or more sexual pleasure as any other kind of sexual behavior.
28. I often become sexually excited when I think about cross dressing.
29. I can get just as "turned on" by dressing up in special men's clothing for a play or a party as I would by cross dressing.
30. My sense of critical judgment seems to be reduced when I'm cross dressed.
31. I feel as if I have a different personality when I'm cross dressed.
32. Very few activities give me as pleasant a sense of exhilaration as does cross dressing.
33. Sometimes I become sexually excited by reading or seeing ads or pictures of beautiful feminine clothing, shoes, or makeup.
34. I sometimes become sexually excited when I shop for women's clothing, shoes, or makeup.
35. I have pleasant fantasies about cross dressing almost every day.
36. I sometimes become sexually excited when I read about cross dressing.
37. I'd choose to be cross dressed at least 90% of my life if I could do it without hurting anyone else.
38. I often think about how pleasant it would be to live full time as a woman.
39. I have the goal of living full time as a woman for at least one year or longer sometime in the future (check here _____ if you have already done so).

40. I'd like very much to attend a 10-day cross dressing meeting where I could remain cross dressed the entire time.
41. When having fantasies about cross dressing I often have strong ideas about sadism or masochism mixed with cross dressing.
42. I don't think I could completely give up cross dressing even if I really wanted to so long as any opportunity existed to cross dress.
43. Creating a small amount of pain in yourself can add to the enjoyment of cross dressing.
44. When in my best cross dressed appearance I can pass practically anywhere so long as I don't use my voice (or even if I do).
45. I spend over $100 monthly on my cross dressing (clothing, makeup, books, club dues, workshops, etc.).
46. I spend over $200 monthly on my cross dressing.
47. I spend over $300 monthly on my cross dressing.
48. At times, cross dressing has had serious harmful effects on my relationships with loved ones or those closest to me.
49. All things considered, cross dressing has been a positive and helpful part of my life despite occasional difficulties.
50. At least once, I have given up all cross dressing for a period of one year of longer.
51. I consider myself to be primarily a preoperative or postoperative transsexual.
52. My behavior has been exclusively or almost exclusively heterosexual.
53. My behavior has been consistently bisexual.
54. My behavior has mainly been homosexual.
55. I think of myself as having very low sexual motivation for my age.
56. I think of myself of having about average sexual motivation for my age.
57. I think of myself as having above average sexual motivation but not within the the top 10% for my age.
58. I think of myself as having extremely high sexual motivation within the top 10% for my age.
59. When cross dressed my inner sense of identity changes slightly but only in a very superficial way.
60. I sometimes have a fantasy in which I am cross dressed and I become sexually excited while with a man who is dressed like a man.
61. I sometimes have a fantasy in which I am cross dressed and I become sexually excited while with a woman.
62. I sometimes have a fantasy in which I am cross dressed and I

become sexually excited while with a man who is also cross dressed.

63. In general, I prefer heterosexual activity with a woman who takes the initiative in sexual behavior.
64. Sometimes when cross dressed I want to have sex with a man dressed as a man.
65. Sometimes when cross dressed I want to have sex with a woman.
66. Sometimes when cross dressed I want to have sex with another man who is also cross dressed.
67. For maximum enjoyment of cross dressing it is usually essential for me to be out in public.
68. My social behavior becomes much more outgoing when I am cross dressed.
69. I am a more assertive person when I am cross dressed.
70. I am a less assertive person when I am cross dressed.
71. I sometimes think about what it would be like to have my funeral carried out with me cross dressed.
72. When I die I would prefer to be buried cross dressed.
73. I believe that if I were married and my wife died, I would probably prefer not to remarry.
74. At least once, I have given up all cross dressing for a period of five years or longer as an adult.
75. (*Check which is most correct*) Over the years, each cross dressing episode resulted in an orgasm:
    _____ less than 10% of the time
    _____ between 10% and 25% of the time
    _____ between 25% and 50% of the time
    _____ about 50% of the time
    _____ between 50% and 75% of the time
    _____ over 75% of the time
    _____ over 90% of the time

References

Allport, G. W. (1955). *Becoming.* New Haven: Yale University Press.

American Psychiatric Association (1987). *Diagnostic and statistical manual of mental disorders* (3rd ed., revised). Washington, DC: American Psychiatric Association.

Bak, R. C. (1953). Fetishism. *Journal of the American Psychoanalytic Association, 1,* 285–294.

Bak, R. C. (1968). The phallic woman: The ubiquitous fantasy in perversion. *Psychoanalytic Study of the Child, 23,* 15–36.

Baker, R. (1968). *Drag: A history of female impersonation on the stage.* London: Triton Books.

Bancroft, J. H. (1972). The relationship between gender identity and sexual behaviour: Some clinical aspects. In C. Ounsted & D. C. Taylor (Eds.), *Gender differences: Their ontogeny and significance* (pp. 57–72). Edinburgh: Churchill Livingstone.

Bancroft, J. H. (1974). *Deviant sexual behavior: Modification and assessment.* Oxford: Clarendon Press.

Bandura, A. (1977). Self-efficacy: Toward a unifying theory of behavioral change. *Psychological Review, 84,* 191–215.

Bandura, A. (1982). Self-efficacy mechanism in human agency. *American Psychologist, 37,* 122–147.

Barclay, A. M. (1973). Sexual fantasies in men and women. *Medical aspects of human sexuality, 7,* 205–216.

Beigel, H. G. (1963). Wives of transvestites. *Sexology* (July).

Beigel, H. G. (1969). A weekend in Alice's wonderland. *Journal of Sex Research, 5,* 108–122.

Beigel, H. G., & Feldman, R. (1963). The male transvestite's motivation in fiction, research, and reality. In H. G. Beigel (Ed.), *Advances in sex research* (pp. 198–210). New York: Harper & Row.

Beitel, A. (1985). The spectrum of gender identity disturbance. In B. W. Steiner (Ed.), *Gender dysphoria* (pp. 189–206). New York: Plenum Press.

Bem, S. L. (1974). The measurement of psychological androgyny. *Journal of Consulting and Clinical Psychology, 42,* 155–162.

Bem, S. L. (1981a). *Bem sex-role inventory.* Palo Alto, CA: Consulting Psychologists Press.

Bem, S. L. (1981b). Gender schema theory: A cognitive account of sex typing. *Psychological Review, 88,* 354–364.

Bem, S. L. (1981c). The BSRI and gender schema theory: A reply to Spence and Helmreich. *Psychological Review, 88,* 369–371.

Benjamin, H. (1953). Transvestism and transsexualism. *International Journal of Sexology, 7,* 12–14.

Benjamin, H. (1954). Transvestism and transsexualism. *American Journal of Psychotherapy, 8,* 219–230.

Benjamin, H. (1966). *The transsexual phenomenon.* New York: Julian Press.

Bentler, P. M. (1976). A typology of transsexualism: Gender identity theory and data. *Archives of Sexual Behavior, 5*, 567–584.

Bentler, P. M., & Abramson, P. R. (1981). The science of sex research: Some methodological considerations. *Archives of Sexual Behavior, 10*, 225–251.

Bentler, P. M., & Prince, C. (1969). Personality characteristics of male transvestites: III. *Journal of Abnormal Psychology, 74*, 140–143.

Bentler, P. M., & Prince, C. (1970). Psychiatric symptomatology in transvestites. *Journal of Clinical Psychology, 26*, 434–435.

Bentler, P.M., Sherman, R. W., & Prince, C. (1970). Personality characteristics of male transvestites. *Journal of Clinical Psychology, 26*, 287–291.

Betelheim, B. (1962). *Symbolic wounds.* New York: Macmillan.

Blanchard, R. (1985a). Typology of male-to-female transsexualism. *Archives of Sexual Behavior, 14*, 247–261.

Blanchard, R. (1985b). Research methods for the typological study of gender disorders in males. In B. W. Steiner (Ed.), *Gender dysphoria* (pp. 227–257). New York: Plenum Press.

Blanchard, R. (1985c). Gender dysphoria and gender reorientation. In B. W. Steiner (Ed.), *Gender dysphoria* (pp. 365–392). New York: Plenum Press.

Blanchard, R., Clemmensen, L. H., & Steiner, B. W. (1987). Heterosexual and homosexual gender dysphoria. *Archives of Sexual Behavior, 16*, 139–152.

Bolles, R. C., & Fanselow, M. S. (1982). Endorphins and behavior. *Annual Review of Psychology, 33*, 87–101.

Bowlby, J. (1969). *Attachment and loss*, Vol. 1: *Attachment.* New York: Basic Books.

Bowlby, J. (1973). *Attachment and loss*, Vol. 2: *Separation.* London: Hogarth Press and Institute of Psychoanalysis.

Bradley, S. J. (1985). Gender disorders in childhood: A formulation. In B. W. Steiner (Ed.), *Gender dysphoria* (pp. 175–188). New York: Plenum Press.

Breger, L. (1974). *From instinct to identity.* Englewood Cliffs, NJ: Prentice-Hall.

Brierley, H. (1979). *Transvestism: Illness, perversion, or choice.* New York: Pergamon.

Bryne, D. (1977). The imagery of sex. In J. Money & H. Musaph (Eds.), *Handbook of sexology* (pp. 327–350). New York: Excerpta Medica.

Bryne, D., & Lamberth, J. (1971). The effect of erotic stimuli on sex arousal, evaluative responses, and subsequent behavior. In: *Technical Report of the Commission on Obscenity and Pornography*, Vol. 8 (pp. 41–67). Washington, DC: U.S. Government Printing Office.

Bryne, D., Fisher, J. D., Lamberth, J., & Mitchell, H. E. (1974). Evaluations of erotica: Facts or feelings? *Journal of Personality and Social Research, 29*, 111–116.

Buckner, H. T. (1970). The transvestite career path. *Psychiatry, 33*, 381–389.

Buhrich, N. (1976). A heterosexual transvestite club. *Australian and New Zealand Journal of Psychiatry, 10*, 331–335.

Buhrich, N. (1981). Psychological adjustment in transvestism and transsexualism. *Behavior Research and Therapy, 19*, 407–411.

Buhrich, N., & Beaumont, T. (1981). Comparison of transvestism in Australia and America. *Archives of Sexual Behavior, 10*, 269–279.

Buhrich, N., & McConaghy, N. (1970). Three clinically discrete categories of fetishistic transvestism. *Archives of Sexual Behavior, 8*, 151–157.

Buhrich, N., & McConaghy, N. (1976). Transvestic fiction. *Journal of Nervous and Mental Disease, 163*, 420–427.

Buhrich, N., & McConaghy, N. (1977a). Clinical comparison of transvestism and transsexualism: An overview. *Australian and New Zealand Journal of Psychiatry, 11*, 83–86.

Buhrich, N., & McConaghy, N. (1977b). The clinical syndromes of femmiphilic transvestism. *Archives of Sexual Behavior, 6*, 397–412.

Buhrich, N., & McConaghy, N. (1977c). Can fetishism occur in transsexuals? *Archives of Sexual Behavior*, 6, 223–236.

Buhrich, N., & McConaghy, N. (1985). Preadult feminine behaviors of male transvestites. *Archives of Sexual Behavior*, 14, 413–418.

Bullough, V. L. (1974). Transvestites in the Middle Ages. *American Journal of Sociology*, 79, 1381–1394.

Bullough, V. L. (1976a). *Sexual variance in society and history*. New York: John Wiley & Sons.

Bullough, V. L. (1976b). *Sex, society and history*. New York: Science History Publications.

Bullough, V. L. (1987). A nineteenth-century case of transsexualism. *Archives of Sexual Behavior*, 16, 81–84.

Bullough, V. L., Bullough B., & Smith, R. (1983). A comparative study of male transvestites, male to female transsexuals, and male homosexuals. *Journal of Sex Research*, 19, 238–257.

Cauldwell, D. O. (1956). *Transvestism*. New York: Sexology Corporation.

Cohen, B. (1980). *Deviant street networks*. Lexington, MA: D. C. Heath.

Cooley, C. H. (1902). *Human nature and the social order*. New York: Scribner's.

Croughan, J. L., Saghir, M., Cohen, R., & Robins, E. (1981). A comparison of treated and untreated male cross-dressers. *Archives of Sexual Behavior*, 10, 515–528.

Diamond, M. (1965). A critical evaluation of the ontogeny of human sexual behavior. *Quarterly Review of Biology*, 40, 147–175.

Diamond, M. (1977). Human sexual development. In F. Beach (Ed.), *Human sexuality in four perspectives* (pp. 22–61). Baltimore: Johns Hopkins University Press.

Diamond, M. (1979). Sexual identity and sex roles. In V. L. Bullough (Ed.), *The frontiers of sex research* (pp. 39–56). Buffalo: Prometheus Books.

Diamond, M. (1982). Sexual identity, monozygotic twins reared in discordant sex roles and a BBC follow-up. *Archives of Sexual Behavior*, 11, 181–186.

Docter, R. F. (1985). Transsexual at 74: A case report. *Archives of Sexual Behavior*, 14, 271–277.

Driscoll, J. P. (1960). *The transsexuals* (master's thesis). San Francisco: California State University, San Francisco.

Dupont, H. (1968). Social learning theory and the treatment of transvestite behavior in an eight-year-old boy. *Psychotherapy*, 1, 44–45.

Ellis, H. H. (1936). *Studies in the psychology of sex*, Vol. 7: *Eonism and other supplementary studies*. New York: Random House.

Epstein, S. (1973). The self-concept revisited: Or a theory of a theory. *American Psychologist*, 28, 404–416.

Feinbloom, D. (1976). *Transvestites and transsexuals*. New York: Dell.

Fenichel, O. (1930). The psychology of transvestitism. In O. Fenichel (Ed.), *Collected papers* (first series, pp. 167–180). New York: Norton.

Fischer, J., & Gochros, H. L. (1977). *Handbook of behavior therapy with sexual problems*. New York: Pergamon Press.

Fiske, D. W., & Maddi, S. R. (1961). *Functions of varied experience*. Homewood, IL: Dorsey.

Fleming, M., Steinman, C., & Bocknek, G. (1980). Methodological problems in assessing sex-reassignment surgery: A reply to Meyer and Reter. *Archives of Sexual Behavior*, 9, 451–456.

Freud, S. (1905). *Three essays on the theory of sexuality*. New York: Basic Books (reprinted 1962).

Freud, K. (1971). A note on the use of the phallometric method of measuring mild sexual arousal in the male. *Behavior Therapy*, 2, 223–228.

Freund, K., Sedlacek, F., & Knob, K. (1965). A simple transducer for mechanical plethysmography of the male genital. *Journal of the Experimental Analysis of Behavior*, 8, 169–170.

Freund, K., Langevin, R., & Barlow, D. (1974). Comparison of two penile methods of measuring mild sexual arousal. *Journal of Behavior Research and Therapy, 12,* 355–359.

Freund, K., Langevin, R., Satterberg, J., & Steiner, B. (1977). Extension of the gender identity scale for males. *Archives of Sexual Behavior, 6,* 507–519.

Freund, K., Steiner, B. W., & Chan, S. (1982). Two types of cross gender identity. *Archives of Sexual Behavior, 11,* 49–63.

Gagnon, J. H. (1973). Scripts and the coordination of sexual conduct. In J. K. Cole & R. Dienstbier (Eds.), *Nebraska symposium on motivation* (pp. 27–59). Lincoln: University of Nebraska Press.

Gagnon, J. H., & Simon, W. (1973). *Sexual conduct.* Chicago: Aldine.

Gebhard, P. (1969). Fetishism and sadomasochism. *Science and Psychoanalysis, 15,* 71–80.

Geer, J. H. (1980). Measurement of genital arousal in human males and females. In I. Martin & P. H. Venables (Eds.), *Techniques in psychophysiology.* New York: John Wiley & Sons.

Geer, J. H., & Fuhr, R. (1976). Cognitive factors in sexual arousal: The role of distraction. *Journal of Consulting and Clinical Psychology, 44,* 238–243.

Gosselin, C., & Wilson, G. (1980). *Sexual variations.* New York: Simon and Schuster.

Grant, V. W. (1960). The cross-dresser: A case study. *Journal of Nervous and Mental Disease, 131,* 149–159.

Green, R. (1969). Mythological, historical, and cross-cultural aspects of transsexualism. In R. Green & J. Money (Eds.), *Transsexualism and sex reassignment* (pp. 13–22). Baltimore: Johns Hopkins University Press.

Green, R. (1974). *Sexual identity conflict in children and adults.* New York: Basic Books.

Green, R. (1978). Sexual identity of thirty-seven children raised by twenty-eight homosexual or transsexual parents. *American Journal of Psychiatry, 135,* 692–697.

Green, R. (1979). Childhood cross-gender behavior and subsequent sexual preference. *American Journal of Psychiatry, 136,* 106–108.

Green, R. (1985). Gender identity in childhood and later sexual orientation. *American Journal of Psychiatry, 142,* 339–341.

Green, R. (1987). *The "sissy-boy syndrome" and the development of homosexuality.* New Haven: Yale University Press.

Green, R., & Money, J. (Eds.) (1969). *Transsexualism and sex reassignment.* Baltimore: Johns Hopkins University Press.

Griffit, W., & Kaiser, D. L. (1978). Affect, sex, guilt, and the reward-punishing effects of erotic stimuli. *Journal of Personality and Social Psychology, 36,* 850–858.

Grinker, R. R., Werble, B., & Drye, R. (1968). *The borderline syndrome: A behavioral study of ego functions.* New York: Basic Books.

Gutheil, E. (1954). The psychological background of transsexualism and transvestism. *American Journal of Psychotherapy, 8,* 231–239.

Hamburger, C., Sturup, G. K., & Dahl-Iverson E. (1953). Transvestism: Hormonal, psychiatric and surgical treatment. *Journal of the American Medical Association, 152,* 391–396.

Harlow, H. F. (1958). The nature of love. *American Psychologist, 13,* 673–685.

Harry Benjamin International Gender Dysphoria Association, Inc. (1985). Standards of care: The hormonal and surgical sex reassignment of gender dysphoric persons. *Archives of Sexual Behavior, 14,* 79–90.

Harter, S. (1983). Developmental perspectives on the self- system. In P. H. Mussen (Ed.), *Handbook of child psychology* (4th ed.), Vol. 4 (pp. 275–386). New York: John Wiley & Sons.

Hilgard, E. R. (1977). *Divided consciousness: Multiple controls in human thought and action.* New York: John Wiley & Sons.

Hirschfeld, M. (1910). *Die transvestiten.* Berlin: Pulvermacher.

Hoenig, J. (1985). The origin of gender identity. In B. W. Steiner (Ed.), *Gender dysphoria* (pp.11–32). New York: Plenum Press.

Hoenig, J., & Kenna, J. C. (1979). EEG abnormalities and transsexualism. *British Journal of Psychiatry, 134*, 293–300.

Holtzman, W. H., Thorpe, J. S., Swartz, J. D., & Herron, E. W. (1961). *Inkblot perception and personality*. Austin, TX: University of Texas Press.

Hoyer, N. (1933). *Man into woman: An authentic record of a change of sex*. New York: Dutton.

Hunt, D. D., & Hampson, J. L. (1980). Follow-up of 17 biologic male transsexuals after sex reassignment surgery. *American Journal of Psychiatry, 137*, 432–438.

Imperato-McGinley, J., Peterson, R. E., Gautier, T., & Sturla, E. (1979). Androgens and the evolution of male gender identity among male pseudohermaphrodites with 5 alpha-reductase deficiency. *New England Journal of Medicine, 300*, 1233–1237.

Imperato-McGinley, J., Peterson, R. E., Stoller, R., & Goodwin, W. E. (1979) Male pseudo-hermaphroditism secondary to 17 -hydroxysteroid dehydrogenase deficiency. Gender role change with puberty. *Journal of Clinical Endocrinological Metabolism, 49*, 391–395.

James, W. (1910). *Psychology: The briefer course*. New York: Holt.

Jorgensen, C. (1967). *A personal autobiography*. New York: Bantam Books.

Jovanovic, U. J. (1971). The recording of physiological evidence of genital arousal in human males and females. *Archives of Sexual Behavior, 1*, 309–320.

Jucovy, M. E. (1979). Transvestism: With special reference to preoedipal factors. In T. B. Karasu & C. W. Socarides (Eds.), *On sexuality* (pp. 223–241). New York: International Universities Press.

Kagan, J. (1955). Differential reward value of incomplete and complete sexual behavior. *Journal of Comparative and Physiological Psychology, 48*, 59–64.

Kaplan, H. B. (1980). *Deviant behavior in defense of self*. New York: Academic Press.

Kaplan, H. B. (1986). *Social psychology of self-referent behavior*. New York: Plenum Press.

Kelly, G. A. (1955). *The psychology of personal constructs*, 2 vols. New York: Norton.

Kernberg, O. (1976). *Object relations theory and clinical psychoanalysis*. New York: Jason Aronson.

Kinsey, A. C., Pomeroy, W. B., & Martin, C. E. (1948). *Sexual behavior in the human male*. Philadelphia: W. B. Saunders.

Kluver H., & Bucy, P. C. (1939). Preliminary analysis of functions of the temporal lobes in monkeys. *Archives of Neurology and Psychiatry, 42*, 979–1000.

Kohlberg, L. (1966). A cognitive-developmental analysis of children's sex-role concepts and attitudes. In E. E. Maccoby (Ed.), *The development of sex differences* (pp. 82–173). Stanford, CA: Stanford University Press.

Koranyi, E. K. (1980). *Transsexuality in the male*. Springfield, IL: Charles C. Thomas.

Lambley, P. (1974). Treatment of transvestism and subsequent coital problems. *Journal of Behavior Therapy and Experimental Psychiatry, 5*, 101–102.

Langevin, R. (1985a). The meaning of cross-dressing. In B. Steiner (Ed.), *Gender dysphoria* (pp. 207–219). New York: Plenum Press.

Langevin, R. (Ed.) (1985b). *Erotic preference, gender identity, and aggression in men: New research studies*. Hillsdale, NJ: Lawrence Erlbaum Associates.

Langevin, R., Ben-Aron, M. H., Coulthard, R., Day, D., Hucker, S. J., Purins, J. E., Roper, V., Russon, A. E., & Webster, C. D. (1985). The effect of alcohol on penile erection. In R. Langevin (Ed.), *Erotic preference, gender identity, and aggression in men: New research studies* (pp. 101–111). Hillsdale, NJ: Lawrence Erlbaum Associates.

Latham, A., & Grenadier, A. (1982). The ordeal of Walter Cannon. *Psychology Today, 16*, 64–72.

Laub, D. R., & Fisk, N. (1974). A rehabilitation program for gender dysphoria syndrome by surgical sex change. *Plastic Reconstructive Surgery, 53*, 388–403.

Lecky, P. (1945). *Self-consistency: A theory of personality*. Long Island, NY: Island Press.

Levine, S. B. (1984). Letter to the editor. *Archives of Sexual Behavior, 13*, 287–289.

Levine, S. B., & Shumaker, R. E. (1983). Increasingly Ruth: Toward understanding sex reassignment. *Archives of Sexual Behavior, 12*, 247–261.

Lothstein, L. M. (1979). The aging gender dysphoria (transsexual) patient. *Archives of Sexual Behavior, 8*, 431–443.

Lothstein, L. M. (1980). The postsurgical transsexual: Empirical and theoretical considerations. *Archives of Sexual Behavior, 9*, 547–564.

Lothstein, L. M. (1982). Sex reassignment surgery: Historical, bioethical and theoretical issues. *American Journal of Psychiatry, 139*, 417–426.

Lukianowicz, N. (1959). Survey of various aspects of transvestism in light of our present knowledge. *Journal of Nervous and Mental Disease, 128*, 36–64.

Maccoby, E. E., & Jacklin, C. N. (1974). *The psychology of sex differences*. Stanford, CA: Stanford University Press.

McGuire, R. J., Carlisle, J. M., & Young, B. G. (1965). Sexual deviations as conditioned behaviors: A hypothesis. *Behavior Research and Therapy, 2*, 185–190.

Mandler, G. (1975). *Mind and emotion*. New York: John Wiley & Sons.

Mandler, J. M. (1984). *Stories, scripts, and scenes: Aspects of schema theory*. Hillsdale, NJ: Lawrence Erlbaum Associates.

Marks, I. M., Gelder, M. G., & Bancroft, J. H. (1970). Sexual deviants two years after electric aversion. *British Journal of Psychiatry, 117*, 173–176.

Marquis, J. W. (1970). Orgasmic reconditioning: changing sexual object choice through controlling masturbation fantasies. *Journal of Behavior Therapy and Experimental Psychiatry, 1*, 263–271.

Masters, W. H., & Johnson, V. E. (1966). *Human sexual response*. Boston: Little, Brown.

Masterson, J. F. (1981). *The narcissistic and borderline disorders*. New York: Brunner/Mazel.

Mead, G. H. (1934). *Mind, self and society*. Chicago: University of Chicago Press.

Mellon, S. L. W. (1981). *The evolution of love*. San Francisco: W. H. Freeman.

Meyer, J. K. (1974). Clinical variants among applicants for sex reassignment. *Archives of Sexual Behavior, 3*, 527–558.

Meyer, J. K., & Reter, D. J. (1979). Sex reassignment. *Archives of General Psychiatry, 36*, 1010–1015.

Meyer-Bahlburg, J. F. L. (1977). Sex hormones and male homosexuality in comparative perspective. *Archives of Sexual Behavior, 6*, 297–306.

Meyer-Bahlburg, J. F. L. (1979). Sex hormones and female homosexuality. *Archives of Sexual Behavior, 8*, 101–119.

Miller, G. A., Galanter, E., & Pribram, K. H. (1960). *Plans and the structure of behavior*. New York: Holt.

Money, J. (1974). Two names, two wardrobes, two personalities. *Journal of Homosexuality, 1*, 65–70.

Money, J. (1977). Determinants of human gender identity/role. In J. Money & H. Musaph (Eds.), *Handbook of sexology*. New York: Excerpta Medica.

Money, J. (1984). Paraphilias: Phenomenology and classification. *American Journal of Psychotherapy, 38*, 164–179.

Money, J. (1987). Sin, sickness, or status. *American Psychologist, 42*, 384–399.

Money, J., & Ehrhardt, A. A. (1972). *Man and woman, boy and girl*. Baltimore: Johns Hopkins University Press.

Money, J., & Musaph, B. (Eds.), (1977). *Handbook of sexology*. New York: Excerpta Medica.

Money, J. & Primrose, C. (1968). Sexual dimorphism and dissociation in the psychology of male transsexuals. *Journal of Nervous and Mental Disease, 147*, 472–486.

Mussen, P. H. (Ed.) (1983). *Handbook of child psychology* (4th ed.). New York: John Wiley & Sons.

Neisser, U. (1967). *Cognitive psychology.* New York: Appleton-Century-Crofts.

Newman, L. E., & Stoller, R. J. (1973). Nontranssexual men who seek sex reassignment. *American Journal of Psychiatry, 131,* 437–441.

Newton, E. (1972). *Mother camp.* Englewood Cliffs, NJ: Prentice-Hall.

Ovesey, L., & Person, E. (1973). Gender identity and sexual psychopathology in men: Homosexuality, transsexualism, and transvestism. *Journal of the American Academy of Psychoanalysis, 1,* 53–72.

Ovesey, L., & Person, E. (1976). Transvestism: A disorder of the sense of self. *International Journal of Psychoanalytic Psychotherapy, 5,* 221–235.

Paitich, D., & Langevin, R. (1976). The Clarke Parent–Child Relations Questionnaire: A clinically useful test for adults. *Journal of Consulting and Clinical Psychology, 44,* 428–436.

Paitich, D., Langevin, R., Freeman, R., Mann, K., & Handy, L. (1977). The Clarke SHQ: A clinical sex history questionnaire for males. *Archives of Sexual Behavior, 6,* 421–435.

Pauly, I. B. (1969). Adult manifestations of male transsexualism. In R. Green & J. Money (Eds.), *Transsexualism and sex reassignment* (pp. 37–58). Baltimore: Johns Hopkins University Press.

Person, E., & Ovesey, L. (1974a). The transsexual syndrome in males: I. Primary transsexualism. *American Journal of Psychotherapy, 28,* 4–20.

Person, E., & Ovesey, L. (1974b). The transsexual syndrome in males: II. Secondary transsexualism. *American Journal of Psychotherapy, 28,* 174–193.

Pirke, K. M., Kockott, G., & Dittmar, F. (1974). Psychosexual stimulation and plasma testosterone in man. *Archives of Sexual Behavior, 3,* 577–584.

Podolsky, E., & Wade, C. (1960). *Transvestism today.* New York: Epic Publishing Co.

Prince, V. (1973). *The transvestite and his wife.* Los Angeles: Argyle Books.

Prince, V. (1976). *Understanding cross dressing.* Los Angeles: Chevalier Publications.

Prince, V. (1978). Transsexuals and pseudotranssexuals. *Archives of Sexual Behavior, 7,* 263–272.

Prince, V. (1980). *Transvestia,* Vol.100. Chevalier Publications: P.O. Box 36091, Los Angeles, CA 90036.

Prince, V., & Bentler, P. M. (1972). Survey of 504 cases of transvestism. *Psychological Reports, 31,* 903–917.

Przybyla, D. P. J., & Bryne, D. (1984). The mediating role of cognitive processes in self-reported sexual arousal. *Journal of Research in Personality, 18,* 54–63.

Purins, J. E., & Langevin, R. (1985). Brain correlates of penile erection. In R. Langevin (Ed.), *Erotic preference, gender identity, and aggression in men* (pp. 113–133). Hillsdale, NJ: Lawrence Erlbaum Associates.

Randell, J. B. (1959). Transvestism and trans-sexualism: A study of fifty cases. *British Medical Journal, 2,* 1448–1452.

Rector, F. (1981). *The Nazi extermination of homosexuals.* New York: Stein and Day.

Rekers, G. A. (1977). Assessment and treatment of childhood gender problems. In B. B. Lahey & A. E. Kazdin (Eds.), *Advances in child clinical psychology,* Vol. 1 (pp. 267–306). New York: Plenum Press.

Rekers, G. A., & Jurich, A. P. (1983). Development of problems of puberty and sex roles in adolescence. In E. C. Walker & M. C. Roberts (Eds.), *Handbook of clinical child psychology* (pp. 785–812). New York: John Wiley & Sons.

Richards, R., & Ames, J. (1983). *Second serve: The René Richards story.* Briarcliff Manor, NY: Stein and Day.

Rogers, C. R. (1951). *Client-centered therapy.* New York: Houghton Mifflin.

Rook, K. S., & Hammen, C. L. (1977). A cognitive perspective on the experience of sexual arousal. *Journal of Social Issues, 33*, 7–29.

Rosen, A. C., & Rehm, L. P. (1977). Long-term follow-up in two cases of transvestism treated with aversion therapy. *Journal of Behavior Therapy and Experimental Psychiatry, 8*, 295–300.

Sarbin, T. R. (1952). A preface to a psychological analysis of the self. *Psychological Review, 59*, 11–22.

Shore, E. R. (1984). The former transsexual: A case study. *Archives of Sexual Behavior, 13*, 277–285.

Simon, W. (1973). The social, the erotic, and the sensual: The complexities of sexual scripts. In J. K. Cole & R. Dienstbier (Eds.), *Nebraska symposium on motivation* (pp. 61–82). Lincoln: University of Nebraska Press.

Simon, W., & Gagnon, J. H. (1986). Sexual scripts: Permanence and change. *Archives of Sexual Behavior, 15*, 97–120.

Snygg, D., & Combs, A. W. (1949). *Individual behavior*. New York: Harper & Row.

Spence, J. T., & Helmreich, R. L. (1981). Androgeny versus gender schema: A comment on Bem's gender schema theory. *Psychological Review, 88*, 365–368.

Sperber, M. A. (1973). The "as if" personality and transvestism. *Psychoanalytic Review, 60*, 605–612.

Steiner, B. W. (Ed.) (1985a). *Gender dysphoria*. New York: Plenum Press.

Steiner, B. W. (1985b). The management of patients with gender disorders. In B. W. Steiner (Ed.), *Gender dysphoria* (pp. 325–350). New York: Plenum Press.

Steiner, B. W., Blanchard, R., & Zucker, K. J. (1985). Introduction. In B. W. Steiner (Ed.), *Gender dysphoria* (pp. 1–10). New York: Plenum Press.

Steiner, B. W., Sanders, R. M., & Langevin, R. (1985). In R. Langevin (Ed.), *Erotic preference, gender identity, and aggression in men: New research studies* (pp. 261–275). Hillsdale, NJ: Lawrence Erlbaum Associates.

Stoller, R. J. (1967). Transvestites' women. *American Journal of Psychiatry, 124*, 333–339.

Stoller, R. J. (1968a). *Sex and gender*. New York: Science House.

Stoller, R. J. (1968b). Differential diagnosis: Transvestism and transsexualism. In J. O. Sutherland (Ed.), *Sex and gender*. London: Hogarth.

Stoller, R. J. (1971). The term "transvestism." *Archives of General Psychiatry, 24*, 230–237.

Stoller, R. J. (1974). *Sex and gender*. New York: J. Aronson.

Stoller, R. J. (1975). *Perversion: The erotic form of hatred*. New York: Dell.

Stoller, R. J. (1976). Sexual excitement. *Archives of General Psychiatry, 33*, 899–909.

Stoller, R. J. (1982). Transvestism in women. *Archives of Sexual Behavior, 11*, 99–115.

Stoller, R. J. (1985a). Normal human sexuality and psychosexual disorders. In H. I. Kaplan & B. J. Sadock (Eds.), *Comprehensive textbook of psychiatry*, 4th ed., Vol. 1. Baltimore: Williams and Wilkins.

Stoller, R. J. (1985b). *Observing the erotic imagination*. New Haven: Yale University Press.

Stoller, R. J. (1985c). *Presentations of gender*. New Haven: Yale University Press.

Storms, M. D. (1981). A theory of erotic orientation. *Psychological Review, 88*, 340–353.

Talamini, J. T. (1982). *Boys will be girls*. Washington, DC: University Press of America.

Walinder, J. (1967). *Transsexualism: A study of forty-three cases*. Goteborg: Scandinavian University Books.

Warner, W. L. (1949). *Social class in America*. Chicago: Science Research Associates.

Wise, T. N., & Meyer, J. K. (1980). The border area between transvestism and gender dysphoria: Transvestite applicants for sex reassignment. *Archives of Sexual Behavior, 9*, 327–342.

Wise, T. N., Dupkin, C., & Meyer, J. K. (1981). Partners of distressed transvestites. *American Journal of Psychiatry, 138*,1221–1224.

Zuckerman, M. (1971). Physiological measures of sexual arousal in the human. *Psychological Bulletin, 75*, 297–329.

Zuger, B. (1966). Effeminate behavior present in boys from early childhood: 1. The clinical syndrome and follow-up studies. *Journal of Pediatrics, 69*, 1098–1107.

Zuger, B. (1978). Effeminate behavior present in boys from childhood. Ten additional years of follow-up. *Comprehensive Psychiatry, 19*, 363–369.

Index